TIN CAN SAILOR

LIFE ABOARD THE USS STERETT, 1939–1945

C. RAYMOND CALHOUN

NAVAL INSTITUTE PRESS/ANNAPOLIS, MARYLAND

© 1993
by the United States Naval Institute
Annapolis, Maryland

Library of Congress Cataloging-in-Publication Data

Calhoun, C. Raymond, 1913–
   Tin can sailor: life aboard the USS Sterett, 1939–1945 / C. Raymond
Calhoun.
     p. cm.
   Includes index.
   ISBN 1-55750-108-4
   1. Calhoun, C. Raymond, 1913–   . 2. Sterett (Destroyer).
3. World War, 1939–1945—Naval operations, American. 4. World War,
1939-1945—Personal narratives, American. 5. World War, 1939–1945—
Campaigns—Pacific Area. 6. United States. Navy—Biography.
7. Seamen—United States—Biography. I. Title.
D774.S74C35 1993
940.54'5973—dc20   93-14743
                                                 CIP

Printed in the United States of America on acid-free paper ∞

9 8 7 6 5 4 3 2
First printing

To those gallant sailors

of the USS *Sterett* (DD 407)

who gave their lives

during the Third Battle of Savo Island

on 13 November 1942.

CONTENTS

PREFACE

IN RETROSPECT, my years aboard the destroyer USS *Sterett* marked the most privileged period of my Navy career. The assignment occurred at a critical time, historically and personally. No other span of service proved to be as valuable in helping me to mature. It was exciting, inspirational, and gratifying.

As the war in the Pacific progressed, the *Sterett* never hesitated to wade in with flag flying and guns blazing to engage the enemy, whatever the odds. The ship was truly unique in many respects, and I will need some divine assistance to do justice to that uniqueness. It grew out of the personal and professional relationships that developed among her crew. I never encountered anything like it on any other ship.

A special bond existed among *Sterett* shipmates. The enlisted men got along well with each other, with the chiefs, and with the officers. The chiefs were outstanding, the backbone of the ship: veteran career men, experts in their specialties. They were blessed with self-assurance, and they maintained good relationships with both seniors and subordinates. The officers were close and compatible. They supported one another, did not vie for special treatment, were enthusiastic and dedicated, and looked upon the crew as friends and teammates. The prevailing atmosphere aboard the *Sterett* was one of mutual trust and respect. Comdr. J. D. Jeffrey, a former shipmate and a good friend, remarked in a recent letter that "the ship itself was nothing but a thin-hulled shell housing a lot of metal parts, without the crew. . . . They, as much as the metal around them, were the *Sterett*." I agree with that comment but would add that the metal that surrounded us was exceptionally tough and had been expertly welded together.

While hospitalized in 1943–44 with a paralyzed right hand, I wrote a sketchy narrative about my experiences aboard the *Sterett*. It was a form of therapy for the wounded arm, but also a way of recording the story of the men who served on a gallant ship. I hoped to use it someday as the skeleton of a book. But the events of forty-odd years deferred the project until I attended the biannual *Sterett* reunion in 1987 in Bremerton, Washington. I wanted to discuss the idea of writing a book on our old ship with George Respess, a retired chief petty officer for whom I had always had great respect. To my sad surprise, I learned that Respess had passed away only a few weeks before the reunion. It was then apparent that the preparation of a narrative about the *Sterett* had to begin as soon as possible, before more shipmates moved on to their ultimate destinies. I was the after-dinner speaker at the reunion banquet that year, and my subject was the history of the *Sterett*. In concluding, I told those in attendance that if they would help by sending me firsthand accounts of the ship's history after my detachment in April 1943, I would try to put together a book covering the *Sterett*'s entire life span. They assured me that they would cooperate, and I embarked on the effort that now reaches its end in these pages.

More than fifty *Sterett* veterans have contributed anecdotes and narrative accounts for this story. I have drawn on their letters freely, quoting from them when appropriate to present the events aboard the *Sterett* through the eyes of others. The letters, and countless personal conversations with the men of the *Sterett* at ship's reunions and in their homes in Virginia Beach, Charleston, Myrtle Beach, Savannah, Suffolk, Glenwood, and Milford, provided details about life aboard the ship and confirmed the veracity of our reconstruction of events. Several personal diaries were made available, with their invaluable personal insights. It should come as no surprise that the resulting text is not uniform stylistically; but I hope that because it is based on such diverse sources, this story is not just a yarn spun by Cal Calhoun but rather a cross-section of the *Sterett*'s experience that more accurately reflects the attitudes and actions of those who served aboard her. It does not pretend to be a fully documented and precise history, although its authenticity has been reinforced by careful perusal of ship's logs, action reports, and historical texts by many distinguished authors. This narrative is based on recollections, especially those of the principal author. I have transcribed conversations as I remember them, and except for minor changes in punctuation and deletions for the sake of brevity I have quoted the letters and diaries of my *Sterett* friends without alteration. Accordingly, I accept full responsibility for the general authenticity of the narrative. But any errors aside, this is an accurate first-person account of life aboard the *Sterett* from her commissioning in August 1939 until she was stricken from the Navy register in November 1945.

Much has been written about the Guadalcanal Campaign and the critical role played in it by U.S. naval forces. A common thread in all of these accounts is the issue of conflicting or unconfirmed claims of damage done to the enemy. This book cannot resolve this issue, but it does state the facts about the damage inflicted by the *Sterett* during the night action of 13 November 1942 as they appeared to those who were in the gun director and on the bridge. The account of the Third Battle of Savo Island presented in this book reflects countless personal conversations with the principal participants over the half-century since 13 November 1942. What is described here is what the captain, executive officer, gunnery officer, assistant gunnery officer, torpedo officer, assistant damage control officer, rangefinder operator, director trainer, bridge telephone talker, and chief gunner's mate all agreed that they saw in the course of the battle. Their observations confirm that the *Sterett* damaged its Japanese battleship target in the bridge structure with some thirty-six 5-inch shell hits, and in the area of her engineering spaces with two torpedo hits. Our cruiser target was hit by forty-two 5-inch shells in the forecastle and forward gun mounts, and our destroyer target was hit by eight 5-inch shells—four in the bridge structure and four in the after gun mounts, which apparently detonated at the same time as two *Sterett* torpedoes, resulting in a huge explosion. All of us believed that we had destroyed it.

Although she was awarded a Presidential Unit Citation for outstanding performance in the Third Battle of Savo Island, that was by no means the ship's only starring role. The *Sterett* was a key participant in the victorious surface engagement at Vella Gulf in August 1943, came under heavy sustained air attacks countless times during the next two years, and distinguished herself by heroic conduct while on radar picket station at Okinawa in April 1945. Not many destroyers managed to place themselves in harm's way more often than the USS *Sterett*.

One of my main concerns was to give full credit to the officers and men who served aboard the *Sterett* after my detachment in April 1943. That task was made easier by the valuable contributions of many of those who served during that period. The true measure of success in my task, however, will be whether the reader finishes this book with the conviction that the *Sterett*'s performance was consistent with the highest traditions of the U.S. Navy throughout her lifetime. Accordingly, I close with a special salute to Frank Gould, "Champ" Blouin, and "Gordy" Williams, who commanded this magnificent little destroyer through the multitude of actions in which she participated from 10 April 1943 until the war's end.

ACKNOWLEDGMENTS

URING MUCH OF THE PAST THREE YEARS, the writing of this book has required that I recall to mind the personal experiences of the years 1939–1945, without question the most exciting years of my life. Dwelling in that sanctuary of memories has enabled me to enjoy again the company of my shipmates from the USS *Sterett* (DD 407). It has been an enriching interlude, and I am grateful for it.

Tin Can Sailor represents the combined efforts of many people, each of whom contributed something unique and essential to the story. I want to acknowledge here the gifts offered by every one of them, although it is likely that I will inadvertently miss mentioning some deserving person. To any such individual I offer my apology and promise a personal letter of thanks if and when the omission comes to my attention.

Number one on my priority list is my wonderful wife, Betsy. For the entire period of book gestation she endured a status akin to widowhood; I disappeared into the study day after day, emerging only at mealtimes to utter generally unintelligible comments about ships, boats, guns, and such. Without her help and inspiration there would have been no book. To my daughter, Susan, another loving supporter, I am indebted for astute editorial suggestions, all gratefully accepted, and for a professional manuscript typing job that merits a "Well Done."

Sterett shipmate J. D. Jeffrey has been a tower of strength and a prolific contributor to the manuscript. His research effort at the National Archives, his many letters to me, his visit to our North Carolina home to offer his assistance in moving the project to a successful conclusion, his writing efforts in producing the account of the Battle of Vella Gulf and other important events, and his several candid discussions with me concerning the substance of the story were all invaluable. His self-motivated compilation of the personnel roster (Appendix 2), which lists the name of every individual (832 in all) who ever served aboard the *Sterett*, was a greatly appreciated contribution.

Gordy Williams kindly offered his excellent eyewitness account of the *Sterett*'s kamikaze experience (previously published in *Shipmate* magazine, March 1988). With permission of *Shipmate* I have quoted it almost in its entirety. Frank Gould furnished both written and oral comments regarding the Vella Gulf engagement, which were very helpful. Vice Adm. Champ Blouin had several personal conversations with me about his experiences aboard the *Sterett*, and later embellished those remarks in several long letters. His observations about the people who were fortunate enough to serve with him were especially considerate. Perry Hall and his wife, Pat, made a special trip to North Carolina to spend several days scanning and commenting on the bundle of letters that *Sterett* veterans had submitted for use in constructing the story of their ship. He also provided accounts of his personal experiences, which are quoted in the text. Tim Cleere contributed his diary, which disclosed a keen understanding of strategy and tactics. Several of his penetrating observations are quoted in the book. Roy Cowdrey, Carl Hibben, Bob Hightower, Gordon Hanna, L. G. Keenum, Doc Scharbius, Doc Lea, Red Hammack, Felix Gebert, Neal Fugate, and Leonard Woods all made generous and valuable written submissions. Felix also handled the mailing of letters to each of those who had provided anecdotal material, requesting authorization to quote their comments. In addition, the following also responded to the call for individual recollections of *Sterett* history: E. J. Andrews, J. R. Choban, W. P. Connors, W. H. Deuel, C. W. Edwards, G. Gates, P. Grimm, G. S. Husby, F. E. Janzen, A. Lester, A. Leisinger, H. E. Lineberry, C. H. LeFebvre, W. Myer, S. Montenegro, R. H. Priest, D. W. Palmer, R. R. Terrano, C. J. Violette, and F. T. Woolard.

Alice Creighton, Head of Special Collections at the Nimitz Library, Dean Allard, Director of the Naval Historical Center, and Capt. Vic Delano, class of '41 secretary, were all cooperative and gracious in responding to my request for specific research assistance. Their help is much appreciated.

A special note of thanks goes to Frank McWhorter, brother of Comdr. Thomas O. McWhorter, and to Tom's widow, Ina K. Rundles, for their generous permission to quote from Tom's unpublished manuscript *Stand and Fight*, which describes so vividly the treatment of the *Sterett*'s wounded on the morning of 13 November 1942. All of my shipmates and I are indebted to Tom for his heroic service on the *Sterett* and for his eloquent description of life aboard our ship while he was a member of her ship's company.

Naval Institute Press Director Tom Epley, to whom I first addressed a letter of inquiry concerning this book, was the critical element in providing "Lift-Off." His evident interest and encouragement were responsible for my decision to move ahead with the project. Two other Naval Institute Press staff members played significant roles in the book's development. Acquisitions Editor Mark Gatlin deserves special mention for his patience, his suggestions regarding the scope of the narrative, and his perseverance and trust throughout a long and frustrating metamorphosis. Managing Editor Mary Lou Kenney provided innovative and constructive guidelines for final revision and editing and then wisely selected freelancer J. Randall Baldini as the manuscript editor. Their efforts were supported by a number of outside readers (all unknown to me except for Comdr. Ed Stafford and Carlo E. Coletta) whose insights and constructive criticism led to major improvements.

Finally, a sincere expression of gratitude to the officers and men of the *Sterett*. They provided me with continuing support and made the writing of this narrative a privilege and a pleasure.

CHAPTER 1

SHAKEDOWN

THE SEARCHLIGHT FROM THE JAPANESE BATTLESHIP swept down our column from the *Cushing* to the *San Francisco*, where it came to rest. Every ship ahead of the *San Francisco* had been disclosed to the enemy in that one rapid sweep of blinding blue-white light. Everyone opened fire at once. In the waters of Iron Bottom Sound, the world exploded. Tracers whistled overhead so close that I felt I could touch them if I raised my hand. The noise and concussions were deafening, but even in that din I recognized the sound of the *Helena*'s 6-inch guns as she blasted a salvo straight into the Japanese searchlight. It was extinguished in an instant, but her guns kept firing. They seemed to stutter as they went off—"B-B-Boom! B-B-Boom!" We saw them hit their mark repeatedly.

Enemy shells splashed on both sides of the *Sterett*. Our own tracers hit squarely on the forecastle of our target. It was illuminated in a most unique way: the *Sterett*'s guns had been loaded with star shells for our first salvo, and we had fired them to hit rather than to illuminate. Hit they did, and when they detonated the "stars" inside broke out of their casings and burned brightly on the deck of the target. She soon caught fire in the vicinity of her number two turret. We hit her again and again and could have done more damage had the *O'Bannon* not overtaken us and obstructed our line of fire. Seeing her move up rapidly on our starboard quarter, we checked fire and swung our guns up ahead, looking for another target.

The short lull gave me a chance to look around at the terrific fight that was under way. In every direction ships were shooting, burning, or exploding—and some were doing all three. On our starboard quarter, the *Atlanta* was almost completely enveloped in red flames. I wondered how anyone could survive that inferno. One enemy salvo crashed down her port side, hitting her 5-inch gun mounts and causing spectacular explosions. But still she fought furiously, sending a constant stream of tracers out toward the enemy. Ahead of us a destroyer was on fire—I thought it was the *Laffey*—while another unidentified friend burned to our rear. But several Japanese ships were also blazing brightly.

Overhead were star shells and aircraft flares galore, all exceptionally bright and long-burning. There seemed to be at least one of their pyrotechnic parachutes hanging in the sky above us at all times. The fires and explosions all around us also cast a brilliant light over the whole area. Tracers still zipped past my head, some from the port side and some from up ahead. I watched several of them approach. Each looked as though it would hit us squarely in the gun director, until in an instant it thundered or whistled past. It was a damned uncomfortable thing to watch. I turned away and looked for a new target. From the rangefinder station, Jack Shelton observed that both the *Cushing* and the *Laffey* appeared to be severely damaged and out of action. That placed the *Sterett* in the van of the formation—if indeed there was a formation left.

I pressed my chest-set telephone contact button and began to describe the scene to the gun captains as best I could. Seconds later there came a sudden, blinding flash. The whole gun director shook, and we were showered with shell fragments. I could hear them and feel them bounce off my padded talker's helmet. One of them neatly clipped the telephone button out from under my finger, leaving me just the stub of a pin to press in order to keep my microphone open. In the moment of comparative silence that followed, I asked whether anyone in the director crew had been hit. They responded quietly and calmly—first Byers, seated only inches to my left, then Jeff, who was a foot or so in front of me, and then Shelton, from the very front of the director.

"Yes, I am."

"Yeah, I think so."

"Yes, in the back."

"Anyone in bad shape?" was my next question. Jeff and Shelton both thought they were OK, but Byers said he had been hit in the neck, and that really concerned me. I reached out with my left hand to touch the back of his neck. I could feel a puncture wound, but because there was no spurting arterial bleeding I told him it did not seem too serious. I asked if anyone felt that he needed immediate treatment. Instantly, all three answered with a loud and definite "No!" So we sat there more alert than ever, looking for fresh targets. We were on the prowl again.

EVEN IN OUR WILDEST FANTASIES in the spring of 1939, none of us imagined that by November 1942 we would find ourselves aboard a little destroyer called the *Sterett* slugging it out at murderously close range against a Japanese cruiser—with a battleship and a destroyer to follow. In April 1939 President Roosevelt conducted a formal review of the U.S. fleet in New York. The USS *Tennessee* (BB 49) made the transit from the Pacific for the occasion, and I was serving aboard that venerable man-of-war on my first tour of duty after graduating from Annapolis with the class of '38. I had enjoyed my tour on the *Tennessee*, but by the time of the visit to New York I wanted a transfer from the big-ship to the little-ship Navy. Duty in destroyers had become my preference two years before, when my Naval Academy class had gone on a summer cruise in ships of that type. Now the Navy was rapidly expanding to meet the growing threat of war, and the nucleus of officers required to man those new ships had to come

Lt. Comdr. Atherton Macondray *(left)* and Lt. Watson T. Singer, the *Sterett*'s first commanding and executive officers, established a "can do" spirit and a winning attitude, both of which lasted throughout the ship's lifetime. (Author's collection)

from the fleet. I hoped to be reassigned to one of the brand-new destroyers that were just coming off the building ways.

The orders arrived and fulfilled my hopes. I was to "proceed to Charleston, S.C., and report to the Commandant, Sixth Naval District, for duty in connection with the fitting out of the USS *Sterett*, at the Navy Yard, and on board that vessel when commissioned." On 1 May I left the *Tennessee* and took a train to Charleston. The next day, a Sunday, I took a cab to the Navy Yard to look at this new destroyer that was soon to become my home.

The *Sterett*'s appearance was a far cry from that of the *Tennessee*. The latter's gleaming brightwork, fresh light-gray paint, smartly uniformed quarterdeck watch, and spotless white teakwood decks marked her as a proud man-of-war. Looking at this lifeless ship, I felt a twinge of regret. My mind's eye had envisioned a sleek craft, with perhaps a clipper bow and rakish mast and stacks. After all, this was one of a new class of destroyers with state-of-the-art design features, and I had expected something more compatible with the "greyhound of the sea" image of the "tin can" Navy. This ship was definitely not attractive. She had a stubby stack and a high, straight, ungraceful bow. The large white numerals "407" painted on each side of the bow, just aft of her housed anchors, did nothing to enhance her appearance. Steam hoses, electrical leads, water lines, and an array of tools and pumps cluttered her topside. Finally, my gaze shifted to her squat stern, where the black letters "STERETT" disclosed her name. Whatever her good qualities, beauty was not one of them. I wondered what life would be like on this new destroyer. Always an optimist, I told myself that appearances are superficial. At least she looked rugged and seaworthy.

The first *Sterett* officer I met was Lt. (jg) James Clute, Naval Academy class of '34 and the *Sterett's* first lieutenant. Jim was a 6-foot, 1-inch former varsity pitcher with a droll sense of humor. He called me at the hotel that evening, having guessed that I might have arrived. We had dinner together, and he filled me in on the other officers, who had already reported. The commanding officer was Lt. Comdr. Atherton Macondray, USNA '21, a Virginia gentleman; the executive officer was Lt. Watson T. Singer, USNA '25, a tall, square-shouldered, gruff veteran of the China Station; the gunnery officer was Lt. Frank Winant, USNA '30, blonde, short, and slight, a graduate of the Navy's postgraduate school in naval ordnance; the chief engineer was Lt. Frank P. Luongo, USNA '30, a graduate of the Navy's postgraduate course in marine engineering; and the communications officer was Ens. Richard Hughes, USNA '37. I was the assistant engineer, and because I was the junior officer I also served as the "George," handling all of the additional duties—mess treasurer, welfare officer, and officer-in-charge of the landing party—that no one else wanted.

All of the officers from the captain to Dick Hughes (whom I had known and liked at the Academy) were friendly and helpful. The common background of Annapolis provided a strong bond among us, and we soon became a closely knit team. As the junior ensign I was the butt of some good-natured ribbing, but the attitudes and actions of my messmates conveyed a sense of trust and acceptance. The most outstanding character among the officers belonged to "Watso" Singer. He was a great teller of sea stories, a fine seaman and ship handler, and a tough disciplinarian. He was also a self-professed "black sheep" who often entertained us with tales of his escapades as a bachelor ensign in China. Watso possessed great courage and an uncanny capacity for common sense. In the two years that we spent as shipmates aboard the *Sterett*, I never knew him to be unfair. The men loved him. He was exacting in his insistence on top-flight performance and industrious in his role as executive officer. More important, he was the kind of stern and uncompromising mentor I needed at that time. I was intent on performing at my best while aboard, but just as intent on raising hell when I went ashore. Watso must have seen something in me that reminded him of his own wild days. When I needed tough discipline, he willingly supplied it. In only a few months he

The USS *Sterett* as she appeared in September 1939. (U.S. Navy Photo)

managed to convince me that I was on the road to disaster and turn me completely around.

For the first three months we were kept busy checking the installation of equipment, the loading of supplies, and the organization of personnel, who arrived in increasing numbers every day. Within a couple of weeks, all of our chief petty officers and the majority of our first- and second-class petty officers had arrived and were hard at work checking their department inventories. Frank Winant supervised the gunnery installation, inspected the fuse setting mechanisms in the shell hoists, ran tests on the fire control circuitry, and assessed the operation of the main battery director. Jimmy Clute was engrossed in the acquisition of our deck force equipment, including a full suit of manila lines for mooring, zinc chromate, red lead, paint, brushes, brooms, cleaning gear, tools, foul weather clothing, and a thousand other items. Dick Hughes supervised the placement of our radio and sonar equipment. I worked with Frank Luongo, tracing out steam, oil, and water lines and preparing sketches of their "as is" installation. We also checked on the installation of pumps, valves, boiler tubes, reduction gears, and myriad other details to ensure that everything in the engineering department was properly hooked up and ready for operation.

Meanwhile, Captain Macondray made it clear to us that our *Sterett* (DD 407) would begin her naval service under the banner of a proud name and a heroic tradition. She had been christened in honor of Andrew Sterett, who in 1801, commanding the schooner USS *Enterprise*, captured a fourteen-gun Tripolitan cruiser and her eighty-man crew in the Mediterranean. Congress awarded a sword to Lieutenant Sterett and commended his crew for their bravery. This history added an unmistakable luster to the privilege of belonging to the ship's company of the new *Sterett*. Although she was not very pretty, we were determined that this ship would live up to her name.

The *Sterett* belonged to the twelve-ship *McCall* class. She was designed for 36.5 knots and sported superheated, high-pressure boilers, twin screws, geared turbines, and a range of ten thousand sea miles. Her armament at commissioning would comprise sixteen 21-inch torpedo tubes in four quadruple mounts (the most ever mounted in destroyers); four 5-inch, 38-caliber dual-purpose guns; and four 1.1-inch antiaircraft mounts (although by the time she was commissioned it had been decided to replace these with 20-mm guns, which were more dependable). She displaced 1,500 tons, was 341 feet long and 34 feet, 10 inches in the beam, drew 9 feet, 10 inches, and had a rated horsepower of 42,800. The *Sterett's* statistics were a lot more impressive than her looks, and they served to reassure us that she would make a formidable opponent for any enemy she might encounter. It would be up to those who manned her to ensure that she came out a winner.

The *Sterett*'s hard-working chief petty officers were the backbone of the ship. (Author's collection)

The *Sterett* was commissioned at Charleston, South Carolina, on 15 August 1939, while the world was filled with rumors of war in Europe. Hitler blustered and threatened aggression with sinister belligerence. England and France were unable to prevent him from taking what he wanted, and two weeks after our ship was commissioned we received the secretary of the navy's message to all naval ships: "Germany has entered Poland, fighting and bombing in progress. You will govern yourselves accordingly." We were not quite sure what that last sentence meant, but aboard the *Sterett* we were convinced that the war would not be contained and that sooner or later we would be in it. On 6 September 1939 President Roosevelt announced the establishment of a Neutrality Patrol to report the presence of any belligerent ships within two to three hundred miles of the East Coast. The situation lent a new sense of urgency to our efforts to make the ship and her crew as battle-efficient as possible, for none of us thought that we would remain neutral very long.

By early June I had become acquainted with most of our leading petty officers, and I made a habit of dropping by the chief petty officer's mess to chat with them at least once a day. They were with few exceptions wise, mature, and competent men. Jackson and Baker were probably the oldest of the lot. George R. Jackson was the chief torpedoman; a veteran of World War I, he had fought at the Battle of the Marne and had a calm, unflappable demeanor. He confided to me that he had enlisted in the Navy to escape from a woman who had "done him wrong." He soon became the "scoutmaster" for all the younger sailors, and his contribution to morale was immeasurable and widely recognized up and down the chain of command. William J. Baker was the chief quartermaster and an excellent navigator. I never heard him raise his voice to anyone, yet he never had a problem with discipline. The other chief petty officers (their names are listed in Appendix 2) were all outstanding team players who wanted to make the *Sterett* shine.

Most of the junior enlisted men were required to participate in the Navy's self-education program, which was similar to a series of correspondence courses. Well-organized and clearly written study materials outlined weekly assignments that were designed to impart the theoretical knowledge needed for advancement up the ratings of one's chosen category. Periodic tests were graded by the appropriate division officers. An individual's progress generally kept pace with the availability of promotion vacancies created by an expanding Navy. The Great Depression had raised the quality of enlisted personnel. The average recruit had three years of high school education, and reenlistment rates hovered between 70 and 80 percent. It was a joy to be associated with the *Sterett's* enlisted men. They were smart, alert, and enthusiastic.

From August to October the *Sterett* and her crew were fitted out, organized, and trained. She went to sea as a commissioned ship for the first time on 6 September 1939 so that we could familiarize ourselves with her maneuvering characteristics. She was very responsive to the rudder, and the surges of power that were apparent as we accelerated made her feel strong and alive. All of us shared the conviction that the Charleston Navy Yard had provided us with a superior fighting ship. The skipper seized the opportunity to conduct general quarters, fire, collision, abandon ship, and man overboard drills. There was little confusion, thanks to several scheduled instruction periods in port over the preceding weeks. We returned to the yard that afternoon. The skipper brought the ship alongside the pier, and while it was not a spectacular landing it was not a bad one either. Our first day at sea was a success.

During the next several weeks we experienced numerous difficulties with the main reduction gears and the boiler safety valves, which popped open whenever the engines were under stress. But the contractors dispatched representatives to ride with us, and they and Frank Luongo quickly worked out the problems. The *Sterett's* engineering plant became as dependable as a railroad conductor's watch.

Our shakedown cruise commenced in October with a visit to Newport, Rhode Island, where we received our full torpedo complement (sixteen 21-inch "fish"). Next we stopped in Norfolk to repair damage sustained during our first North Atlantic gale and then proceeded to Veracruz, Mexico, to join the other ships of Destroyer Division 15 (the *Lang*, the *Wilson*, and the *Stack*) for a brief period during their surveillance of

The battleship *North Carolina*, as seen from the deck of an unidentified destroyer. This was the scene observed on almost any day from the deck of the *Sterett* during her many months in the wintry North Atlantic. This was a relatively calm sea—it was often much rougher. (U.S. Navy Photo)

the German liner *Columbus*, which had sought refuge in a neutral port. The *Sterett* resumed her shakedown cruise in early December, visiting Guantánamo Bay, Mobile, and Savannah. In Savannah we learned that the *Columbus* had made a run for it but was intercepted by the British destroyer *Hyperion*. The German crew had set the *Columbus* afire and scuttled her rather than turning her over to the British.

We returned to Charleston on 20 December 1939. The shakedown cruise marked our first sustained period of at-sea watch standing, and all officers qualified as top watch-standers. The cruise also demonstrated to Dick Hughes (and to his shipmates) that he was subject to chronic seasickness. He earned our respect and admiration by never missing his turn on watch, even though he always had to bring a bucket with him. Anticipating a transfer to Pensacola to train as a naval aviator, he looked forward to an early end to his problem. We all wondered at the logic of that view.

The first several months of 1940 were spent operating along the East Coast. As part of the Neutrality Patrol, we often chased down foreign merchant ships, established their identities, and reported their locations, courses, and speeds. The North Atlantic in any season is cold, bleak, and

The *Sterett*'s ship's company in San Diego, June 1940. Officers, *from left to right*, Calhoun, Hughes, Winant, Macondray, Luongo, Clute, and Scofield. (Author's collection)

rough; remaining at sea in the winter was itself an ordeal. Our enlisted men were in danger of being washed overboard every time they came topside. Unfortunately, coming topside was the only way they could get from their living quarters aft to their watch-standing stations forward. The common experience of combating a hostile sea welded us together. There were countless times when the entire bridge watch consisted of a lone officer (the officer of the deck) and five sailors (quartermaster, signalman, helmsman, engine-order telegraph operator, and telephone talker) who held the fate of the ship in their hands. Each had an important job to do, and each appreciated and depended on the others. We came to know one another and to respect our shipmates for their dependability and competence. To be out on the wing of a destroyer's bridge in a blinding snowstorm with a sturdy sailor standing next to you, both of you straining to see through a swirl of white into the inky darkness—such shared experiences built a level of camaraderie unique to life aboard a destroyer. Several times during a watch like that, one of your companions would bring out a cup of steaming coffee—"How about a cup of joe, Mr. Calhoun?" And later you would return the favor. When conditions were exceptionally bad, Watso or the skipper would join us. No wonder we felt close to one another.

In the spring the high command ordered the *Sterett* to deploy to Pearl Harbor. On 12 May 1940 our Panama Canal pilot took us into the Gatun Locks in company with the *Hammann* (DD 412), another new destroyer. We made the transit from Gatun to the Miraflores Locks and thence to Balboa and the Pacific without incident. The weather was sunny and warm, and I thought how wonderful it was to leave the bleak North Atlantic behind. As we steamed north from Panama to San Diego we passed through thousands of miles of calm, aquamarine waters, with gentle swells and hundreds of huge sea turtles. It was like moving into another world, and the peace of the Pacific seemed to have an impact on the human relationships aboard ship. We now considered ourselves veteran sailors.

ON 2 JULY 1940 the *Sterett* arrived at Pearl Harbor for duty as a unit of the Pacific Fleet. As we approached the channel buoys I could see Aloha Tower, which issued the traffic control instructions for the busy harbor of Honolulu. We anchored in one of Pearl Harbor's little bays near Pearl City, and the captain spent the rest of the day making courtesy calls on the senior officers in our chain of command. I was impressed with the number and variety of ships in that huge base: battleships, carriers, cruisers, destroyers, submarines, oilers, supply ships, and other auxiliaries. Ship's boats flitted about like a swarm of water bugs. We had joined the Navy at last, and we felt the pride of belonging.

Within a few weeks of our arrival, Waikiki (with its Royal Hawaiian and Moana hotels), Aloha Tower, the Section Base, Ford Island, Battleship Row, the Navy Yard, West Loch, and Diamond Head all became familiar names and sights to us. From my viewpoint, the most important development was the departure of Dick Hughes, who was bound for Pensacola. I moved up to the post of communications officer, and Ens. Hugh B. Sanders, USNA '39, relieved me as assistant engineer. We cruised down to the vicinity of Jarvis Island, crossing the equator for the first time on 23 July 1940. All of us became "shellbacks." Our initiation was memorable: all "pollywogs" were subjected to the same ordeal, officer and enlisted alike. First we were tried for a variety of "offenses." After the inevitable guilty verdict we were sentenced to a shave and a haircut by the Royal Barber (which involved a fuel-oil shampoo and some especially nasty-looking, foul-smelling shaving cream), a swimming lesson in Neptune's pool (with two or three of the biggest, toughest instructors, who proceeded to half-drown the victims), and finally a trip on our hands and knees through a gauntlet of paddle-wielding sailors who appeared to consider it a matter of honor to deliver a bell ringer with every swat. It was legalized mayhem—but I never knew anyone to be really hurt by it, and it always was accompanied by a spirit of fun and good sportsmanship.

When we returned to Pearl Harbor a short time later, our operating schedule took on a predictable pattern. We would get under way on Monday morning, proceed to a designated area, conduct assigned operations until Friday evening, and return to Pearl Harbor on Saturday morning. Sometimes we went in company with our division mates the *Lang*, the *Wilson*, and the *Stack*. We conducted individual ship exercises (ISE) for a couple of days—air and surface gunnery shoots, ship-handling tests, man overboard drills, and damage control exercises. After a full program of ISE, we spent the next several days operating with the division as a tactical unit. Steaming in column three hundred yards apart (often at night at speeds of 20 knots or more, with the ships darkened), we learned how to judge the distance to the ship ahead by the size of the image in the field of our binoculars. It was more of an art than a science, and we took pride in our ability to maintain station accurately. It called for heads-up ball, and there was certainly nothing boring about it.

This first deployment also drew the wardroom officers closer together. We got to know each other aboard ship as well as ashore, where we often had dinner together or went to a show. Only Jim Clute and I were bachelors, but because none of the wardroom wives had come to Honolulu one or more of the remaining officers would accompany us on shore leave from time to time. Usually we went ashore on Saturday afternoon, spent a couple of hours on the beach, ate dinner at the Moana or the Royal Hawaiian, gathered with friends from other ships in the lounge, and took part in bull sessions until the wee hours of the morning before returning to the ship. Sundays were perfect for quiet trips around the island, picnics, beach parties, or just for basking in the glorious sunshine for which Waikiki is so famous. Our operating schedule moved us around to other islands in the Hawaiian chain. The island of Hawaii, with its awe-inspiring volcano, was my favorite port of call. On one trip to the summit Jim Clute and I watched nervously as Watso, with the kind of nonchalance engendered by one too many martinis, walked to within inches of the crater to peer down inside. I refused to go closer than three or four feet.

Eventually, it came time for our navy yard refit. The *Sterett* returned to San Diego on 8 December 1940 for a brief but extensive overhaul; this gave me just enough time to return to Charleston and marry Virginia Taylor of Winston-Salem, North Carolina—the wisest move of my entire Navy career.

The ship returned to Pearl Harbor on 27 January 1941. For the next four months we concentrated on destroyer operations, focusing on anti-submarine warfare (against our own target sub) and on air-defense training (in which our target was a towed sleeve). We also engaged in torpedo firing exercises, but we rarely fired the "fish" for fear that we might lose one; they occasionally sank instead of surfacing at the end of their run. The loss of a torpedo usually resulted in a letter of reprimand for the torpedo officer and unfavorable comments on the skipper's report of fitness. The Navy's high command tended to blame any damage to expensive weaponry on personnel error. Consequently, the preparation and maintenance of such equipment were accorded the greatest concentration and care. Our highest priority in torpedo firing exercises was not hitting the target but rather recovering the torpedo.

Meanwhile, the complexion of our shipboard duties underwent a significant change. Our new division commander, Comdr. Don P. Moon, shifted his command pennant to the *Sterett*. Suddenly we were a flagship, and I became the communications officer to the division commander as well as to my ship. I soon learned that the words *work* and *busy* had an entirely new range of meanings. The commodore was a vigorous, ambitious workaholic, and it took a full head of steam to keep up with him.

One night during tactical maneuvers, with all fleet units darkened, the destroyers *Aylwin* and *Farragut* collided. It happened quite close to us, and we could see that the *Aylwin* was on fire in the vicinity just forward of her bridge. Captain Macondray brought the *Sterett* as close as possible to the cripples and sent a rescue party. When it reached the *Aylwin* their own damage control party already had the situation in hand. Our boatload of volunteers placed themselves under the command of the

Aylwin's first lieutenant and remained aboard for about two hours, helping to fight the fire and shoring up bulkheads that had been weakened by the collision. When they returned to the *Sterett* and reported that the major fire hazard they encountered was the accumulation of many coats of paint, Captain Macondray lost no time in initiating a paint-chipping program. Commodore Moon mandated the same action for the other ships in our division, and before long it was a standard procedure for the entire Pacific Fleet.

The *Sterett's* officer complement increased by two in this period as Ens. T. O. McWhorter, USNA '41, and Ens. P. G. Hayden joined our ranks. Tom McWhorter's enthusiasm and friendly manner made him popular immediately with both the officers and the crew, and he was named our torpedo officer. Gardie Hayden, a handsome reserve officer from Appleton, Wisconsin, conveyed a sense of quiet competence; he became the assistant first lieutenant, under Jim Clute.

The desk log for the forenoon watch on 2 May 1941 contains the following entry: "0812—Lt. Comdr. A. Macondray, USN, was relieved of command of this vessel by Lt. Comdr. J. G. Coward, USN, in accordance with Bureau of Navigation dispatch 281418 of March 1941, and was detached this date.—/s/ P. G. Hayden." All hands regretted the departure of Atherton Macondray. He was an outstanding destroyer commanding officer and had set the tone and established the standards for the *Sterett's* development. We knew that we would miss his even disposition and his infallible sense of fairness. We turned to the new skipper with hope and confidence.

Jesse G. Coward was a completely different entity. My first impression was that we had exchanged the good humor of Atherton Macondray for a sour martinet. But as I was to learn a hundred times over the next thirty years, looks are often deceiving. Beneath Jess Coward's serious mien resided a fair and compassionate personality, as well as a good sense of humor. His dedication to the naval service and his can-do attitude were contagious, and he imparted to all of us a renewed desire to go in harm's way. He was a fighter, looking ahead to the day when he could take the *Sterett* into action. Every day he made it clear that we had to prepare for the battles that lay ahead. The *Sterett* volunteered for every task that came along, and we found ourselves sharing a new pride in the ship's growing reputation as a star performer on the first team. The atmosphere in the wardroom was upbeat and positive. The mess deck and the CPO mess reflected the same attitude.

The presence of the division commander and his staff aboard the *Sterett* made a difference from the moment that Commander Moon first stepped aboard. We liked his staff, but the commodore was aloof and preoccupied. Our enlisted men seemed to like him, a fact that made me think he possessed certain qualities that for some reason he preferred to conceal from the officers. Perhaps he thought we would benefit from a good dose of hazing; but whatever his reasons most of the officers appeared to be wary and ill at ease around him, Atherton Macondray and Watso excepted. Jess Coward initially seemed uncomfortable too, as though he expected some kind of trap. I found this quite understandable: the commodore had a habit of springing surprise drills on the officer-of-the-deck, and his manner conveyed a sense of skepticism and distrust.

Commander Moon proved to be one of the most interesting people I ever met. He was unpredictable, constantly asking questions about the ship's position, course, speed, tactical maneuvers, cruising range, fuel consumption, and seaworthiness. His questions always served a purpose, and it was essential to stay one step ahead of him. Yet at times his actions seemed somewhat strange. For example, at night it was not unusual to find him reading in bed and listening through headphones to the fleet broadcast of the FOX schedules, messages addressed to any and sometimes all naval ships and units that were transmitted on an hourly schedule and a prescribed frequency in five-letter groups of Morse code—not everyone's idea of entertainment. Once as we approached Pearl Harbor at night he told Jim Clute, the officer-of-the-deck, to take a compass bearing on the star Polaris. That may have made sense to some navigational experts, but it was beyond our ken.

Don Moon was also a prolific message writer, and it was a rare day when the *Sterett's* signalmen and quartermasters were not exhausted by nightfall. Their heavy work load soon started to affect their morale. After about three weeks of watching them transmit four-hundred-group dispatches by flashing light, I decided to surprise the commodore by confronting him with the total group-count of outgoing message traffic for the month. I expected that when he realized just how much visual traffic he was generating, he might ease up a bit. Accordingly, one morning when we were engaged in ISE I went down to the radio shack and enlisted the help of Chief Radioman Lillard in collecting and tabulating the total visual group-count for the past thirty days. It took about two hours to do the job, but when we finished the adding machine tape must have stretched for ten feet—and the total was astronomical, somewhere above ten thousand. Convinced that this would startle the squadron commander (it had certainly impressed me), I climbed the ladder to the bridge, where he was engrossed in watching one of our division mates through his binoculars. I approached him and stood quietly, waiting for him to acknowledge my presence. In a few minutes he put his glasses down and looked at me. "Did you have something for me?" "Yes, sir," I said. "I thought you might be interested to know how many groups of visual traffic have been handled by the *Sterett's* signal gang in the past thirty days."

By now he had noticed the adding machine tape trailing from my hand and was obviously interested. "All right, how many?" He did not bat an eye when I mentioned the total, instead asking, "How did you arrive at that figure?"

"By running a tape of the group-counts from our message files," I replied.

"How long did that take?"

"About two hours."

"Did you run the tape yourself?"

"Yes, sir."

He nodded. "Go do it again."

Well, I thought, he's hazing me, but this might still work. I had of course only one possible response, so I mustered the cheeriest "Aye aye, sir!" that I could manage and went below to count up the message units all over again. When I finished, the second total came in six groups under the first. I trudged back up to the bridge, where "the Dipper" (as we sometimes referred to him) was now eating lunch. "Well," he asked, "did you get the same total?" "No, sir. It's six groups less." He immediately shot back, "So that first total you brought me was inaccurate?" "Yes, sir." Now he fixed his eyes on me for perhaps three or four seconds. Then the slightest suggestion of a smile came to his face. He said, "I am aware that I have been pushing the signal gang pretty hard. I wanted it to be the best in the fleet, and the best way to achieve that is to make them work at it." That ended the episode, but later that afternoon he addressed a message to the commanding officer extolling the performance of the *Sterett*'s signal gang during the past month. It had been worth the effort, and Leading Signalman Jeffery and his men were visibly encouraged by Don Moon's words of praise.

While at Pearl Harbor we suffered another major loss: Watso was promoted to lieutenant commander and promptly reassigned to a repair ship. He had been a giant in guiding the *Sterett*'s development as an efficient man-of-war. Like Atherton Macondray, he deserved a share of the credit for her performance in the difficult days ahead. I felt Watso's loss very keenly and wondered how we could ever function without him—but of course we did. Lt. "Red" Everett came aboard as the new executive officer. He was a small man with a temper that seemed to match his red hair and a very "regulation" attitude. After a short acquaintanceship, he became one of us. The *Sterett* took all these changes in stride.

CHAPTER 2

ATLANTIC OPERATIONS

ON 14 MAY 1941 the *Sterett* was returning to Pearl Harbor after division tactical exercises. The commodore had had a great time putting us through our paces, and we felt pretty good about our performance. I was on the bridge and could see several heavy ships standing out the channel. We pulled off to the right and stopped, watching their progress out of the channel with some impatience. In the lead was the battleship *Mississippi*, and pretty soon one of her signalmen trained a light in our direction and began to flash our call, "DD 407." Jeffery jumped to our signal light and responded. The dots and dashes now spelled out the words "follow me." Captain Coward immediately took a course to put us behind the *Mississippi*, and within about fifteen minutes we found ourselves headed south, five hundred yards behind the broad stern of the battleship. I could not imagine why the *Mississippi* would direct the *Sterett* to follow her. We were accompanied by a cruiser and two other destroyers from our division, the *Lang* and the *Wilson*. As Pearl Harbor gradually receded over the northern horizon, I realized that we would not enter port that weekend.

Then the squat-sterned behemoth ahead of us flashed another message: "Come alongside to receive guard mail." The skipper kicked her ahead fifty feet to the right of the *Mississippi's* wake until our bow overlapped her stern. A husky boatswain's mate 2/c named Byers was our best pitcher when it came to heaving lines. Standing in our bow, he threw the coiled line toward the battleship's stern; the monkey-fist arched through the air and came down in the midst of her line handlers. They quickly hauled it in and attached a small waterproof bag to it. On signal, our sailors hauled it back aboard the *Sterett*. I had gone down to the forecastle to receive the mail. It consisted of two letters, one addressed to the commander of Destroyer Division 15 and the other to the commanding officer of the USS *Sterett*. I hurried to the bridge with them, delivered the first to the commodore, and handed the second to the captain, who quietly opened and read it. Then he gave it back to me, saying, "Cal, file this, and note its classification. It should be closely held, on a need-to-know basis." I saw that it was stamped "Secret" and hurriedly read it.

We had been assigned to screen the *Mississippi* and the cruiser *Savannah* through the Panama Canal as reinforcements for the Atlantic Fleet. President Roosevelt was concerned that the British could not handle the

German threat without the support of the U.S. Navy. The redeployment was to be kept secret; there would be no communication by radio, mail, or direct contact with personnel ashore when we made our canal transit. We were to paint out our bow numerals, cover the ship's name, and obliterate any other identifying marks or symbols. Of course my shipmates were all curious about our destination. Since Red Everett was the navigator, he had to know, but I told no one else. The crew came up with a wide range of possibilities, including the occupation of Tahiti, but within a few days a consensus emerged that we were headed to join the Atlantic Fleet in case it became necessary to capture Martinique, where units of the French fleet had taken refuge.

Commodore Moon made the voyage to the canal memorable. He must have felt that if we had been left to the devices of the individual commanding officers, the officers and men of the three destroyers would have wasted a lot of valuable time. In any case, he originated and delivered to the *Sterett's* signal gang a series of lengthy messages on two unrelated subjects, the first of which was the establishment of an intership athletic contest—what we dubbed "the Moon Olympics." For the next six days each destroyer would hold seven athletic contests (standing broad jump, running broad jump, standing high jump, running high jump, chin-ups, push-ups, and the hop, skip, and jump) and signal the results to the commodore. Commissioned and chief petty officers competed against their opposite numbers on the other ships, while enlisted men participated according to their ratings, so that we had to announce a winner in each event in each rating: the best seaman, the best fireman, the best radioman, the best signalman, the best torpedoman—the list seemed endless.

At first the whole idea seemed laughable, especially when I tried to envision some of the older chiefs—some in their late fifties—and the more senior officers taking part. I fully expected Captain Coward either to protest or to put out no more than a token effort in order to get off the hook. I was wrong. When asked how he felt about the competition he said, "When the commodore says 'Jump' I'm going to jump, and this time he said 'Jump' literally!" When news of the skipper's reaction spread throughout the ship, everyone's attitude changed (with the exception of Jim Clute, whose favorite response to any proposal involving physical exercise was to borrow from Mark Twain and declare that he was going to lie down until the proposal evaporated). Almost to the man, we determined that the *Sterett* was going to win this contest.

There was apprehension about the consequences of doing the running broad jump on the deck of a heaving destroyer, but it proved unwarranted. The weather remained calm, and our creative carpenter's mates fabricated mattress- and sawdust-filled jumping pits that greatly reduced the risk of injury. Each day a crowd of cheering spectators turned out to encourage their division mates to do their best. We all assembled to support Jess Coward as he performed these events, probably for the first time since his days at Annapolis. We were all delighted with his good sportsmanship, and when he told Commodore Moon, "Commodore, if you don't compete in this we're gonna think you're chicken," our admiration rose to a new level. Lo and behold, Don Moon did compete, just as a matter of principle, and acquitted himself quite well.

The Moon Olympics passed into history, and no world records were broken. The *Sterett* came in second. (I think the *Wilson* finished first; we accused them of having recruited a bunch of "ringers" before leaving Pearl Harbor.) Once more a heavy load of visual traffic descended on the shoulders of our signalmen, but by this time nothing could faze them. They were the best, and I am willing to admit the possibility that Don Moon's work load had improved their skills.

The second subject pursued by the commodore was a ship-handling exercise. What rendered it unique was the manner in which it was to be executed. We would soon enter "Turtle Country," that area along the California-Mexico coast where for several hundred square miles we would find hundreds of large sea turtles on the surface, basking in the warm sun. Each ship was to rig out its boat boom and stream from the end a steel hoop ten feet in diameter (held in a vertical position, with only a small portion of its circumference submerged) to which was fastened a pouch made out of cargo netting. The idea was to rig out essentially a big turtle net and then, by maneuvering carefully, scoop a turtle into it. In his messages the commodore described in great detail how, when a turtle was first sighted, the officer-of-the-deck was to hoist a special flag to alert all ships to the fact that his vessel was engaged in a turtle capture and would be maneuvering radically as needed to capture her target. The message warned that these creatures had to be approached with deliberate speed and stealth lest they become alarmed, for then they would certainly submerge.

For several days the destroyers of Division 15 could be seen zigzagging all over the ocean. The problem was not finding a target but rather deciding which one to pursue. Nonetheless, the turtles' early warning systems proved absolutely infallible. We did not catch a single one. Commodore Moon was not pleased. His critique of the exercise made that point clear, and his opinion of our ship-handling skills was not enhanced by our performance.

All of us were aware of the additions to our inventory of professional skills that resulted from Don Moon's ingenious schemes; it was just that sometimes his creativity seemed to border on the bizarre. The Moon Olympics certainly made every member of our ship's company more aware of his own physical condition and the need to improve it. Yet I think most of us agreed with Jim Clute's comment about the commodore's efforts to provide a little recreation: "Well, he didn't just tell us to recreate, he recreated our asses off!"

WE FINALLY ARRIVED AT THE CANAL ENTRANCE after dark on 2 June 1941. The Army's coastal batteries were not at all happy about allowing these darkened and unidentified ships to enter; but somehow the Navy managed to explain our presence, and we made the transit in six hours. By morning on the third we were steaming toward Guantánamo Bay, where our arrival had been anticipated and stirred little if any interest. There we awaited the arrival of the battleship *Idaho*, the cruiser *Brooklyn*, and the destroyers *Stack*, *Wainwright*, and *Winslow*, all of whom had followed us from the Pacific. Then the whole group moved north—two battleships, two cruisers, and six destroyers. Southeast of Delaware Bay, the *Mississippi* pointed her signal light in our direction. "DD 407, you are detached. Proceed to Philadelphia Navy Yard and await further orders." To me this was a welcome message. I would be going home.

The *Sterett* remained in Philadelphia for only a few days before moving down the coast to Charleston. Her navy yard overhaul was badly needed. The technicians there fixed a number of mechanical problems that were beyond the abilities of the ship's personnel and also updated our weapons. We received improved sonar gear, new Y- and K-gun depth charge launchers, and 20-mm machine guns; two of our four torpedo tube mounts were removed to compensate for the additional weight of our new ASW/AAW armament. In the meantime the situation in Europe continued to worsen. Hitler invaded Russia, and the Germans appeared to be almost invincible in their conquests. Their U-boats took an increasingly heavy toll on Allied shipping on the other side of the Atlantic. Tom McWhorter was sent off for a month of instruction at the Torpedo School at Newport, and Dr. McGinnis reported aboard as our first ship's doctor. Previously only one medical officer had been assigned to each squadron, but the events of the early convoy escort days, when it became apparent that submarine warfare would inflict heavy personnel casualties, demonstrated that each escort needed her own doctor. Instead of sharing him with seven other ships, we had one to ourselves.

When the *Sterett* arrived in Casco Bay in mid-August 1941, Tom McWhorter returned aboard to learn that his Naval Academy roommate, Craig Spowers, was in port aboard the *Reuben James*, an old four-stack destroyer of World War I vintage. Although the *Sterett* was on four-hour readiness status, Jess Coward seemed pleased to allow Tom to visit the *Reuben James* as Craig's guest and to remain aboard for dinner. Tom returned in a pensive but cheerful mood. He was appalled at the condition of the old ship, which was rusting away and, in Tom's words, "held together with bailing wire and chewing gum." His obvious concern for his friend's safety was a measure of Tom's deep sense of compassion.

For the next few months we performed escort duties in the cold North Atlantic, where the sea and the weather are always the "other" enemies. The U.S. Navy had just transferred fifty old four-stack destroyers to the Royal Navy and in return acquired base rights to Argentia, Newfoundland (and to British facilities in Bermuda and Trinidad), for escort of convoy operations. The *Sterett* became a frequent visitor to that northern anchorage, and most of us came to believe that there was no such thing as fair weather in Argentia. By October, the tempo of convoy operations had accelerated considerably. Eastbound ships were formed into convoy units in Argentia and escorted by a mixture of Canadian and U.S. destroyers and corvettes for the first several hundred miles of their eastward journey until they arrived at a predesignated midocean meeting point, where they were turned over to British escorts. In a move intended to release the British garrison there for deployment to the Mediterranean, our Marines had occupied Iceland on 8 July 1941; that rugged outpost then served as a haven for U.S. naval forces. But in October a large eastbound convoy, escorted by Canadian corvettes, was attacked by submarines about four hundred miles south of Iceland. A group of five U.S. destroyers, including the USS *Kearny*, which had departed Iceland a few days earlier on another assignment, was ordered to the aid of the ships under attack. In the ensuing melee, the *Kearny* was torpedoed, and seven men were lost. Aboard the *Sterett* we heard about the *Kearny*'s fate and realized more keenly than ever that we were at war. This was no game but rather a life-and-death struggle that the people of the United States did not even realize was in progress. The *Kearny* incident was broadcast to the world, and President Roosevelt took the opportunity to remind everyone that we had resolved to help our British friends by delivering the supplies they needed to defend themselves. German attacks were not about to stop us. The American people took the news in stride, and aboard the *Sterett* we accepted it as an inevitable development.

The *Kearny* was hit on 17 October. In the early hours of the twenty-ninth, the *Reuben James* was sunk. Like the *Kearny*, she had been engaged in escorting a convoy, doing her best despite inadequate and antiquated armament and detection equipment to protect her charges against a wily enemy equipped with the most devastating naval weapon system then known. For the German U-boat commanders, attacks on the convoys represented a low-risk, high-profit exercise. To Tom McWhorter, the *Reuben James* was a great personal loss. Ens. Craig Spowers had gone down with his ship. Tom's grief touched all of us and strengthened our determination to make the *Sterett* the best, most pugnacious destroyer in the U.S. Navy.

The *Sterett's* operational luck had been remarkably good compared to that of other escort ships. We had not been assigned to any of the really slow convoys; they were the ones who took it on the chin. Our assignments had involved the faster troop convoys as well as carrier operations, in which speed was essential. U-boats simply were not fast enough to maneuver into attack positions at high speeds of advance. It was always possible that a German sub might accidentally find herself in just the right spot for an attack; but we always zigzagged, and whenever possible we were routed away from areas where submarines were known or suspected to be operating. None of us was foolish enough to wish to experience a U-boat attack, but we did wish for action and the chance to even the score for the *Kearny* and the *Reuben James*. Tom McWhorter drilled his torpedo gang daily. We had no doubt that if the chance came, the *Sterett* would give a good account of herself. Meanwhile, the North Atlantic winter was a bruising, pervasive foe, and we knew we were lucky just to be alive.

Felix Gebert, once a mainstay of the *Sterett's* electrical gang and now a resident of Coal City, Illinois, wrote recently of his impressions of the *Sterett's* Atlantic convoy duties:

> I remember walls of mountainous waves on all sides, and they posed a real problem for those of us who had to come topside and cross over the main deck to relieve the watch in the forward engine room. More than once I got caught on the catwalk (an elevated steel-mesh walkway mounted on stilts about six feet above the main deck) when a huge wave of green water crashed over my head. There was nothing to do but hang onto the lifelines, holding my breath, with my feet and legs hanging free, while I waited for it to pass. Then came the challenge of making a mad dash for the engine room hatch. If you had the roll and pitch calculated correctly, you could jump down from the catwalk, dash across about fifteen feet of main deck, spin open the wheel on the hatch cover, jump over the hatch combing, and land with your feet on the rung of the ladder, then grab the underside hatch wheel and spin it shut as you were descending the ladder. It was a neat trick. Of course, it was always a little bit harder leaving the engine room. There was no chance to observe and time the seas, and more often than not I got caught in the open hatch with a big green sea pouring down over my head and shoulders into the engine room.

We earned a respite from the worst of the North Atlantic weather when we were assigned to operate out of Bermuda. We were to screen and act as plane guard for the USS *Long Island* during her initial training and flight operations. The first of the CVEs, the *Long Island* was a converted Moore-McCormick freighter, and her class of vessel offered a quick and inexpensive solution to the problem of providing close ASW air cover for convoy escorts. Working with her was a definite change of pace from fast carrier operations and would not have been our preference as a permanent assignment, but it gave us a welcome breather. We arrived at Port Royal Bay, Bermuda, on 21 November 1941, and I still recall the pleasant panorama we saw as we pulled into our anchorage: all of the houses were white or pastel with terra-cotta roofs, and they looked delightfully clean in the bright sunlight. Red Everett was ill during most of our Bermuda duty, so Frank Luongo filled in as navigator. Red was soon detached for hospitalization, and Frank became our new executive officer. Hugh Sanders moved up to become chief engineer.

The *Sterett's* deck log for 7 December 1941 reads: "0-4—Moored starboard side to USS *Wilson*, port side to USS *Stack*, in division nest less USS *Lang*, alongside USS *Altair*; order of ships: USS *Altair*, USS *Lang*, USS *Sterett*, USS *Stack* in Port Royal Bay, Bermuda Islands. No. 3 boiler in use for auxiliary purposes. Ships present: various units of U.S. Atlantic Fleet, district craft, and local British craft.—/s/ P. G. Hayden, Ensign, U.S. Naval Reserve." It started out as a lovely day, with clear skies and bright sunshine. Not until sometime in the early afternoon did we receive that famous message: "Pearl Harbor under attack by enemy aircraft. This is not a drill." It was hard to believe, but as radio reports began to pour in we realized with sinking hearts that we had been caught completely by surprise and had absorbed devastating losses. At first we did not want to believe that either—surely when the official damage reports came in we would learn that we had hurt the attackers as much as they had hurt us. But this was not the case. As the gravity of our losses became apparent, we wondered where the enemy would strike next. My thoughts turned to my former shipmates on the *Tennessee*, for she was among those that had been caught. Hugh Sanders had similar concerns for his friends on the *West Virginia*. We all wondered how it could have happened and were shocked by the apparent failure of our ships to defend themselves adequately. Above all else came the realization that we were at war. Our lives and our country's survival were now in constant jeopardy.

The flow of radio traffic during the next twenty-four hours was overwhelming, and I was up all night decoding urgent and priority messages. Some were addressed to us, but most were not. We "broke" many of the latter out of curiosity about what was happening. Classmate Charlie Pond, the communicator on the USS *Wilson*, helped to supplement the *Sterett's* radio surveillance, and between us we were able to piece together a good summary. Of course, Commodore Moon expected to be kept as well informed as any fleet commander, and to the extent that it was possible I believe he was.

Now all of us wished to be back in the Pacific. We were outraged—at the deliberate deception of the Japanese, at the manner in which they had attacked without warning when we were supposedly at peace with them, and at the attitude of the American media, who clamored for full disclosure of the damage done to our ships. Did they not understand that disclosing the extent of our losses would serve the enemy's interests? We were sad, disgusted, and angry. More than anything else, we wanted to fight.

By 10 December we were on the way to carry out our first wartime mission. Several major units of the French fleet had been bottled up in the harbor of Martinique. The carrier *Bearn*, the light cruiser *Emile Bertin*, and the training cruiser *Jeanne d'Arc* had been at Guadeloupe since mid-1940. Concerned that the French might turn these ships over to their German conquerors, Admiral Greenslade had convinced Admiral Roberts of the French fleet to give the United States ninety-six hours notice of any intended ship movement and to allow U.S. Navy surface and air patrols to maintain surveillance within French territorial limits. But amid the confusion resulting from the Japanese attack on Pearl Harbor, reports were received that a French cruiser (the *Barfleur*) had eluded our patrols and left Martinique. In the afternoon of 10 December the carrier *Wasp*, the cruisers *Brooklyn*, *Nashville*, and *Savannah*, and the destroyers *Lang*, *Stack*, *Sterett*, and *Wilson* (Destroyer Division 15) got under way and headed south at high speed for Martinique. The entire ship's company was keyed up. We knew that the French ships were no match for our task group, but they could give us a pretty fair scrap—and we looked forward to the chance to retaliate. We would rather have fought the Japanese, but since they were not at hand we were perfectly happy to tangle with any available foe. We stripped the *Sterett* of practically every comfort and heaved overboard anything that could conceivably become a fire hazard. We worked over our guns and fire control equipment, checked our ammunition, positioned it for easy access, prepared the wardroom as a dressing station for the wounded, and briefed our damage control parties one last time. Then we waited.

The night before our arrival we were told to prepare to intercept a breakout by the French ships in the morning. Long before dawn we stood at our battle stations, ready for anything. But daylight brought only serenity. There was no thundering gunfire, no sign of the French ships—just the splendid beauty of Martinique, a lush, green island in a turquoise sea. We waited. We steamed in a giant square. We patrolled the coast, blocking all exits. Finally a message from the *Wasp* reported that her planes had spotted our quarry, still safe and sound at anchor. I wondered if they had all had a good night's sleep while we scurried across the Caribbean.

We remained near Martinique for a couple of days, and very little information filtered down to our level. We concluded that our authorities were at work negotiating some kind of deal with the French. At last an agreement was reached: they would demilitarize their ships and hold them at Martinique for the duration of the war. I thought of those French sailors who would be stuck there away from home for all that time. Then it occurred to me that at least they were still alive, and that was a hell of a lot better than the fate of the more than two thousand bluejackets who had been killed at Pearl Harbor. I wasted no more sympathy on the French. More than ever, we lamented the fact that we were not in the Pacific, where our comrades needed us and where we had a better chance of seeing surface action.

On 21 December we were ordered to accompany a couple of cruisers and an escort carrier back to the States. The flattop was to go into Norfolk, and the other ships were bound for Portland, Maine. We griped about having to continue on to Casco Bay after going all the way to the entrance buoys at Norfolk; but on the morning of the twenty-fourth, just as we were about to turn around and leave the Virginia capes in the distance to spend our Christmas at sea, we received a message from the officer in tactical command (OTC): he wanted us to proceed to Norfolk with him and remain until 26 December. It was the most wonderful Christmas present possible.

We left Norfolk on the twenty-sixth for Casco Bay and Argentia. On 10 January 1942 we departed again in company with the carrier *Wasp*, the old battleship *Texas*, the cruisers *Tuscaloosa* and *Wichita*, and our division mates *Lang*, *Stack*, and *Wilson* to escort four transports carrying the first contingent of American troops to the United Kingdom. The OTC in this case was Rear Adm. "Ike" Giffen, one of our scrappiest flag officers and the father of "Skip" Giffen, an immensely popular and highly respected classmate. We fully expected that the U-boats would be deployed to ambush such a critical convoy, because the potential propaganda value of a successful attack on our first attempt to send troops to England was tremendous. But we had a quiet trip—either because we had been routed around German sub concentrations or because the enemy simply could not find us. We met our Royal Navy relief escort at a midocean meeting point some three or four hundred miles south of Iceland on 23 January. When our British friends appeared and signaled, "May I have my ships now?" we realized that the Royal Navy escort consisted of two of the old four-stack destroyers we had just given them. We were annoyed: two escorts, even modern ones, were clearly inadequate. The remainder of their trip took them through the most hazardous waters of all—the western approaches to the British Isles. It seemed to us aboard the *Sterett* that either they were desperately short of escorts or they were not as concerned about our soldiers as we were. In retrospect, I am sure the former was the case. Fortunately, the transports arrived at Londonderry, Ireland, safe and sound a few days later.

After delivering our charges to the Royal Navy we entered Reykjavik on 25 January. It was bitterly cold, and the wind blew at gale velocity for the duration of our stay. As Jim Clute said, that "breeze" felt as though it came straight from the North Pole. Four days later the Coast Guard cutter *Alexander Hamilton* was torpedoed about ten miles south of Iceland. The *Sterett*, the *Stack*, and several other destroyers were dispatched immediately to locate and destroy the U-boat. We passed the torpedoed ship, still afloat, a few miles outside the harbor entrance. It had started to snow that afternoon, and by nightfall we were in a real blizzard. Standing on the wing of the bridge, I strained to see ahead and to keep my teeth from chattering. As soon as we reached the location of the attack we formed a search formation, in line abreast. Even though we were only about fifteen hundred yards apart, we could not see the ships on either side of us. Captain Coward, Jim Clute, and I—each of us holding a cup of steaming coffee with both hands in an effort to stay warm—peered ahead through the swirling white flakes and repeatedly wiped the snow from our eyes, hoping to catch sight of a surfaced sub. In that weather, any sane U-boat commander would have kept his craft submerged. Nevertheless, at about midnight one of our companions from another ship reported that he had just passed a surfaced submarine on an opposite course, so close aboard that he was unable to turn sharply enough to go after it. Without hesitation, Jess Coward swung the *Sterett* around to try to catch the U-boat before she submerged. We had moved only a few hundred yards on our new course when we picked up a sonar contact. Jim assisted the captain with interpretation of the contact, and we dropped a full depth-charge pattern on what we firmly believed to be the sub—no doubt she had crash-dived after passing through our line. The *Sterett's* stern bounced high out of the water with each concussion as the charges detonated at a depth of fifty feet. Even on the bridge the shock was severe, and I could imagine the intensity of those explosions close against the outer shell of a submarine. We circled around and continued to search for our quarry but were unable to regain contact. I was convinced that we had sunk that sub, but Jess Coward and Jim both agreed that we had only managed to shake her up a bit. They were right. Meanwhile, the *Alexander Hamilton* had sunk while being towed back to Reykjavik.

The two torpedomen responsible for loading the Y- and K-guns were named Keenum and James. Keenum, the older of the two, was of average size, but James was depicted by Tom McWhorter as "a horse of a man" at 6 feet, 2 inches and 220 pounds. In a recent letter, Keenum described the fight this way:

> We immediately got into the thick of it shortly after dark. All of us torpedomen were in heavy foul weather clothing. We were manning the depth-charge racks, K-guns, and Y-gun. James and I were

on the Y-gun, using a davit with tackle to hoist the charges up to load. The seas were running very rough, with green water breaking over us on the main deck every few minutes. I probably weighed about 150 pounds soaking wet, even with all that heavy clothing, so big James bore the brunt of controlling those charges. He and I were often off our feet swinging free under the charges we were trying to load. At the same time, the spare charges in the storage racks had been dislodged and were rolling around loose on the deck. Fortunately some of the Repair Party (who were helping out everywhere) came to our aid, and it all turned out OK.

Tom McWhorter's recollections also make it clear that these were brave, tough men who had repeatedly risked their lives to deliver that depth-charge attack. We were all proud of their actions, Jess Coward included. After we had expended our depth charges, he directed the torpedo gang to report to sick bay, where the doctor issued each man a welcome dose of "medicinal" whiskey. It was only a token gesture, but it said a lot to those men about their skipper's regard for them.

A few days later we were assigned to escort a big convoy into New York. This gave us our first real opportunity to observe our new division commander, three-striper Bill Warlick, in action. The *Sterett* was stationed on the starboard flank of the convoy, which was in column formation. Because we were at our special sea details I was the officer-of-the-deck. We were actively patrolling station, maintaining a speed slightly faster than that of the convoy and steering a few degrees on either side of the base course. It was standard practice, designed to widen our sonar coverage. The division commander looked somewhat unhappy; he walked over to the captain, who was standing next to me, and said something to him. Jess Coward looked flustered. Turning to me he said, "Mr. Officer-of-the-Deck, patrol station!" It was obviously intended as an order, one to be complied with immediately, and it was delivered with force. And because the skipper normally addressed me as "Cal" I was even more aware of a sense of urgency. However, I did not have the slightest idea what it was he wanted me to do. "But captain," I said, "we are patrolling station." He reacted swiftly and angrily: "Damn it, I said patrol station!"

All I knew was that he expected (and apparently felt that he needed) some immediate show of response. It seemed to me that he was saying, "For God's sake, do something!" As soon as that thought entered my head, I said, "Oh! Yes, sir! All ahead full—hard right rudder, come to course. . . ." The change brought us about twenty degrees to the right of our previous course. The skipper looked relieved. "That's better," he said. Then he and the commodore walked away, chatting pleasantly, and I was left on my own to bring these more radical moves in line with the convoy's progress. Never again did I patrol station in any but the most aggressive manner. So far as I could tell, both the captain and the commodore quickly forgot the incident. I did not—it was a useful lesson.

The *Sterett* was assigned a six-day availability at the Brooklyn Navy Yard, and we made the most of it, going to nightclubs with Jim Clute before his transfer to a new destroyer (the USS *Bailey*) then under construction at Staten Island. We also lost Frank Luongo to a new ship, and we knew we would feel the absence of those two stalwarts very keenly. They were not only shipmates but also competent and dependable pros who had contributed a great deal to the organization and training of the *Sterett*'s crew. Those of us who remained benefited from their service throughout the *Sterett*'s lifetime. Lt. Frank Gould now came aboard as our new executive officer, and I moved up to the post of gunnery officer.

Our New York interlude ended much too soon. The *Sterett* departed with the carrier *Wasp* for a period of intense training in the vicinity of Casco Bay. The *Sterett* and *Wasp* had already developed a good working relationship during previous assignments. Capt. "Black-Jack" Reeves of the *Wasp* was a hard taskmaster who made it clear that he would accept nothing less than outstanding performance from his destroyer escorts. Aboard the *Sterett* we made it a matter of personal pride always to provide the *Wasp* with the best services that any escort could render. We were especially careful to anticipate every *Wasp* maneuver and never to leave her uncovered and vulnerable to submarine attack. The result was the development of a *Sterett* doctrine for carrier operations—"Hard right rudder, all ahead flank, make turns for 29 knots!" It was a matter of attitude, and our relationship with the *Wasp* continued to flourish.

Jim Clute's departure necessitated several other changes in personnel assignments. Ens. Hillard Marver, a new arrival, became assistant gunnery officer, and Tom McWhorter took on the job as communications officer but also retained (at his request) his assignment as torpedo officer. Tom threw himself into the communications job with typical McWhorter enthusiasm and turned in his usual fine performance. Marver was quiet and reserved—a counterbalance to the rest of us, who were inclined at times to be more boisterous than was appropriate for wardroom decorum.

We arrived in Boston on 16 February to find the *Queen Mary* there, loading soldiers. At once we concluded that we were about to escort her somewhere but had no idea what our destination might be. At 1100 on the eighteenth we left from South Boston Pier and anchored in President's Road, where we waited until our new charge got under way an hour or two later. She departed at high speed with ten thousand troops aboard and the *Sterett* in hot pursuit. We had to make 30 knots to get ahead of her to our screening station. The weather was rough and getting

USS STERETT

The *Sterett* departs Brooklyn Navy Yard in early February 1942 bound for Boston and a brief but rough escort assignment with the *Queen Mary*. Note that the after two 5-inch gun mounts have been enclosed (although gun number three has only a canvas top). (U.S. Navy Photo) ahead of her to our screening station. The weather was rough and getting rougher by the hour.

The majestic, enormous *Queen* continued to accelerate. The *Sterett* had to labor from the outset just to keep up with her, and our companion escort, the *Stack*, was having just as hard a time. Throughout the night of the eighteenth our bow reared up wildly and then suddenly plunged down and down until we slammed into the sea with a bone-wrenching crash. Then the ship would slowly rise, shuddering and shaking the whole way as she shook the water off. On the bridge, walls of green water broke over our heads and battered us constantly as we tried to hold on to a rail or anything solid to keep from being dashed against a bulkhead. I did not see how we could possibly be of any use to that giant vessel unless she encountered a U-boat on the surface, in which case the conditions would have made it extremely difficult to achieve any effective gunfire. By noon on 19 February we were barely able to hang on at 31 knots. Perhaps because she realized the futility of our situation, and just when it looked like we would have to cry "uncle," the *Queen* released us. As she disappeared over the horizon she sent a very nice message to thank us for our services. All of us wished her well and prayed for her safe arrival whatever her destination.

On 23 February 1942 we were in the Atlantic with the *Wasp*, just east of the coast of Maine. She was engaged in flight operations, launching and recovering aircraft, and the *Sterett* was up ahead as a screen against submarine attack when I saw a *Wasp* plane from the returning group crash into the icy water several miles ahead of the carrier. We immediately headed for the spot where we had seen it splash. By the time we arrived, no more than ten minutes later, there was absolutely nothing left; we searched the area for several hours with one of our division mates but found nothing. We had to abandon the search and return to our screening stations. When I went ashore in Portland several days later I learned that the missing pilot was Frank D. Case, Jr., one of my best friends. Frank was the president of our Naval Academy class, a star football and lacrosse player, and one of the finest men I have ever had the privilege to know. Since our last names both began with the letter C we were often in the same division or group, especially during the summer cruises. We had even taken girlfriends on double dates to Academy social functions. I recalled all of those incidents of good comradeship and mourned his loss. Deaths in routine operations were the hardest to take. Those in combat were no less sad, but they seemed easier to rationalize.

While we were still at sea with the *Wasp*, the skipper called me into his cabin. "Cal," he said, "we have to send an officer to gunnery school. You'll leave for Norfolk as soon as we get in this afternoon." The course was a hands-on, accelerated program conducted aboard the old battleship *Wyoming*. It was designed especially for destroyer gunnery officers and continued for about one month. The students were rotated through each of the stations on the gun director so that they could better appreciate the duties performed by each member of the director crew. We took part in a series of concentrated firing exercises at both air and surface targets under the close supervision of expert instructors, who critiqued each student's performance immediately after each practice.

On 18 March the *Wyoming* was in the Chesapeake conducting gunnery exercises. My class had just been dismissed for lunch when a Navy PBY landed nearby, and the pilot signaled that he had come to pick up an officer named Calhoun. I hurried to the quarterdeck, where a boat awaited me. I jumped in and in a few minutes was hauled by the seat of my pants into the gently bobbing PBY. Half an hour later I was at the Norfolk Naval Air Station. The *Sterett* had arrived that morning for a three-day availability at Portsmouth Navy Yard in advance of an extended period away from home. The PBY delivery was Jess Coward's way of giving me an extra day with my bride. It was typical of the consideration he demonstrated constantly for his *Sterett* shipmates.

During the next three days we accomplished some structural repairs and received a few minor alterations. On 23 March we left Norfolk and proceeded to Casco Bay with our old friend the *Wasp*. Before departing, however, we also received one other very important addition: Lt. A.A.W. Scharbius, M.C., USNR, reported for duty as the *Sterett's* medical officer. He was to be my roommate, and I should let him relate the story of his arrival:

> I remember I reported aboard our destroyer after chasing her up to Casco Bay then finally down to Norfolk, where she was undergoing an overhaul in March 1942. I had just ten days of active duty behind me as I scrambled up the gangway, barely remembering to make the proper salutes, which was about the only thing I knew. I was directed to the wardroom, where I presented myself to Captain Coward. His first question was, "Do you get seasick, doctor?" Apparently I was relieving their previous medical officer (McGinnis I think his name was) who, though immensely popular, had the misfortune to suffer from chronic mal de mer and could hardly make a sick call, let alone chow down. I gulped and answered with supreme, if totally uncertain, confidence that I was immune. This was based on a bit of sailing on small boats as a youngster, and several Atlantic crossings on the old SS *Leviathan* on which I worked during summer vacations while at college, which probably never rolled more than three degrees while I sailed on her.
>
> That night, lying in the upper berth, I was lifted right up against the overhead at 2 A.M. by a riveting machine that some idiot was suddenly inspired to operate on the deck immediately above me.

Worse, I came into intimate contact with some lightly insulated steam pipes right over my bare belly. I had been looking forward eagerly to sea duty up to this time. Some weeks later, plowing through a mid-Atlantic storm, I began to wonder what the hell I was doing out here. And I was a *volunteer* reservist!

Bill Scharbius would have made a welcome addition to any wardroom, and he quickly adapted to the life of a destroyerman.

CHAPTER 3
THE BRITISH HOME FLEET

ON 26 MARCH 1942 the *Sterett* left Casco Bay for Scapa Flow, the base for the British Home Fleet, along with the *Wasp*, the new battleship *Washington*, the cruisers *Wichita* and *Tuscaloosa*, and the destroyers *Wainwright, Plunkett, Madison, Lang,* and *Wilson*. It was a strong force, provided to help the British prevent a breakout of German heavy ships into the Atlantic. No longer was the U.S. Atlantic Fleet to be restricted to escort of convoy operations. We were going into harm's way, ready to take on the enemy's biggest and best.

The Atlantic was its usual bleak and miserable self. Just one day out, we received a stern reminder of the constant threat of the sea. Aboard the *Sterett* the first indication of trouble came in the form of a voice radio message from the flagship (the USS *Washington*) reporting a man overboard. The seas were very rough; it would have been difficult to keep a swimmer in sight, let alone recover him. Despite extra lookouts no one was able to spot the victim, and it began to appear that the original report was in error. All ships then were asked to muster their crews and report whether anyone was missing. With negative reports in hand from every ship, the chief of staff sent a messenger to tell Admiral Wilcox that all hands were accounted for. When the Marine orderly entered the admiral's cabin to inform him of the messenger's presence, the admiral was not there. Only then did it become clear: the man overboard was the admiral himself. Search planes were launched from the *Wasp* despite the poor conditions, and one of them was also lost. Rear Adm. Ike Giffen now became our task group commander, and we continued our journey to Scapa Flow.

On 3 April the British cruiser HMS *Edinburgh* met us shortly after daybreak and escorted us into Scapa Flow the next day. The fog and mist gave an even more somber tone to the general appearance of the place. Many British men-of-war were anchored in the harbor, and the barrage balloons overhead testified to the fact that we were within range of some kind of German aircraft. In plain view was the superstructure of the HMS *Royal Oak*, which had been sunk by a German U-boat. We all felt a certain admiration for that submarine skipper, for he had penetrated a dense antisub net in the middle of the entire fleet, conducted a successful attack, and escaped. As we proceeded to our assigned berth we received a visit from a Home Fleet boarding officer. Straddling our lifelines, a young lieutenant commander of the Royal Navy saluted smartly and requested permission to come aboard. His uniform was of Gieves quality and fit perfectly but was very "salty": the gold braid was tarnished, and the cuffs and elbows were reinforced with black glove leather. He wore full Wellington boots and carried under his arm a brass telescope wrapped in leather and engraved with the words "To Viscount Kilbourne" and the royal seal of King George. He gave a nice little speech of welcome to Captain Coward, and it appeared that our Royal Navy comrades were happy to see us. Scapa Flow was the main base of operations for the entire British Home Fleet. It was packed with warships of every description, all flying the White Ensign. A cold and dismal anchorage, it had nothing to offer the shore-goer in the way of a liberty port but the tiny settlement of Lynesse, where we were told there was a pub or two. However, the warm, friendly attitude of our British comrades more than made up for the lack of facilities ashore.

We moored alongside the Royal Navy's destroyer tender HMS *Tyne*. We had just secured to her when a disreputable-looking Royal Canadian Navy trawler came alongside our starboard quarter and secured her lines to us. Her young skipper, bearded and looking very seamanlike, came aboard. I met him as he walked forward on the *Sterett*'s main deck. "Good morning," he called, coming up to me with his hand extended and with a disarming smile. "I looked over and saw you standing in a little while ago and asked my quartermaster, 'Do I see the Stars and Stripes flying on that destroyer over there?' When he confirmed that you were Yanks, I couldn't wait to get over here to welcome you on behalf of the Royal Canadian Navy. You can't imagine how wonderful it is to see these beautiful U.S. destroyers joining us over here." I took him up to meet Captain Coward, who immediately asked if he and his crew would like to remain alongside the *Sterett* until their scheduled departure two days later, and in the meantime to make full use of our washrooms and eat their meals in our general mess. His gratitude was both genuine and touching. He and his men had not had either a freshwater shower or a decent meal in weeks. So the *Sterett*'s sailors adopted the Canadians and became good friends. In the process we learned how lucky we were by comparison. That little trawler had served as a convoy escort for two years in the North Atlantic, destroying one U-boat and discouraging many others from attacking. We were impressed with her mettle, and when she shoved off two days later we assured her skipper that whenever he found himself in port with the USS *Sterett* he was welcome to moor alongside for as long as he liked.

Meanwhile, the officers and men of the HMS *Tyne* treated us to a superb brand of hospitality. We spent the first week alongside her, and every afternoon one of her officers came aboard the *Sterett*, rounded up all the officers who were not on duty, and took them aboard the *Tyne* for drinks. Despite the fact that their drinks were served without ice, the Scotch whiskey was excellent, and our little afternoon gatherings were tremendous fun. Usually they involved a lot of singing (not very good, but loud) and good-natured ribbing. One day perhaps a week after our arrival, Commodore Moon—now reassigned as our squadron commander and embarked in the *Wainwright* (DD 419)—assembled all of our squadron's officers on deck. He told us that he had noticed the heavy flow of U.S. naval officers to the *Tyne* every afternoon, and he told us that he did not want to see any more of us going aboard her with "a thirsty look on our face." We all complied with his directive: we continued to go aboard, but we made certain that we did not look thirsty.

Occasionally a movie was shown on the *Tyne* or the HMS *Dunluce Castle*, an old tub that was used as a barracks and station vessel. We also attended a British USO show featuring English stage stars. I remember that a Royal Navy rear admiral volunteered to go onstage and allowed himself to be used as a buffoon, to the delight of the mostly enlisted audience. It was the kind of performance that, although attended by hilarious and undignified behavior, produced respect for the admiral's good humor and stage presence.

But we also had work to do at Scapa Flow. Our ships were to be assimilated into whatever Home Fleet operations best suited our armament and capabilities. Thus we had to learn their way of doing things, a process that our hosts seemed eager to facilitate. The day that we arrived, ten British signalmen came aboard to teach their American counterparts how to communicate with the Royal Navy. They were to live on the *Sterett* and be treated just like our own men. I was delighted with these men: they were all competent professionals with ten or more years of experience behind them, and they adapted quickly to our routines. Our sailors liked them and admired their proficiency. Their training enabled them not only to read and translate tactical signals, but also to understand the tactical maneuvers required to execute the commands received. On ships of the U.S. Navy at that time, only the officers had to learn what the ship needed to do in order to execute a signal command. Suddenly we had a team of signalmen who could advise the officer-of-the-deck on specific tactical responses. This was a boon to us, and it demonstrated how our Navy could more fully utilize the capacities of our bluejackets.

Without question, the British tars found much about our ships for which to be thankful. The food was perhaps the most welcome of these advantages. Thumbing through Quartermaster Cleere's diary recently, I came across this passage: "The ten English sailors aboard are really enjoying the quantity, quality, and variety of food they are eating. I guess it is no joke that food is not too plentiful in England. One limey said they were eating like the lords and ladies of London, and it's probably true."

Combined British–U.S. operations out of Scapa Flow began on 7 April. With several British destroyers, we practiced screening the HMS *Duke of York* and the USS *Washington*. For communication purposes we were referred to as the HMS *Steadfast* to hide the fact that elements of the U.S. Navy were present at Scapa Flow. "Steadfast" was a good alias, denoting a sense of dependability of which I hoped we would prove worthy. While the ship engaged in daytime tactical maneuvers, we put the crew through all kinds of drills. Gunnery practice received a lot of attention, and at least once a day I managed to exercise the 5-inch crews at the loading machine for about a half-hour. The Home Fleet had one neat arrangement that I envied: a few miles from the harbor entrance was stationed a small tug with a target sled in tow. Every ship that went past that tug was free to shoot its guns at the target. The tug would then mark the fall of shot and signal the results to the ship. There was no wait and no voluminous report to be made. The *Sterett* fired her 5-inch guns whenever she went past that corner, and the practice allowed the crew to develop self-confidence and familiarity with the process of gunfire, including the noise and concussion. It prepared us for what lay ahead.

Each afternoon as we approached the harbor entrance, the flagship hoisted a signal addressed to its destroyers: "Scatter!" At that moment all the destroyers in the screen—often as many as twenty—headed hell-bent and at flank speed for the opening in the antisubmarine net, which was held open just long enough for the returning ships to enter. This hole was only wide enough to allow at most two destroyers to enter together, abreast of each other. The exercise amounted to a game of "chicken" played out under the amused and approving eye of the officer in tactical command. It called for a precise sense of timing and relative movement, confidence in one's engineering gang, and a lot of fortitude. The risks of collision were high; and in light of the cautious attitude of the U.S. Navy brass, our skippers were not very well prepared for this wild game. I could hardly blame them, because I doubt that our flag officers could have been as forgiving as their Royal Navy counterparts were when damage occurred in these mad dashes. (This is no reflection on U.S. Navy flag officers—congressional reaction would have been very negative.) When I asked one skipper what would happen to the C.O. if a collision ensued from one of the "scatter" exercises, he said, "Oh well, that happens now and then. It's treated as a normal operational casualty, you know. No fuss!" The philosophy of the British seemed much more likely to produce aggressive ship-handling skills among their destroyer captains than our cautious approach; perhaps we learned something from it.

On several occasions the *Sterett* spent two or three days moored alongside the HMS *Tyne* to make use of her services as a tender. Among her many capacities as a support vessel, the *Tyne* possessed an "attack teacher"—an antisubmarine training facility that was in essence a mock-up of a destroyer's bridge complete with wheel, rudder-angle indicator, compass, and underwater detection equipment. Thanks to specially prepared recordings, student sonar operators and conning officers were able to hear the sounds of an actual sonar contact and the development of that contact to the point of a successful attack. Students also made sonar contact with a simulated sub maneuvered by a control team, conducted an attack (which they could watch as it developed on a visual display) using all of the normal ship control devices, and determined whether their attack solution would have worked in a real situation. It was the next best thing to training with a live submarine, and we made maximum use of it. Our British instructor was a tall Leslie Howard look-alike who acted as though he considered us to be among the world's most ignorant people. He fancied himself an infallible authority on the Doppler principle, which describes how sound rises in pitch as it approaches the listener and falls as it moves away, and claimed to be able to distinguish the exact speed of an approaching submarine by this means alone. We soon grew tired of his scolding: "No, no—cawn't you heah the Doppla? You have *up* Doppla!" But we soon managed to disregard his arrogance and came away from each class a little better prepared to cope with U-boats.

EVER SINCE OUR ARRIVAL we had wondered what kind of war mission awaited us once we learned to work smoothly with our British friends. Our old companion the *Wasp* and two members of our destroyer group, the *Lang* and the *Madison*, had made a quick dash into the Mediterranean in mid-April to deliver Spitfire aircraft to the beleaguered island of Malta. That British bastion had been under constant attack by German bombers for many months, and we knew from press reports that it was running critically low on fighters. The fresh Spitfires delivered by the *Wasp* had inflicted significant losses on the Germans, and we speculated that we might be utilized for a similar mission.

On 29 April we moved down to Greenock, Scotland, arriving there the next day. As we moved through the channel en route to our assigned berth, we could see for the first time evidence of the attacks perpetrated by the Luftwaffe against the people of the British Isles. Bombs had destroyed whole blocks of homes, while dockside naval installations had escaped with minimal damage. Describing this scene in his diary entry, Chief Quartermaster Tim Cleere wrote: "I used to be pretty skeptical about those press reports which claimed that the German bombers always hit the residential areas, churches, and schools, but all the signs here indicate just that. We saw one church that was a complete wreck. It is said that five thousand people have been killed in this vicinity by the German air raids."

We sent liberty parties ashore on 30 April and 1 May. Glasgow was only about twenty miles away, and most of our bluejackets managed to get there for a firsthand look at one of Scotland's busiest ports in wartime. I had visited Edinburgh on one of my middie cruises, so I elected to forgo a visit to Glasgow to save my money; but those who went returned with the sobering realization that the British had taken a savage beating—and that they were absolutely determined to win the conflict. Tim Cleere came back with these observations:

> A truck driver took a bunch of us into Glasgow. It was a wild ride over hairpin curves, and I would have been better off to have waited for the train, but we did enjoy the scenery along the highway. Nearly everyone in Glasgow wore some kind of uniform, many of them from other Allied countries. Even most of the girls were in uniform. My impression was that Britain is making a mighty effort to win this war, and I think the United States could learn something from these people. They are all very cheerful, and you have to wonder how they can be that way, with all they have endured. It was a sight to see the hands of some of the girls who are now employed in an auto factory. They were mechanics' hands, so stained with carbon and grease that they probably would not come clean, no matter how long or how hard they scrubbed. I wondered if American girls could do the same, and like it. This is absolutely total war over here. The blackout at night was not so bad, because of the bright twilight, but it was an experience to walk through a darkened city, and I mean darkened! We had taken our flashlights (and gas masks) ashore with us, and it was a good thing. I'm glad I wasn't hungry, because the only food available in the restaurants was fish and chips. Meat comes only once a week over here—in the Navy they feed it to us three times a day!

On 2 May 1942 our favorite flattop, the *Wasp*, arrived in Greenock. We noted that she was loaded with Spitfires and immediately figured that we were about to escort her somewhere to deliver them to a friend in need. At 0500 the next morning we departed Greenock in company with the *Wasp*, the carrier HMS *Eagle*, our squadronmate the USS *Lang*, and the British destroyers HMS *Intrepid* and HMS *Echo*. As we had guessed, our destination was the Mediterranean. A single Hudson bomber provided air cover for us during most of the daylight hours. The sea state picked up the next day, and our ride became rougher as the day wore on. The British destroyers seemed to have an even tougher time because their bridge structures were more exposed than ours.

On the sixth we were met by three British destroyers from Gibraltar. They relieved us of our screening duties so that we could run ahead to refuel and meet the heavy ships as they came through the straits. Obviously they did not want the *Wasp* and the other heavies to stop at the Rock. We sighted Cape St. Vincent Light, on the southern tip of Portugal, at about 0330 on 7 May. As we turned to the east we encountered a gale-force head wind and had to slow to 15 knots. We did not get to Gibraltar until just before dark, accompanied by the *Lang, Intrepid*, and *Echo*.

A small minecraft patrolled Gibraltar's submarine net, and just before the gate opened for us the minesweeper dropped several depth charges across the entrance. The British were taking no chances on a sub penetrating the harbor defenses while we were entering. As soon as the gate closed behind us, depth charges were again dropped across it. We proceeded at once to moor at the fueling dock, with the *Lang* securing to our starboard side. While we refueled we also received provisions—including fresh vegetables, which we had not seen in quite some time. We noted that the HMS *Renown* was present in the harbor and wondered if she might join us for our run into the Med.

The *Sterett* and the *Lang* left Gibraltar just before midnight and patrolled outside for about two hours as the *Renown* and the rest of the escort force sortied. We joined their screen. I had the deck for this evolution, and I remember how nerve-racking it was to attempt to position ourselves ahead of the heavy ships without the help of radar as they steamed eastward at 20 knots in the pitch-black night. But as we converged on them the phosphorescent bow wave of the *Renown* became visible, and we took station ahead of her without difficulty. We caught up with the *Wasp* at about 0800 on 8 May and found that we were one of ten destroyers assigned to the screen. That seemed adequate to us, and we spent the day at general quarters, anticipating a reception committee of German bombers. Apparently they had no indication of our presence, and the only threat we encountered was a submarine contact by the HMS *Intrepid*. She dropped six depth charges, and we just kept on going.

At first light on 9 May the two carriers turned into the wind, launched several of their own fighters, and then began to send out the Spitfires. I was on the bridge as officer-of-the-deck and found myself imagining how those young RAF pilots must have felt as they took off from a carrier flight deck for the first time—a fact that in itself warranted some concern. As they left the carriers they were still some three to four hundred miles west of Malta, and there was a good chance that they would have to fight their way to the landing field. In their new role on that island, they would be called upon to fly up and defend it from attack every day. Everyone aboard the *Sterett* saluted them for their courage and their flying skills that morning. The *Wasp* and the *Eagle* launched sixty-three Spitfires. One crashed into the sea shortly after takeoff; it sank immediately, leaving only a few small pieces of wreckage on the surface. The pilot was not recovered. Another developed engine trouble and had to turn back. He landed safely on the *Wasp*—no small feat, considering that the plane was not configured for carrier landings and that the pilot probably had never made one before. Tim Cleere's diary noted that the pilot had to make a long run up the flight deck, but the bottom line was that he landed safely. Our hats were off to him.

Once the Spitfires were on their way, the task force headed back to Gibraltar as quickly as possible. We continued to expect German air attacks and so remained at our battle stations all day; but once again our luck held. The *Sterett* entered Gibraltar at about 0100 on the tenth to refuel. The heavy ships continued on their way, and we were to dash after them and resume our screening duties just as soon as we were able. While there, we were told that the Spitfires had arrived over Malta in the midst of an air raid and had fought their way in, shooting down some thirty German planes in the process (a figure I could never confirm). We all felt good about that news and were delighted to hear shortly thereafter that Prime Minister Churchill had sent a congratulatory message to the *Wasp*, asking, "Who said a *Wasp* can't sting twice?"

I was out on deck shortly after daybreak when two British destroyers came in and moored astern of us. I can still recall how much I admired the way in which they were handled. The line of our pier ran generally east to west. The two ships entered the harbor on a northerly heading, turned east for a few minutes, then simultaneously spun 180 degrees to the left. They slipped into their assigned berths without having to do anything other than backing their engines and throwing their mooring lines to the pier. It was a minor and routine maneuver, one that their crews no doubt had executed many times before, but it served to demonstrate the kind of smart and precise ship-handling skills our hosts made use of every day while we were a part of the Home Fleet—skills honed by the game the escorts played so gleefully every day as they returned to Scapa Flow and reacted to the "scatter" signal. I envied their abilities and hoped that as the war progressed we would learn to handle our destroyers with the same flair and precision. Just a few months later, when we joined the invasion fleet near Guadalcanal, I could see unmistakable signs that my wish had come true.

Shortly after the arrival of the two British "cans" the *Sterett* finished fueling and got under way to leave the harbor. As we maneuvered to clear a huge mooring buoy our starboard quarter drifted against the side of a barge that was anchored nearby, and her anchor chain hooked our starboard propeller. Almost before Captain Coward knew that we had made contact, we had managed to wrap about fifteen turns of anchor chain around our starboard shaft. The chain parted, but it took only a few minutes to realize that we were not going anywhere until we removed it: the resulting vibrations were unacceptable. To add insult to injury, we had sounded one long blast on our whistle as we cleared the pier, and the whistle stuck in the open position. We must have awakened every soldier and sailor on the Rock, and perhaps a fair number of the citizens of neighboring Spain, before we managed to shut it off. To make this "Chinese fire drill" (as J. D. Jeffrey called it) complete, we almost collided with a four-engine flying boat that taxied across our path as we struggled back to our berth.

After several hours of feverish work, a British diver removed the chain. We got safely away at last, caught up with our companions, and settled down to the familiar routine of providing antisubmarine protection to the *Wasp*. It had been a humiliating day, an illustration of how easily a little carelessness in mundane circumstances can tarnish an otherwise outstanding performance in hazardous circumstances. I am certain that Jess Coward felt badly about the fiasco of our departure, and Commodore Warlick made his displeasure quite obvious with a couple of blistering expletives. But it did not seem to cloud the skipper's outlook for long; after all, it was a highly successful strike, and we were justly proud of our small part in it.

Back in Greenock for a couple of days, we moored just a few yards astern of a pair of British destroyers, the HMS *Icarus* and the HMS *Escapade*. The skipper of the former, in a hand-written message that I still have today, invited us to a cocktail party aboard his ship: "The Captains and Officers of HM Ships *Icarus* and *Escapade* request the pleasure of the Company of the Captains and Officers of the United States Ships *Wilson* and *Sterett* to cocktails at 1800 this evening. It is suggested that numbers may be signaled so that suitable arrangements can be made for your comfort." Appropriate numbers were signaled, and late that afternoon a small contingent from our host ships came aboard to escort us to the party. Every officer from both the *Wilson* and the *Sterett* who was not actually on watch attended the get-together. It was an event I will never forget, because it exemplified the camaraderie that seemed to blossom every time officers of the Royal Navy and the U.S. Navy met.

By this time my roommate Bill Scharbius had already established himself as a character, and the two of us had become fast friends. He was popular with everyone on board, and on this particular afternoon he paired off with his Royal Navy counterpart, the doctor of the *Icarus*. As we walked over to the British ship Bill and his partner took the point position ahead of us and exchanged uniform caps as a gesture of friendship. The British doctor's hat size must have been at least 8½: his cap came all the way over Bill's ears, and only by setting it on the back of his head was my roommate able to see where he was going. Meanwhile, Bill's cap looked like a fly on a billiard ball, perched on top of the British doctor's head. The two of them walked arm in arm down the pier, and the tone of the party had been set.

We boarded the *Icarus* and found that she was a former French ship that the Home Fleet had acquired after the fall of France. Most of her signs and all of her instruction pamphlets were still in French, but her British officers and many of her crew were fluent in the language. Besides, as her gunnery officer said to me, "After all, a gun is a gun, whether French or English"—and I suppose the same could be said for a destroyer. The cocktail party proceeded amid a hubbub of friendly voices and a continuous exchange of sea stories. We talked about our leaders, Roosevelt and Churchill, about the conduct of the war, about where our ships had been, and about what we thought would happen next. Our hosts did not want us to return to our own ships, and even turned back their wardroom clock an hour in an effort to prolong our visit. Finally we returned to the *Sterett* and the *Wilson* for dinner, inviting them to come aboard for pie and coffee. They accepted with obvious pleasure (an indication of their appreciation of the superior quality of U.S. Navy food as well as their good-fellowship), and after partaking of generous helpings of both they insisted that we return to their ships to continue the party. Most of us accepted, and when the flow of Scotch whiskey resumed they involved us in a game designed to separate the men from the boys. The participants gathered in a small circle and drained their glasses. In turn, each man was required to stand in the center of the circle, place both hands on top of a walking stick held upright on the deck, bend from the waist, place his forehead on his hands, circle the stick three times, and walk out the wardroom door. The winner of this insanity was the last individual who could still walk through the door. When one of our hosts had to drop to his knees and crawl to get through the door, Jess Coward wisely declared them to be the winners of "the Battle of Greenock," and we retired to the safety of our own flag and our own bunks. Our British brothers in arms certainly played as hard as they fought, and as we departed we felt a closer kinship with them.

Bill Scharbius was already much more than the ship's doctor, although that role was large enough on any ship let alone a destroyer. He was an early Tom Selleck in appearance, with black hair and a bushy mustache. His medical ministries earned him the sobriquet "One Shot" because it appeared that one shot of whatever elixir he dispensed from his little sick bay always cured the common cold, which was the most common malady aboard the *Sterett* at that time. He interested himself with every facet of shipboard life and frequently stood deck watches with me. He had excellent eyesight, and I found him to be a great junior officer-of-the-deck until the skipper heard of his interest in operational matters and suggested that he be made a part of our regular watch list. Then Doc took refuge behind the Geneva Convention, which exempted medical personnel from military duties. Most important, he was a very creative individual with a completely independent and innovative viewpoint, and he did not hesitate to question old procedures and traditional attitudes—all positive attributes that the wartime influx of reserve officers contributed to the Navy.

At dinner in the wardroom one evening, Doc addressed the skipper: "Captain, why is it that the other ships in our squadron are making ten thousand gallons of fresh water a day, while we are only able to make eight thousand? I thought, for example, that the *Stack* was a sister ship. Well, sir, she's making over ten thousand gallons a day, and as I look at our crew I see that they need that extra water. They really aren't keeping themselves as clean as they should, and when I complain to them about their poor personal hygiene they tell me that they're on water hours, and can't take baths except at very odd and inconvenient times. I'm really concerned about their welfare, captain, and I wonder if there's anything we can do about it."

The skipper turned to the chief engineer and said, "Chief, that's a question for you, and I'd also like to know how the *Stack* makes more fresh water than we do."

Clearly embarrassed and annoyed, the chief replied, "Well, I can assure you that the *Stack* is not making more water than we are, and the doctor is wrong about our rated evaporator capacity. Our plant is designed to make eight thousand gallons a day, and we're doing consistently better than that."

"Well, Doc, I guess you've just been misinformed," said the captain. "I too wish we could make more fresh water, but that's just part of destroyer life, and we have to make the best of it." Doc nodded in agreement, and the conversation turned to other things.

Once my roommate and I returned to our stateroom, I remarked that I had spent several months in engineering and knew the chief's figure of eight thousand gallons was wrong. I offered to ask him to check the figure the next morning, so that he could have a chance to correct a bad mistake. Doc responded that this was his problem, that he had already decided to check the manufacturer's instruction manual to confirm the capacity figure, and that if he found that the rated capacity was in fact ten thousand gallons he would confront the chief engineer with that information in the captain's presence. He added that the chief had been less than cooperative on several occasions regarding minor alterations he had asked for to improve morale, and that perhaps this was a good opportunity to impress the chief with the fact that considerations of the crew's welfare deserved a higher priority than he appeared to give them.

The next evening at dinner, Doc again called down to the skipper: "Captain, this afternoon I went over to the *Stack* and talked with their chief engineer. He showed me the Griscom-Russel Evaporator instruction book, and it definitely indicates that the rated output of our plant is ten thousand gallons, not eight thousand. And furthermore, they are making about eleven thousand gallons daily by using a newly recommended procedure, employing boiler-water compound in some way that I didn't quite understand."

"Chief, I want to see you in my cabin immediately after dinner," said the captain. That was the last time the subject ever came up at the table. However, the chief engineer spent the next day aboard the *Stack*, and within two days the *Sterett* was also making eleven thousand gallons of fresh water daily. Our crew suddenly became cleaner and healthier, and for that Bill Scharbius deserved most of the credit.

In the letter he wrote almost eighteen years ago in response to a notice about a *Sterett* reunion, Bill penned this description of his service aboard DD 407:

I'm sure you all remember that crossing to Scapa as vividly as I do. My orders seemed to read destroyer duty, but this was submarine stuff, as we always seemed to be more under than above the surface of the angry seas. As a fully qualified surgeon with a hell of a lot of expensive and hard-earned training behind me, I felt ashamed to take Uncle Sam's money (not that I ever refused any actual offering from the paymaster), for I think the *Sterett* had the healthiest damn crew in the entire Navy. I couldn't even make headlines like some of the pharmacist's mates on other ships who were taking out appendixes with bowie knives and bent spoons. A few residual cases of gentlemen's diseases left over from glamorous Norfolk, an occasional runny nose, and a bit of seasickness were about all that ever came my way. And even those poor patients I soon learned to leave to the tender ministrations of my worthy Chief O'Briant, who had twenty years more experience behind him, and knew more about medicine as it is uniquely practiced in the Service than I shall ever know in a lifetime of civilian practice. O'Briant dispensed pills, drops, advice, and torpedo juice, with the practiced skill of a circus magician. My head swam with admiration, and with a resigned sigh I quickly gave up and let him run the show, always secretly hoping that someone would break a leg or develop a rupture, but I suppose he would have taken that over as well, with his customary dexterity.

By great coincidence, not many weeks ago while on a visit to England and Scotland I drove down through the western Highlands, past Glasgow, and found myself along the waterfront in Greenock where we once put in briefly on our way down through the Irish Sea bound for Gibraltar and the Med. The town looked exactly the same, and the beer was just as warm, some thirty years later. But I thought of our old ship, and here I am, for some crazy reason, writing about a few of my old reminiscences. Maybe I've forgotten the bad parts, as one does with time, but I loved that old ship. Most of you guys are just a blur now, though a few faces and a few names stand out, but there wasn't one man, from the lowliest boot up to and including the skipper, that I didn't like. I sound like Will Rogers, who said much the same thing and which I always thought was a lot of crap, for I sometimes almost enjoy disliking some people.

In mid-May came orders directing most of the squadron to return to the States. Aboard the *Sterett* we were ecstatic. But aboard the *Wainwright* everyone was unhappy except Commodore Moon, who had chosen to fly his broad command pennant there and who had volunteered for duty with the Murmansk convoys. His request had been approved, and now as the rest of the squadron was headed home the men of the *Wainwright* discovered that they would be on escort duty in the coldest, nastiest sea traversed by the Allied convoy system. I doubt that there was a coward among them, but no one in his right mind could have looked forward to such an assignment with much pleasure. The *Sterett* was directed to transfer the rest of her 5-inch ammunition to the *Wainwright* as soon as possible. We would be able to replenish our stock when we reached New York, but the *Wainwright* would find few such opportunities—and where they were headed the German Air Force, operating from its Norwegian bases, could subject them to almost continuous air attacks for several days.

The *Wainwright*'s gun boss was my Academy roommate, Vern Soballe. The *Sterett* moored alongside the *Wainwright* to expedite the ammunition transfer, and I climbed over the lifelines to shake Vern's hand and wish him well. He predicted that he and his shipmates would soon be salt-encrusted, frozen heroes. When I told him that by off-loading our entire 5-inch inventory we would be giving him three more projectiles than powder cartridges, he said, "No problem. If we get down to those last three bullets, I'll throw the damn things at 'em." There was not much that could upset Vern, and when we backed clear a short time later I was sure that he would prove to be a formidable foe against anything the Germans could muster. Meanwhile, the *Sterett* was homeward bound.

CHAPTER 4

GUADALCANAL LANDINGS

ONCE AGAIN WE CROSSED THE STORMY ATLANTIC. Our companions on the way back were the *Wasp*, the cruiser *Brooklyn*, and the destroyers *Lang*, *Nicholson*, *Trippe*, and *Ingraham*. It was a bruising and tiring ride, and the fog was so thick that I was constantly amazed at how well the ships were able to keep station despite the poor visibility. We made extensive use of towing spars to avoid collisions as we moved through the fog in closed-up formations: dragged by each ship a specific distance astern, the spars sent up a plume of spray for the next ship in line to follow. We held a good speed of advance, and although I am sure there were plenty of U-boats along our route, none got a decent shot at us. We reached Norfolk on 27 May and immediately entered Portsmouth Navy Yard for repairs and the installation of our first radar.

Shortly after our arrival the captain encountered me on the pier, where I was supervising the unloading of our 40- and 20-mm ammunition. "What are you doing here?" he asked. "I thought you were going on leave to Winston-Salem." When I told him that I thought it was my responsibility to get the ammunition off-loaded first, he said, "Well, I agree with you, but I hereby relieve you of that responsibility. I'll supervise unloading of the ammo. You shove off and get on your way home. You don't have much time." I thanked him and left, aware once more of his compassionate concern for his shipmates.

On 5 June we left Norfolk and headed south for the Panama Canal. There was little doubt that we were headed to rejoin the friends we had left behind in the Pacific the previous year. Most of us felt that we would see our fair share of combat there, and we had determined beforehand that when our chance came we would prove ourselves equal to the challenge. Our fire control technicians solved the mysteries of radar operation and became proficient in its use. We had received only air-search and fire control radars, which showed targets as small blips on a straight line. We did not have a plan view of the water's surface like that provided by the more sophisticated surface-search model. Still, the fire control radar was a godsend because it enabled us to determine positively that there was a target out there, that it was on a specific bearing, and that it was a precise number of yards away. Against an enemy who did not have that capability, it was a tremendous advantage. Chief Fire Controlman Chapman was a major factor in our capacity to exploit this new equipment. As we headed south I held routine drills on tracking targets by radar for our director crew. We found to our delight that we could track surface as well as air targets using only the fire control radar. Cross-checking our radar readouts with the visual rangefinder, we quickly gained confidence in the accuracy of the radar ranges: they and the visual ranges were almost identical most of the time. Jack Shelton, our "first team" rangefinder operator, became very radar-proficient, and within weeks we learned to shoot as well at night as during daylight.

Our companions on this trip were the *Wasp*, the battleship *North Carolina*, the cruisers *Quincy* and *San Juan*, and the destroyers *Lang*, *Stack*, *Wilson*, *Farenholt*, and *Buchanan*. Tom McWhorter described our return to Pacific waters in his "Stand and Fight":

> It was with some pleasure that we again felt the slow swells of the Pacific under our feet, and we thought back over the long days and nights in the Atlantic, when there was no respite from violent rolling and pitching; when thirty-five-degree rolls were commonplace (and even some of forty-eight degrees); of green water, freezing cold, beating against the bridge and spraying in sheets high over the director platform; of balancing our plates on our laps as we tried to eat in the wardroom while hanging on by our legs; of the struggle it was to try to stay in our bunks at night, let alone to get some sleep; of the U-boat alarms in the middle of the night that sent us running to our battle stations as we fastened up our life jackets— with a subconscious thought of that cold, black water. We were glad to be back in the Pacific where the real naval war was—but also where you could see what you were fighting, and where the water was warm enough that a man would have a fighting chance of survival if his ship was shot out from under him.

Quartermaster Tim Cleere's diary entry for 12–18 June reads: "En route San Diego. Weather is swell. Each day we are given a taste of what an air attack looks like with the planes from the *Wasp* doing their stuff. Fueled at sea from *Quincy* on the way up. It could never have been calm enough in the Atlantic to do that sort of thing."

On 18 June we arrived in San Diego. Several former U.S. President Line ships were at the piers. It seemed likely that they were preparing to carry troops somewhere, and that the *Sterett* would be asked to escort them. No one officially confirmed our conjecture, but when we saw that Marines were going on board we concluded that they were the assault force for an amphibious landing. Two other facts stand out in my recollection of that visit to San Diego: I was promoted to the grade of full lieutenant (a block promotion of the whole class of '38), and Doc Scharbius left us for Pensacola and a course in aviation medicine. "One Shot" had contributed much to the "soul" of the *Sterett*. A group of us took him to one of San Diego's nicer clubs for a hilarious final fling the night before his detachment. The new doctor (and of course my roommate) was Lt. Harry C. Nyce, a quiet, unassuming guy from Philadelphia's Main Line. He was a graduate of Duke University, a surgeon with more than two thousand major surgical procedures under his belt and an excellent sense of humor.

On 1 July we left San Diego with the three ex-President liners (*Adams*, *Hayes*, and *Jackson*), one amphibious cargo ship, the carrier *Wasp*, the cruisers *Quincy*, *Vincennes*, and *San Juan*, and the destroyers *Buchanan*, *Farenholt*, *Aaron Ward*, *Lang*, *Stack*, and *Wilson*. We could only guess at our destination, but our course appeared to be aimed at the South Pacific. Because we were with our old friend the *Wasp* we had many opportunities to track aircraft with our fire control radar. We held gunnery and director crew drills every day and made excellent use of the loading machine—an apparatus that used an exact duplicate of a real shellhoist to teach crewmen how to load ammunition into a 5-inch gun breech. It was a great training device, and the gun crews understood that it gave them the chance to become expert loaders. I saw to it that each of the four 5-inch gun crews spent at least half an hour every day on the loading machine.

The long voyage also allowed us to assess the performance of officers and crew at their various battle stations. I knew the *Sterett* was blessed with an exceptional group of gunner's mates, fire controlmen, and rangefinder operators. Frank Winant and Jim Clute had honed their skills, so that by the time I became gunnery officer all I had to do was follow the established routines and supervise the daily drills. These dedicated professionals formed the core of the ship's gun-fighting capacity, and if we could keep our loading crews at an equivalent skill level I was sure that we could take on any enemy. I was especially impressed with the knowledge and intelligence of our director crew. Ens. J. D. Jeffrey had relieved Hillard Marver as assistant gunnery officer when the latter was hospitalized after an auto accident in Norfolk. Jeff had repeatedly demonstrated his dependability and competence. If anything happened to me, he was ready to step into my shoes.

Chief Fire Controlman Chapman was a gem. I once told Captain Coward that I thought Chapman could visualize the inner works of the gun director and pinpoint any malfunction within seconds. His problem-solving skills were already legendary. Prior to our deployment to Scapa Flow, the director's optical system often fogged up because of condensation in the cold North Atlantic. One morning Chapman remarked that with about four dollars from the welfare fund he could eliminate the condensation problem. He then described how he could mount a second-hand hair dryer inside the director casing. No permanent alteration to the casing was required: he simply had to remove a small screw-on access cover, insert the hair dryer, and attach it to the director frame. I gave him the four dollars. He bought the hair dryer and installed it as he had described—and our condensation problem was solved. (We wrote up this procedure and offered it to the Bureau of Ordnance as a suggestion to other ships. BuOrd responded that they "had their best minds working on the problem" and expected to have a solution soon. About a year later, a package arrived from BuOrd containing their "solution." It was a hair dryer, painted gray.)

At the rangefinder was Jack Shelton, a youngster who had come aboard with the original crew in 1939 as a seaman 2/c. By the time we left San Diego he was probably a fire controlman 2/c. He was infallible in his capacity to identify ships and aircraft. He studied and practiced constantly, and his ranges (taken optically in the days before radar with the stereoscopic rangefinder) were always precise. The director pointer and trainer were Donald J. Starr, FC 2/c, and Robert O. Byers, BM 1/c, respectively. Both had steady nerves and excellent visual acuity and were, as far as I could tell, completely unflappable. The director crew was tops.

The gunner's mates were headed by newly promoted Chief Gunner's Mate Hiram Hodge. They formed a dedicated team and maintained the guns in apple-pie order. We were ready to shoot at a moment's notice, always. An excellent leader, Hodge was everywhere, turning up when least expected to observe some maintenance procedure or to supervise a drill. Gunner's mates Vernon J. Arnold, Vernon R. E. Martin, Clarence M. Simmons, and Charles L. Soelch were also the gun captains and were responsible for the training and individual supervision of their gun crews.

As we worked to perfect our gun-loading performance, the roles played by the first loaders were critical. These were the sailors who placed the 5-inch projectiles in the tray of the gun and positioned them for the hydraulic ram that pushed them into the barrel. Because the shells weighed about fifty-five pounds apiece, it took a strong individual to throw one into the tray every five seconds and to sustain that pace for a protracted period. The half-hour that the gun crews spent on the loading machine every day gave them a pretty good workout. But as we steamed across the broad Pacific a spirit of competition developed among the members of the four crews. They were all good, but of course some were better than others. The first loader of gun number two was Big Willie, the well-built mess attendant; he was certainly one of the best. The first loader of gun number four was a young seaman 2/c named Jim Grann, who appeared to belong in the same category as Big Willie. I fostered the sense of rivalry and began a series of weekly loading contests, timing the crews to see which could consistently load one hundred rounds in the fastest time over the course of a week. The prize was usually a carton of cigarettes for each member of the winning crew. I was delighted with their performance and their attitude. I promised them that we would soon tangle with the Japanese Navy, and that that contest would decide whose gunners were the best in the world.

As we sailed westward our priorities shifted. The main focus, dictated by Jess Coward, was on battle-readiness. The uniform requirements in the Pacific were far less formal, and the efforts normally devoted to "spit and polish" projects were now turned toward preparations for combat. It affected everything. Matters of appearance became relatively unimportant. The attitude was more relaxed, and the fact that we had dropped our division commander in Norfolk seemed to lift a burden from Captain Coward's shoulders. His new independence was a boon to him and to us. We also seemed to have a guardian angel in Washington. Before we sailed for the South Pacific we were afraid that the Bureau of Personnel would strip us of most of our veterans in order to man the many new ships then entering the fleet. It did not happen, and our cohesiveness had a great deal to do with our performance in combat over the next four months. We owed a debt of gratitude to someone. I was content to attribute it to God.

On 18 July we sighted Eva Island, one of the Tonga group south of Samoa and our first landfall since leaving San Diego. We entered the harbor and anchored off the town of Nukualofa, on the island of Tongatabu. For the next three days our sailors were to be seen on shore, happy to feel terra firma under their feet again. With typical American curiosity and ingenuity, they rented horses for the purpose of touring the island. In one case a sailor bargained with the owner of a horse, paid the five-dollar fee he demanded, and when he tried to return the steed to his owner discovered that he had purchased the animal. With the liberty boat waiting, the sailor had no choice but to turn the horse loose to graze, saddle and all. *Sterett* sailors claimed for months afterward to be the owners of a horse on Tongatabu. Tim Cleere's diary entry about the visit seemed very appropriate: "Haven't seen Dorothy Lamour yet, but she ought to be along any moment now."

THREE DAYS AFTER OUR ARRIVAL all commanding officers, plus their gunnery and communications officers, were summoned to a conference on board the cruiser *San Juan*. We assumed that we were about to participate in an invasion, but we had no idea where. The conference provided the answer. We were to rehearse a shore bombardment the next day on one of the uninhabited islands in the Tonga chain. Our ultimate target was somewhere in the Coral Sea; we received more specific instructions shortly after we returned to the *Sterett*. We were part of the task force assigned to conduct the first U.S. offensive operation of the war by seizing and occupying Guadalcanal, in the Solomons.

The bombardment rehearsal went off without incident, and we avidly read every scrap of intelligence material we could find about Guadalcanal. Tom McWhorter summarized what we learned:

This area constituted one of high strategic importance. Its naval possibilities long recognized, it had once been referred to by the German Admiral Scheer as "the finest natural fleet base in the world." The Japanese, very receptive to such advice, recognized this fact, and it was from Tulagi, Florida Island (across from Guadalcanal), that they had fought the ill-fated Battle of the Coral Sea.

The Japs had advanced down from the north and had taken Rabaul, New Britain, the northern coast of New Guinea, and all of the Solomons. They were smugly and confidently building an airstrip on Guadalcanal (the progress of which we had been receiving in daily reports). This airstrip, when operational in a few days, would give the Japs command of the air over the New Hebrides, preparatory to invasion, and also command of the air over sections of our supply routes from the east. Observation planes operating out of Guadalcanal would be of immense value to the enemy. The airstrip was almost complete. The time had come for us to deprive the Japs of the fruits of their labors. D-Day was set for 7 August— just eight months after Pearl Harbor.

On 23 July we left Tongatabu and headed in the general direction of the Fiji Islands. We were joined by a number of other ships and started to appreciate the size and strength of the force that the United States had mustered for this first offensive thrust. The *Sterett* seemed to be permanently assigned as a screen and plane guard for the *Wasp*, a job that we knew well and always enjoyed. By 4 August we were in the vicinity of the New Hebrides. Tim Cleere's diary described the next two days: "4 August—At sea. Fueled from the *Cimarron*. Weather is perfect. It was a lucky day, for mail from the States arrived, and I received four letters from Marie. 5 August—At sea. The captain had the crew gather on the fantail and told us some of the plans for the coming invasion. We are going to take over some of the Solomons and very soon. The transports with their accompanying warships made their appearance again today."

My own notes, compiled while hospitalized in 1943, indicate that 5 August was a beautiful day, with a calm sea and a hot, bright sun. We steamed northward with the *Wasp*, five destroyers, and two cruisers. At sunrise we were roughly six hundred miles south of Guadalcanal. Shortly after noon I walked back to our midship machine gun station to have a talk with Chief Torpedoman Jackson. He had an excellent sense of humor, and as we joked with "Doc" Nyce we began to spot other U.S. warships. At first there was just a mast astern of us—then another—and then several. Soon superstructures came into view, and we became aware that we were joining a whole fleet of ships: transports, destroyers, tankers, minesweepers, cruisers, a new battleship, and two big carriers. The carriers we quickly identified as the *Enterprise* and the *Saratoga*. Each was accompanied by a screening force similar to ours—two cruisers and several destroyers. One had the added luxury of a new battlewagon. It was probably the biggest show of seapower ever assembled in the Pacific at that time, and it was awe-inspiring.

By dusk on the fifth we were arranged in one huge disposition, the three carrier groups out in front and the transports (with their supporting cruisers and destroyers) bringing up the rear several miles behind. I was confident that we had sufficient force to take our objective. As we approached Guadalcanal on 6 August the panorama of ships held our interest, and there was a great deal of speculation over what tomorrow would mean for us. I recalled the skipper's briefing. The Marines were to land on Guadalcanal, Florida, Gavutu, and Tulagi islands to wrest those strongholds away from the Japanese troops who held them. The carriers would open the invasion with an air strike before dawn. The heaviest resistance was expected on Guadalcanal, which was the largest and most heavily garrisoned island. We would be screening the *Wasp* and therefore would not go close enough to see the actual landing; but determined air opposition was expected from Rabaul, and we hoped to get in a few shots at enemy aircraft. In fact, we expected an air attack and had been at Condition Two since morning, with half our guns constantly manned. I spent the entire day either on the bridge or in the gun director, wondering why we had not been attacked yet. We were only about one hundred miles from Guadalcanal at dusk. For whatever reason we remained unmolested, and I got a surprisingly good night's sleep.

The quartermaster of the watch woke me at 0400 on 7 August. I dressed and went to the wardroom to join as sleepy-eyed a group as I had ever seen. Herb May and I played acey-deucey and gulped down several cups of coffee before the alarm sounded for general quarters. At my station in the gun director I would have a box seat for the air activities. It was still dark when I poked my head through the director hatch and looked around. The three carriers were barely visible until they began to warm up their planes. Then blue flashes from engine exhausts flickered and burned—first only here and there, but all at once as if at the flip of a master switch they covered two-thirds of each flight deck. The air filled with the roaring, throaty noises of powerful engines, and in just a few minutes the planes began to take off. We could see them circle, rendezvous, form up, and disappear into the northern sky. Our guns were completely manned and ready, and we were eager for action, but the day belonged to our aviators and our gallant Marines.

Shortly after dawn the first planes returned to the carriers. Jubilant pilots circled us, rocking their wings and waving as they passed overhead. The attack had been a complete surprise. Reports from the carriers indicated that all air opposition had been wiped out while still on the ground. Antiaircraft positions had been hit, and the Marines were moving ashore. There was practically no initial opposition on Guadalcanal, but Gavutu and Tulagi were the scenes of fierce battles.

A few minutes after noon the expected Japanese visitors arrived. We did not know how many aircraft had taken off to attack the invasion fleet, but only twenty-five torpedo planes arrived at Guadalcanal. They went after our transport group, and we were told that we lost one medium-sized transport that had already unloaded. All of the enemy planes were shot down, either by antiaircraft fire from ships or by our fighters. To those of us aboard the destroyers accompanying the carriers, it was a keen disappointment to be able to see so little. During the visit by enemy planes, our force commander wisely steered us into a convenient rain squall to keep us out of sight. But we did share in the feeling of elation and pride that prevailed throughout our fleet. We had been a part of the first American offensive operation of the war, and it had been successful. We soon learned from dispatches that the Marines had faced a tough opponent on Tulagi but reported the island completely in their control by the next afternoon. On Guadalcanal they had taken the airfield, which would have been operational in another three days. There was another air raid that afternoon, but our fighters fended them off. The score as we tallied it at the end of the second day was one successful U.S. landing and defense against Japanese retaliatory efforts at a cost of twenty-one fighter aircraft, one transport, and damage to two destroyers.

Tim Cleere's diary for the seventh provides a good indication of the comprehensive understanding and appreciation of the tactical situation with which the *Sterett's* crew viewed these and other operations:

7 August—Coral Sea—General Quarters at 0515 this morning, and everyone raring to go. Only thirty miles from Guadalcanal, and that is close to be taking a carrier group. Let's hope it isn't a mistake. At 0530 the carriers launched their planes, and it looks as though they put up everything they own. All planes roared overhead for awhile, and then sped to their objectives. What a good feeling to know we are doing the dishing out this time. I have a dollar bet that we do have an opportunity to fire at the enemy today. If we don't, it means the Japanese airfield has been wrecked and our planes control the air. Right now it looks as though we are giving them a surprise party. 0600—No bandits yet. The transports must be close in by now. 0800—Lots of good news just received. *Wasp*

just informed us that their fighters alone have shot down thirteen Zeros and four patrol planes so far. No telling how many were wrecked at the airfield. Things look good on the beach, for they have ceased firing the main batteries at the invasion points, and no doubt the Marines are landing. The planes are constantly landing and taking off. The dive-bombers always return minus their bombs, reload, and go off again. No *Wasp* planes have been lost yet. Latest reports say that the troops have made landings at Tulagi at 0800 and that the opposition is diminishing. 1200—Word just received that seventeen bombers have left the Japanese base at Rabaul and are headed this way. 1330—Enemy planes have been sighted, but apparently they are attempting to bomb only those ships that are inside at the invasion beaches. The carriers had lots of fighters up to meet them and I imagine that they were well taken care of. About 1445 a *Wasp* plane crashed in the sea, and about one minute later another crashed into the barrier and toppled over. As there were many planes waiting to land with little gas in their tanks, the damaged plane was gotten rid of in a hurry by pushing it over the stern. Things must still be going well on the beach, for the scout bombers have run out of targets. Another troop landing had been made on the north side of Guadalcanal. At 1830 we secured from General Quarters. Everyone is tired and disappointed at not getting a chance to shoot at the enemy, and I have lost a dollar!

By 9 August the carrier groups had all moved south to reduce their vulnerability to air attack. This gave us a welcome opportunity to refuel. The bad news on the ninth was the message from the *Wasp* informing us that the Japanese had destroyed the cruisers *Vincennes* and *Quincy* and the Australian cruiser *Canberra* during a major surface engagement the night before. The cruiser *Astoria* had sustained severe damage and might also be lost. The message concluded, "Enemy losses not known, but hope they are heavy." We were shocked and puzzled. We had many friends on those ships, and we wondered how many of them had survived. It was sobering news indeed, and it brought home the realization that, success at Guadalcanal notwithstanding, the Japanese Navy was still a formidable foe. Now we wanted more than ever to get a crack at the enemy.

For the next several weeks we operated south of Guadalcanal rendering escort and plane guard services to the *Wasp* while she provided air support to the Marines, who were having no easy time of it. According to General Vandegrift, they whipped the Japanese ashore but took a nightly pounding from Japanese Navy surface units, including battleships. Aboard the *Sterett* we wondered why our own surface units were not sent in to oppose them. On 23 August we received word from the *Saratoga* and *Enterprise* groups that Japanese carriers and transports were on their way down from Rabaul. A nice fight was about to happen, and our group headed north at 25 knots in an effort to join the fray. We did not make it in time to see the enemy, but reports from the *Wasp* said that *Enterprise* and *Saratoga* planes had damaged a carrier, a battleship, five cruisers, three destroyers, and one transport, as well as shooting down eighty-one enemy planes. Unfortunately, in the exchange the *Enterprise* had taken a 1,000-pound bomb on her flight deck. Obviously the "big E" would have to return to some repair facility and get herself patched up, and we did not have any carriers to spare.

MEANWHILE, DAY-TO-DAY LIFE aboard the *Sterett* drew us closer together as we learned more about one another. Harry Nyce proved to be a dedicated medical officer, with foresight and administrative capacity. One of his pet projects was the creation of a team of first-aid experts who could help him deal with a large number of casualties. He recruited about fifteen sailors of all rates who in his opinion had the steady composure, intelligence, and compassion necessary to handle traumatic injuries on a large scale. He conducted training sessions, and when the inevitable accident occurred he delegated first-aid treatment to these individuals (always under his careful supervision). Harry also performed daily rituals to hone his own surgical skills, and I frequently walked into our stateroom to find him tying knots in a short piece of fishing line inside a matchbox—an effort to maintain his manual dexterity. In addition, he interested himself in all phases of shipboard life, and like Bill Scharbius he often stood bridge watches with me to gain a better understanding of the operational aspects of destroyer duty.

Lt. Tiny Hanna and I became fast friends. A William and Mary graduate and former varsity football player, Tiny was our popular first lieutenant. Like most reserve officers, he was eager to serve in whatever way the situation demanded. We seemed to share many of the same values, and I found him to be a real asset to the ship. When he first came aboard in August 1942 he was delivered to us at sea by high line from a tanker. It was understandably not his favorite mode of travel. To effect a high-line transfer at sea, two ships steamed on parallel courses at the same speed. Gradually one converged on the other until they were only about fifty feet apart. Then the transferring ship rigged a high line from its superstructure to a lower point on the receiving ship. The person to be transferred sat in a boatswain's chair suspended from the high line by a pulley wheel, and the crew of the receiving ship pulled the chair across the intervening water by means of a small line attached to the chair. The linehandlers had to keep the high line taut to prevent the occupant of the chair from being dunked in the water. On this occasion I watched with some amusement as the new arrival rode across the heaving ocean. When he arrived safely aboard the *Sterett* and I saw exactly how big he was, I called down from the bridge, "Welcome aboard, Tiny." The nickname stuck.

Lt. Comdr. Frank Gould, USN (class of '31), came aboard as executive officer and navigator in February 1942. I first met him in Charleston, where he was one of the shipyard's most knowledgeable specialists. He was the Navy Yard's ordnance officer, and he was instrumental in setting up the *Sterett*'s trouble-free gunnery installation. As our exec he went by the book but was always fair. He was a source of wise counsel regarding regulations and the legal aspects of personnel disciplinary problems. During our deployment with the British Home Fleet Frank proved to be an excellent navigator, and Jess Coward trusted his judgment. He was also a good-humored messmate but an aggravating acey-deucey opponent: the way he jiggled the dice in the palm of his hand and then abruptly dropped them resulted in an unusually high percentage of winners. I usually protested that technique, to no avail.

Ens. Herb May, USNR, was another mainstay on the *Sterett*'s team. He came aboard in Norfolk in March 1942 just before we deployed to Scapa Flow, and I recall that on the day he reported I asked him to round up a supply of new battle helmets. I did not think that he would be able to cut through the Navy's red tape in time to accomplish his mission. Furthermore, he was new to the base—he did not even know where the supply depot was—and had no means of transportation and certainly no rank to throw around. But when he returned that afternoon in a huge truck (which he had managed to wangle from someone) loaded with enough brand-new helmets to outfit the entire crew, I knew that we had acquired a prize in Herb May. By the time of our departure for the Guadalcanal show, he had become our officer-of-the-deck during general quarters.

THE 5-INCH LOADING CREWS became increasingly competitive during these weeks in the vicinity of Guadalcanal. One morning Chief Hodge asked me to officiate at a loading contest between the crews of guns number two and number four. The contest was to measure stamina as well as speed. Each crew would load four hundred rounds; the winner would be the one that completed the task in the shortest time. This race was a matter of intense interest to the entire ship's company, and a considerable sum of money was riding on it—four thousand dollars, to be exact. I became the custodian of the pot and scheduled the contest to begin at 1400.

At the appointed hour, everyone who was not on watch was at the loading machine. The gun captains drew lots, and gun number two picked the leadoff spot. This was Big Willie's crew, and as first shellman he was without question the key man on that team. With stopwatch in hand, I shouted, "Go!" Big Willie attacked each shell as it came up in the shell hoist, handling them as if they weighed five pounds instead of fifty-five. His movements were fluid and graceful, and there was no wasted motion. The noise of the loading machine took on a cadence of its own as one after another the shells came out of the hoist, were put in the tray, and went into the breech. Big Willie averaged about four seconds per load at first, and I waited for the pace to slow as he grew tired. But it did not slow. It continued for five, ten, even twenty minutes, and within thirty minutes the crew of gun number two had loaded four hundred rounds. Big Willie and his teammates looked as fresh as when they had started.

Now came Jim Grann's turn. He was younger and an inch or two taller than Big Willie, but not quite as muscular. He started out like a sprinter. Again the shells landed in the tray with a regular cadence. But after twenty minutes the pace slowed, and after thirty minutes (still short of the four hundred rounds) Grann was very tired and had trouble moving the shells. Gun number two had won, hands down. I presented the four thousand dollars to Big Willie for distribution to his mates and congratulated both crews. This performance assured us all that when our time came to fight, we would acquit ourselves well.

On 10 September our unit, Destroyer Division 15, was relieved of its duties with the *Wasp* group (Task Force 18) and replaced by Destroyer Division 24. We hated to leave our old friend, and Tom McWhorter expressed our feelings well: "Even though she was a hard taskmaster and a great responsibility, we were somewhat reluctant to leave her. For a full year we had taken her through the worst submarine waters in the world without a scratch. For that length of time the destinies of the *Sterett* and the *Wasp* were the same: Bermuda, Martinique, Argentia, Scapa Flow, the Mediterranean, Malta, the Coral Sea. She was a fine ship, and a friend of ours. We joked to each other about it. 'They can't do that,' we said. 'Why, the *Wasp* won't last a week without the *Sterett* to keep her out of trouble!'"

We were assigned to work directly under Commander South Pacific and proceeded to Nouméa, New Caledonia. Liberty was granted but there was nowhere to go, and after a few days we were glad to get under way again and run up to Espíritu Santo, in the New Hebrides. There we learned that we were to escort two cargo ships (*Fuller* and *Bellatrix*) to Guadalcanal. Our companion escort, the USS *Hull*, had just pulled in to fuel when we left the harbor, making it apparent that we would be the only escort until the *Hull* caught up with us. She did so the next morning, and our four-ship convoy headed north along the eastern side of San Cristobal Island, then turned west and entered Lengo Channel. We arrived off Lunga Point at dawn, and while our two cargo ships proceeded to Guadalcanal and Tulagi to unload we went on antisubmarine patrol and familiarized ourselves with our surroundings. We had a hunch that we would be frequent visitors to "Cactus" (Guadalcanal's code name). At 1700 we proceeded to Tulagi Harbor and anchored to wait for the *Fuller*. We were only a stone's throw from the beach, and many of Tulagi's Marine defenders took advantage of our proximity to ride out in native canoes or landing boats and do business with our ship's service store. They were after such simple little items as toothbrushes, toothpaste, soap, and razor blades. It was a revelation to meet them and to appreciate for the first time what the life of a Marine on one of these islands was like. Those of us who lived aboard ship had a comfortable existence by comparison.

While anchored there we received a red alert warning by radio, indicating that enemy planes were on their way to attack us. We immediately went to general quarters. As we did, the Marines also rang their general alarm, which sounded like a small-town fire gong that one struck with a hammer. At the first clang the boats shoved off and the beach swarmed with Marines, scrambling into foxholes and manning well-concealed anti-aircraft weapons among the palms and undergrowth. They added their voices to the din, yelling "Bring 'em on!" and other less elegant expressions.

We weighed anchor and stood out of the harbor ahead of the *Fuller*, both of us zigzagging at best speed and headed in the general direction of Guadalcanal. When we were halfway across (about eight miles away) we saw the *Hull* and the *Bellatrix* on our starboard bow, also standing out into open water. By this time the sun was close to the horizon, and the entire western sky was ablaze with the red glow of a beautiful South Pacific sunset. Ahead was the flat beach and mountainous interior of Guadalcanal, the peaks of which were hidden by dark, low-hanging thunderheads. It was from this tranquil scene that the planes emerged. About fifteen in all, they hopped over the hills and swooped down on the Marine shore installations. They were float planes of cruiser type, and in no time at all a group of our fighters from Henderson Field took them on. Tracers filled the dusky sky. In short order, two of our fighters scored kills. Their victims burst into balls of brilliant orange-red fire and fell into the water, where they continued to burn with a heavy black smoke. Tracers continued to pour out of one of them even after he hit the surface. I could not help thinking of the scorched and blackened bit of humanity inside that inferno. It was not a very good way to die.

By this time the raiders had started to scurry for home. A flight of four came within range of our guns, and we opened fire on the second in line. As the targets passed aft, the guns followed their movements; I could almost see down the muzzle of the number two 5-inch. The heat and blast of that barrel were damned uncomfortable for those of us in the director. Then one of our shell bursts exploded very close to its target. The plane faltered and fell smoking into the sea—it was one hell of a lucky shot. It was almost dark, so we turned east and headed out Lengo Channel to get clear of the Japanese bombarding force that was expected to arrive later that night. Everyone felt relieved to have had a chance to engage the enemy at last. The *Sterett* had scored her first kill of the war.

The next few days were described by Tom McWhorter:

> The night after the attack we anchored in Tulagi Harbor. The "Tokyo Express" had by this time become a very real thing. Usually composed of one or two cruisers and about four destroyers, this force would enter Savo Sound sometime during the night, make a sweep looking around for our light forces, then bombard Henderson Field and leave at a speed that would get them away from our planes by daylight. The Japanese had good aerial reconnaissance, and would not strike when our heavy surface units were in the area. A few nights earlier the old four-stack destroyers *Gregory* and *Little* had gone out to oppose them and were sunk in a matter of minutes. However, on our first night in Tulagi the Tokyo Express failed to show up. On the next day the cargo ships finished unloading, and we retired back to Espíritu Santo. When we returned to Santo we received a shock that struck us deeply. During our brief absence from Task Force 18, the *Wasp* had been hit by four torpedoes from a Japanese submarine, had burned furiously for a few hours, and had sunk in her patrol area south of the Solomon Islands. We were sick. It seemed ironic that she should have been lost so soon after we left her—and we couldn't dodge the feeling that perhaps it wouldn't have happened if we'd remained with her. Our division had grown so accustomed to the *Wasp*'s modus operandi that we anticipated her every move. That knowledge, or lack of it, on the part of those good destroyermen who had relieved us could well have made the difference. In any case, it was a sobering and depressing piece of news. Again we had reason to hope that we could tangle with the Jap Navy.

CHAPTER 5

GUADALCANAL SUPPORT

O**N 15 OCTOBER 1942** Vice Admiral Ghormley was relieved as commander in the South Pacific by Vice Adm. William F. Halsey. We learned of this shake-up in the high command when the new ComSoPac sent a short message to all ships in his command: "Strike Repeat Strike—Halsey sends." It was typical of the new commander, and it conveyed the posture of U.S. Navy operations from that day forward.

By this time, life aboard the *Sterett* had become rather predictable. There seemed to be three operational modes: the low-risk wait at Espíritu Santo to pick up transport ships bound for Guadalcanal, the moderate-risk escort phase, and the high-risk wait in the Guadalcanal-Tulagi area while the transports unloaded. We spent our time at either battle stations or Condition Two, with half our guns manned. It was often boring, but we realized that vigilance was essential to our survival. We did not intend to be caught flat-footed by Japanese aircraft or a lurking submarine—and certainly not by an enemy surface ship. The crew adapted to the routine easily. Our cooks kept a caldron of soup on the stove, always adding the leftovers from our meals until it became a real gourmet treat; when we had to stay at our guns all day, the soup was delivered to every man at his battle station. We were called to general quarters for dawn alert every day no matter where we were, so the days were long. Lacking anything better to do, Harry Nyce often visited the gun director. On one such occasion we entertained ourselves by imagining that we were at Bookbinder's restaurant in Philadelphia, deciding what to order.

There was no one in the director crew I would have replaced even if given the pick of the entire Navy. Assistant Gunnery Officer J. D. Jeffrey's station was about two feet to my right, while Boatswain's Mate Byers (the director trainer) sat next to me to the left. Byers was a quiet but strong and intelligent individual, the kind of man you would want next to you if you were ambushed by a gang of thugs. We all got to know one another quite well in those months of watchfulness, and an atmosphere of mutual respect developed. There could hardly have been a more compatible ship's company. This translated into high morale and a high state of battle-readiness.

There were also plenty of activities and personalities aboard to provide a daily touch of humor. For example, Chief Gunner's Mate Hodge was a great poker player and once admitted to me that he sent home more than one thousand dollars a month in winnings. I reminded him that gambling was against Navy regulations and that if he were caught he could lose his rating. Not long afterward the skipper told me that he knew there was a big poker game somewhere on the ship—and that Hodge was one of the consistent winners. He was determined to break it up, and if Hodge was part of it he would be demoted immediately from chief gunner's mate to first class. When I repeated Jess Coward's warning to Hodge, he smiled and said that he was sure the skipper would never find the game. As I expected, Hodge had underestimated the captain's intuition and experience. No more than a week later the game was raided by the skipper and the chief master-at-arms. The culprits were apprehended in the galley at about 0200 while we were en route to Santo from Guadalcanal. York, ship's cook and one of the game's veteran players, made a narrow escape. When the captain opened the door to the galley he activated the "darken ship" switch, which shut off the lights in the galley until the door was closed. In those few moments York, a diminutive man, climbed into an empty soup caldron and was never caught. As Captain Coward promised, Hodge was quickly knocked down to first class. But he took it in good humor, saying with a shrug, "The skipper sure is a wise old coot, isn't he? Well, I'll just have to make my rate again."

One day in mid-October while we were in Santo, I went aboard a destroyer tender to arrange for their help in repairing a shellhoist. When I arrived I came alongside a PT boat and was intrigued by the young skipper and his exec, both in worn and faded khakis, who were waiting for their crew to take freshwater showers aboard the tender. The next day aboard the *Sterett* we received a request (in a message addressed to all destroyers present) for a volunteer officer, rank of lieutenant, for duty with that PT boat squadron. I immediately wrote to the skipper to ask for reassignment. Jess Coward called me to his cabin and asked me what I was unhappy about. I told him I was not unhappy with my duty on the *Sterett* but just did not think we would ever see action. He smiled and said, "First, let me say that you aren't going to PT boats if I have anything to do with it, and I do. Second, I can guarantee that if you wait just a little while you're going to get all the action you could possibly want. Request denied!"

ON THE MORNING OF 5 OCTOBER 1942 the *Sterett* was off the entrance to Nouméa, New Caledonia, returning to the anchorage there after an escort run with the supply ship *Betelgeuse* to Guadalcanal. It was a beautiful day, and the calm sea changed color as it neared the encircling reefs from deep blue to blue-green, blending smoothly into the lush green of the dense island undergrowth. The scent of wild honeysuckle seemed to follow us everywhere in the South Pacific, and here it seemed to promise peace and quiet in a safe harbor. Ens. Perry Hall was the junior officer-of-the-deck, and he glanced at the navigational chart to note the course he would have to steer to avoid the defensive minefield.

Satisfied that he understood the entrance pattern, he turned his attention to two new 2,100-ton destroyers ahead, which were about to negotiate the channel. An exchange of call signs identified them as the USS *Fletcher* and the USS *O'Bannon.* Hall looked at them with a touch of envy. They were cleaner and sleeker in line than the *Sterett*, with her stubby one-stack configuration, and they boasted five 5-inch gun mounts instead of our four. These ships were new arrivals—welcome additions to the small force of destroyers that provided close gunfire support for the Marines, antisubmarine and antiaircraft escort services for troop transports and supply ships, and harbor-approach patrols for fleet anchorages like Efate, Espíritu Santo, and Nouméa. As Ensign Hall watched, the two destroyers cleared the reef and at once turned left, heading directly for the harbor entrance. Reacting as swiftly as the ships had turned, he realized that they were unaware of the defensive minefield and were almost upon it.

Once apprised of the crisis, Jess Coward seized the TBS handset and called to the *O'Bannon:* "Reverse your engines—you are standing into danger!" Within a minute or two it was apparent that they had "backed full" and were now stopped. The *Sterett* rushed to the scene and offered to lead the new arrivals safely in to the anchorage. We concluded in light of the momentous events of the next six weeks that Perry Hall's alertness and quick response were significant factors in the attainment of U.S. naval superiority in the region. The balance of naval power was at that point very delicate, and the loss of those two destroyers would have made a difference.

On the night of 11–12 October Rear Adm. Norman Scott's task force—the cruisers *San Francisco, Salt Lake City, Boise,* and *Helena* and the destroyers *Buchanan, Laffey, Duncan,* and *McCalla*—engaged three Japanese cruisers and two destroyers. Both sides lost a destroyer and had two cruisers damaged, one seriously; in addition, the Japanese lost a cruiser and had one destroyer nearly wrecked. Because the enemy force had intended to bombard Marine positions at Lunga Point, the engagement was a success from the U.S. point of view. We received word of the battle aboard the *Sterett* on the twelfth as we neared Guadalcanal, settling into antisubmarine patrol off Lunga Point at dawn. Only a few minutes after our arrival, search planes from Henderson Field reported seeing about one hundred survivors in the water near Savo Island. Two World War I–era destroyers were dispatched to the scene to rescue them. Shortly before noon the old destroyers returned with many forlorn figures wrapped in blankets on the fo'c'sle decks. They were all survivors from the gallant little *Duncan*—among them, my Academy classmate Herb Kabat.

Around noon we received news of approaching enemy aircraft. The cargo ships got under way so as not to be sitting ducks, and we headed northwest into open water. We were of course at general quarters (we had not left our battle stations since our arrival), and every eye was straining skyward in the direction of Savo Island. Suddenly Herb May saw the planes through a break in the clouds; they were almost overhead. He grabbed the skipper by the shoulder and, pointing to a group of twenty-three twin-engine Mitsubishis, yelled, "Christ, captain—look, there's millions of 'em!"

We opened fire with our 5-inch battery. The planes were high, and although our bursts came close enough to bounce them around a couple of times the pilots exhibited excellent discipline. They kept tight formation and never wavered from their course. Their aim was excellent, and we watched a perfect pattern fall smack on Henderson Field. Once the attackers departed, the cargo ships returned to their anchorage and continued unloading. We resumed our antisubmarine patrol and took advantage of the lull to feed the crew. At about 1500 the assault was repeated, this time with twenty-four planes from the southeast. Again our bursts came close, but not close enough to deter the Japanese from their mission. Again a well-placed pattern fell on Henderson Field. The transports continued to unload after the raid, but because of the interruptions they were still in the harbor after sunset.

We were on patrol five miles offshore at 2000 when we saw flashes from the Japanese shore batteries near Point Cruz. Their tracers arched their way eastward to Henderson Field, where we could see shells exploding. We were almost directly opposite that Japanese stronghold and needed no invitation from the Marines ashore (although we received one anyway) to "put the heat on" against those batteries. In a few minutes we opened fire on those flashes of light with our 5-inch guns. From up in the gun director it was beautiful to watch the four tracers of each salvo sail gracefully through the dark, converging as they traveled until they landed together at the target. As each shell hit there came a bright flash and a sudden cloud of smoke and debris. After the tenth or eleventh shell landed, I could no longer see the enemy gun flashes. With no exact target to shoot at, we "walked" our salvos out to the beach until we could see them splash in the water, then moved back inland in one-hundred-yard increments to the maximum range. After expending some three hundred rounds, we stopped firing. We had covered Point Cruz with shells and could see nothing there now but a few small fires.

Suddenly everything around us was illuminated brilliantly by a flare that seemed to be directly over our heads. We realized before the Marine radio report reached us that enemy aircraft had arrived on the scene. We searched the sky for a glimpse of the plane that had spotted us. As I looked out from the gun director I knew that we were clearly visible to any ship within fifteen miles and wished we had some way to put out that damn light. Next we were brought to attention by a radio report that blared from our bridge speaker: "Stand by to repel enemy surface units approaching from the west!" I did not know who had sent the message, but it did not matter much. We were about to become the target of the entire Tokyo Express.

The captain, in a calm voice, radioed the task force commander. "This is *Sterett*. Unless otherwise directed, I am proceeding to intercept. Over." I found myself wondering how many heavy ships we would face and whether we would get a chance to fire our torpedoes before they hit us. There was no way we could surprise them, and we had just expended three-quarters of our 5-inch ammunition. Fortunately, we received an immediate reply: "Do not, repeat, do not intercept. Retire to the east through Lengo Channel. Your friends are getting under way now and will follow you out. Over." I breathed a sigh of relief and thought, Looks like we'll live to fight another day. As we passed through Lengo Channel we could see the gun flashes of the Japanese bombarding force. They were too close for comfort. Then I thought of our Marines: there was no place to which they could retire. They had to sit there and take the punishment.

We remained at general quarters throughout the night. General Vandegrift's morning report confirmed that the bombardment had been very effective and had done significant damage to Henderson Field. He also noted that his men were tired, hungry, and in desperate need of aviation fuel. That was the bad news. The good news was that his patrols had discovered about two hundred dead Japanese soldiers in the area we had shelled. We felt that we had contributed to that body count, but we remained keenly aware that those brave Marines desperately needed naval support beyond what we were able to render. Our admiration for them grew daily. Tom McWhorter described these times in his own inimitable fashion:

> Things were tough on Guadalcanal. The Japs were continually putting reinforcements ashore at night from destroyers; air attacks were stepped up, and the Tokyo Express was an almost nightly occurrence. Messages from the commanding general of the 1st Marines [General Vandegrift] were received daily, reporting operations but also the status of his troops and equipment. It was a little pathetic to read those messages day after day, pleading for more planes, more gasoline, more troops. He would report the results of the previous night's bombardment by the cruisers and destroyers of the Tokyo Express, listing the number of serviceable planes on Guadalcanal; sometimes it would be pitifully few—eighteen or twenty. Some of the planes were old P-40s and P-39s of small value.

A flight of a dozen or so planes would arrive, and some would promptly be destroyed by Jap bombardment. Gasoline was critical at times, especially in the middle of October, and was being flown up by DC-3 transport planes. Some old four-pipe destroyers also were used to carry gasoline. The rate of attrition was high among the few Marine aviators who were carrying the burden in spite of the fact that they were exacting five or six Jap planes for each of our losses, and 50 percent of our pilots were being saved to fight again. General Vandegrift begged for "one more division in order that offensive action may be initiated." He stated that excellent though his 1st Marine Division was, the troops were constantly fatigued by strenuous operations during the day, and bombardment at night. The last remark made us grit our teeth, because the Navy was not yet in position to stop the Tokyo Express. . . .

During all this time the *Sterett* was getting not a moment's rest; it had come to be a very personal war.

The Guadalcanal Shuttle was in full operation. Every trip to the objective area brought about a quick turnaround. It was never-ending, escorting cargo ships one time and assault transports with reinforcements the next. During our time under ComSoPac the *Sterett* escorted every group of reinforcements the Marines received. It seemed that after every successful trip to Guadalcanal, Tokyo Radio would send out a friendly, patronizing broadcast to our Marines, saying: "Marines on Guadalcanal, you are doomed if you insist on waging this losing fight in the Solomons. You are now cut off from all supplies and reinforcements by the big guns of the Imperial Japanese Navy. You will get no more food, and you will starve. Lay down your arms; think of your loved ones back home!" Listening to Tokyo Radio was always good for a laugh; they understood our fighting men less than we understood theirs. Tokyo Rose ran the most popular radio show in the Pacific at that time. She would open by saying in her cheery voice, "Hello, you honorable boneheads in the Solomons. This is your favorite enemy, Ann." Then she would play some good old American records intended to make us homesick and quit. It was a good morale builder.

In our numerous trips "up the slot" we found that Japanese tactics followed a set, unaltered pattern. Air attacks on Henderson Field were regularly at 1145 and 1500 by high-altitude bombers, then at dusk by dive-bombers and Zeroes. The high-altitude bombers were beautiful planes, trim and silvery as they came in from the northwest in perfect formation, dropped their bombs, and veered south over Guadalcanal and then back toward Buka and Rabaul, from whence they had come.

We would shoot at them, but they were too high and wide for accurate fire from us. The Japs never learned. Every time they pulled a high-level raid—always on schedule—they would come in at twenty-five thousand feet. The Marines would be waiting for them with their F-4F Wildcats at thirty thousand feet, dive down on them through their fighter cover, if they had any, and send a large percentage of them to join their ancestors. Japanese losses were high, but they kept coming.

We had our set routines also, dictated by necessity. On our runs to Guadalcanal our task groups would be timed to enter Lengo Channel at about 0500 and arrive off Lunga Point at daylight. We were always at general quarters during these approaches, as we were most of the time in the objective area. It was rather pleasant up on the bridge when steaming through Lengo Channel, though. The channel was about three thousand yards from the beach, and the morning air just before dawn was cool and refreshing and carried a heavy fragrance from the wild honeysuckle and vegetation on the beach. Once at the anchorage the transports and cargo ships would make great haste in unloading, while we patrolled and searched for the Jap submarine that was usually in the area. The ships got under way during air attacks, with attendant loss of time; then they returned to the anchorage to unload until the next raid. At dusk the ships retired out Lengo Channel and on to the south of San Cristobal Island to return at dawn. As soon as we left, the Tokyo Express moved in. Often they were so close on our heels that we could see their guns' flashes as they bombarded the Marines and the airfield. It was a strange setup. The Japs had control at night and we had it in the daytime. It was a bitter pill to run out and submit to letting the Japs bomb with impunity. Our PT boats were on the job in the absence of any of our surface forces, and they would damage a Jap destroyer every once in a while—they even sank a couple of them…

Events moved in rapid succession in the month of October. The Guadalcanal Campaign was already two months old; the Japs were gradually getting their forces together for a supreme effort to recover the important island, and we were reinforcing our troops in an equally determined manner. To be beaten in our first offensive would have been unthinkable.

And so it went. On 15 October on the way back to Espíritu we were shadowed by a four-engine Kawanishi 97 for most of the morning. We went to general quarters in the hope that we might get a shot at him, but he obviously knew his business well: he never came within our maximum gun range. Our escort duties continued. The total Japanese force in the South Pacific at that time was formidable in comparison to ours. Admiral

Yamamoto had five aircraft carriers, five battleships, fourteen cruisers, and forty-four destroyers. We had two carriers, two battleships, nine cruisers, and twenty-four destroyers—a total of thirty-seven combatant ships against their sixty-eight. On 26 October in the vicinity of the Santa Cruz Islands the U.S. Task Force 16, under the command of Rear Admiral Kinkaid and comprising the carriers *Enterprise* and *Hornet*, the battleship *South Dakota*, six cruisers, and fourteen destroyers, engaged a vastly superior force consisting of four carriers, four battleships, ten cruisers, and twenty-nine destroyers. The action was fought entirely in the air, with the ships remaining about 250 miles apart. When the smoke cleared, we had lost the *Hornet* and the destroyer *Porter* and had sustained damage to the *Enterprise*, the *South Dakota*, the cruiser *San Juan*, and the destroyer *Smith*. The Japanese retired with damage to two carriers, a cruiser, and two destroyers. The aircraft tally was one hundred Japanese planes lost to seventy-four of our own. Despite the box score, the enemy had failed to achieve his objective: to deliver a strong force of carrier-based aircraft to Guadalcanal. Ashore, the Japanese Army had been ordered to capture the airfield; in a fierce battle, the Marines defeated the assault on Henderson Field, and our carrier pilots destroyed most of the planes bound for the new Japanese air squadron on Guadalcanal. We continued to hold our own. In the jargon of the active combat zone, Guadalcanal now became known as "Cactus," and Tulagi was "Ringbolt." Cactus seemed to be an especially appropriate name—our forces on that island were prickly, tough, and highly durable.

Our milk runs continued, and when we heard about the action at Santa Cruz we all wished we had been there instead of shepherding the transports. On 4 November 1942 we arrived in the Cactus-Ringbolt area once more, this time with a large force of transports and cargo vessels carrying Army reinforcements. We covered their landing on the eastern tip of Guadalcanal at daybreak and then joined the cruisers *San Francisco* and *Helena* to bombard Japanese positions at Koli Point, where the enemy had landed reinforcements during the previous two nights. Joe Jeffrey recently sent me these *Sterett* log entries from that day:

> 0815—Ship at general quarters maneuvering with USS *San Francisco* off Kokumbona Point, Guadalcanal Island. 0837—USS *San Francisco* commenced firing main battery on Japanese concentration on beach. 1008—Form 18 [in column behind the *San Francisco*] off Koli Point making eastern firing run on Japanese-held shore concentrations. 1010—Commenced firing on Japanese shore concentrations as designated by spotting plane. 1022—Ceased firing. 1025—Commenced firing on western run. 1032—Ceased firing. 1043—Commenced firing on second eastern run. 1048—Ceased firing. Total rounds expended 506; no casualties.

This modest bombardment effort marked our first attempt to use aerial spotting to guide surface gunfire. As soon as we formed up behind the *San Francisco* the air spotter, Lt. Red Johnson, came aboard the *Sterett* to outline communication procedures. We discussed every contingency and agreed on a plan of action. First we tagged along behind the *San Francisco* and the *Helena* while they blasted away at Kokumbona, then we steamed down to a position opposite Koli Point. The beach near the new target area was still littered with small landing craft. A few hundred yards inland and hidden from our view was a native village in which the Japanese had established defensive positions. We opened fire. Each salvo was spotted by Red Johnson, who circled about one thousand feet above our target area in a little cruiser floatplane. He used the radiophone to communicate with Jeffrey in the gun director, and because Jeffrey was the one who normally applied "spots" (corrections to the firing solution) no time was lost. If Red said, "OK, small boy, let's get that gun emplacement over there—spot up two hundred, left ten," Joe would make the corrections with the appropriate knobs. As soon as that was accomplished I gave the order to fire, and off went another 5-inch salvo. As soon as it landed Red reported back, "That got him—good shooting!" or "Didn't quite do it that time—try up another hundred," in which case we corrected our coordinates and sent off another round. This system gave us perfectly coordinated control over our gunnery. Johnson also spotted for the cruisers, and they really hit the Japanese positions hard.

Our gunfire support mission completed, we returned to the eastern end of the island and continued to cover the Army landing operations. During the night a couple of Japanese "cans" were reported off Lunga Point, and we wanted very much to go after them. This time the job was handed to our PT boats; although they chased the destroyers away, they did not inflict any damage. Aboard the *Sterett* we felt that we had missed an opportunity to fight on our own terms.

We received a few air raid alarms on 5 November, but nothing materialized. We concluded that our fighters had probably intercepted the attackers and shot them down. The Army's unloading continued in good order and was finished the next day. We left for Espíritu Santo with the empty transports, expecting to pick up another convoy of support ships. This is the way Tom McWhorter described the situation:

> From the second to the sixth of November, the transports unloaded troops and supplies at our beach at Lunga Point, but the primary purpose of this trip was to form a new beach at Aola Bay, about fifteen to twenty miles east of our main positions. There we unloaded an Army engineering battalion. It was the job of this group to build an airfield at Aola Bay. This spot was chosen for obvious reasons, considering the topography of "Guadal."

Guadalcanal is a mountainous island of volcanic origin some ninety miles in length (east to west) and twenty miles in width. On this relatively small land area are several mountains over six thousand feet high, and two or three of seven thousand or eight thousand feet. On most parts of the northern coast the foothills of these mountains slope down almost to the water's edge. There are two positions on the northern coast suitable for building an airstrip: the first and most desirable is in the vicinity of Lunga Point, where Henderson Field is located. The other is at Aola Bay. An airfield at Aola Bay would serve several very useful purposes. It would provide a standby field sufficiently far from the center of operations that if we were to lose Henderson Field we could maintain an air strength on Guadalcanal to neutralize the Japanese control of Henderson. Another practical use of a second field (other than the obvious advantage of having two fields instead of one) was that it would disperse our planes to minimize damage by aerial bombs and naval bombardment.

Thus the Aola Bay project was undertaken. [It proved later to be a disaster and had to be abandoned.] The combatant ships during the unloading phase were employed in a manner by this time familiar to us: at night when the transports and cargo ships retired to the south of the eastern Solomons, the combatant ships, cruisers and destroyers, formed up and patrolled Indispensable Straits—thus protecting the other ships from possible surface attack by enemy ships approaching from the north and west.

For almost two months it had been the practice to stay at our battle stations during all hours of darkness while in the Solomons area. It was a relief when the task force completed its assigned task and retired eastward through the slot between San Cristobal and Malaita islands, and on southeast to the good harbor of Espíritu Santo.

Soon after our arrival at Santo the *Sterett* received orders detaching her from her long duties as the South Pacific handyman and placing her once again on the "main team." It looked like a fighting outfit when we joined the cruiser Task Force 67.

Although little high-level intelligence flowed through the radio circuits to those of us in destroyers, we were aware of the increasing pace of our efforts to reinforce Guadalcanal's defenders. We sensed that the Japanese were about to make another effort to recapture the island. We did receive the daily reports from General Vandegrift indicating that he considered the situation to be nearing an extremely critical phase. As we steamed back to deliver another load of troops, ammunition, gasoline, and other supplies, we felt that we would soon be in a real scrap—and we were ready for it. On 10 November we left Espíritu with several cruisers and destroyers to join Admiral Turner's amphibious transports and cargo ships at Lunga Point. The sailors of the amphibious ships had been delivering troops and supplies to Guadalcanal for three months, and they had learned the hard way how to increase their unloading efficiency. They made their runs to the beach and brought their craft back alongside their mother ships with skill and precision. Meanwhile, the *Sterett* and the other destroyers established an antisubmarine patrol around the anchored amphibious ships. The operation proceeded throughout the day without interruption. That afternoon the cruiser *Portland* sent her observation planes back to Espíritu Santo. It was a significant move; obviously her skipper wanted to clear the decks for action. After escorting the transports out of the objective area that evening, we returned with the cruisers to make a sweep of Iron Bottom Bay in search of the Tokyo Express. Seeking out the enemy instead of running away from him was good for morale, but on the night of 11 November the Japanese decided not to cooperate. We remained at general quarters until after dawn alert and then led the transport ships back in so that they could continue to unload. Again we patrolled around them and took the opportunity to catch a few hours of shut-eye.

At midmorning on 12 November Admiral Turner sent a message to the entire force about a flight of twelve friendly DC3 transport planes due to arrive at noon. He noted that they would probably approach from the north and warned everyone not to mistake them for enemy aircraft. Captain Coward used our public-address system to pass along to the *Sterett's* crew the gist of the admiral's message. At about 1130, anticipating the customary Japanese raid, we went to general quarters. No attack materialized, but a few minutes before noon our DC3s appeared over Florida Island, right on schedule. As soon as Shelton spotted them, I reminded all of our gun captains over the sound-powered telephone circuit that these were the friendly aircraft we had been cautioned about and again warned them not to fire. I had just finished when I heard the first gunshot from some unidentified ship, and almost immediately a veritable chorus of fire rang out from the entire formation. Simultaneously, we heard the task force commander shout over the TBS, "Cease firing! Cease firing!" It did no good.

The shooting continued until the planes passed overhead. Then an angry Admiral Turner came on the radio and asked those ships that had not fired to identify themselves. Only Jess Coward responded. It was incredible, in light of the special warning the admiral had sent, that all of the other ships had broken their fire discipline. And more disturbing perhaps was the fact that not a single aircraft had been shot down; it was a damn good thing that they were not enemy planes. Admiral Turner then ordered the commanding officer of every ship that had fired on the DC3s to report to him aboard the flagship (the *McCawley*, an attack transport) immediately. One can only imagine what took place when those skippers faced the admiral, who had a reputation for being a formidable opponent under any circumstances. Captain Coward went on the public-address system for a second time to express his appreciation for the tight fire discipline the men of the *Sterett* had exhibited.

EVERYTHING HAS A RELATIVE ORDER OF IMPORTANCE, and as the events of the next twenty-four hours unfolded the incident of the trigger-happy gunners soon faded into insignificance. On the afternoon of 12 November we received a Condition Red warning: heavy air attacks were reportedly on the way. We went to general quarters at once. The transports got under way, and we formed a defensive disposition around them. The cruisers stayed in close, while the destroyers went into a circular screen formation on the periphery. We were on a northerly heading when the attackers first appeared over Florida Island, directly ahead. The *Sterett* was on the starboard flank, or the eastern side of the disposition.

Up in the gun director we used binoculars to scan the horizon for approaching bogies. Shelton, our keen-eyed rangefinder operator, spotted them first. "There they are!" he shouted. "Right over Florida Island—headed east." Their intentions were clear: safely out of range, they meant to head east as far as the channel entrance to Sleepless Hollow and then reverse course, coming in from our starboard beam. By this time, Shelton had identified them as "Betties" (twin-engine bombers) armed with torpedoes. We had our guns on full automatic control, and our director sights framed the lead plane in dead center. They flew to the eastern tip of Florida Island and then reversed course in a wide arc.

At the stereo rangefinder, Shelton checked his visual ranges with those of the fire control radar. As the planes came within our effective range Chief Fire Controlman Chapman turned his knobs and adjusted our estimates of their course, speed, and altitude. In about twenty seconds he called out, "Solution!" That told us that our director computer had solved the gunnery problem and was now generating angles of elevation and bearing that were automatically translated into gun position angles. Hydraulic motors pointed the guns at the proper spots, allowing for the necessary lead angles. The computer also generated fuse settings and transmitted them to the shellhoists in the ammunition handling rooms, where a small rotating ring engaged each shell as it was placed in the hoist. As the first shellman removed the shell from the hoist and slammed it into the gun tray, the fuse was set to detonate at precisely the distance calculated by the computer. Chapman could quickly change the director settings to set the fuses to detonate on impact (for a surface target) or to place the guns in local control, leaving everything to the gun crews.

Now I gave the gun captains the signal they had been waiting for— "Commence firing! Director control. Rapid, continuous fire." The crews loaded the shells and powder cartridges into the guns, and in four seconds the first salvo was on its way. The concussion was terrific, but by now we were used to it. Our first bursts were low and short, so we changed our trajectories. We were the ship closest to the attackers, and our tracers were headed straight at the lead plane. On our third salvo we made our first kill. With a tremendous explosion and a huge cloud of smoke our target fell out of the sky, its tail section completely demolished. The plane hit the water with a crash, skidded, tumbled, came to a stop, and burned like all the fires of hell. We shifted our sights to the next plane in line and immediately hit it squarely. It simply disintegrated in the air— big chunks of airplane splashed into the sea across a wide area.

Now every ship opened fire at one target or another. Because we were between the main body of the formation and the attackers, hundreds of shells streaked over our heads and hit the water ahead of the planes. The sky was filled with antiaircraft bursts, and our fighters flew into the middle of that steel hailstorm with their guns firing at the maximum sustained rate. The Japanese formation broke up and starting dropping torpedoes all over the place. Some fell at such a high speed that they somersaulted, while others ran true but wide. Two passed close astern of us. Two planes that we had hit fell into the water after they had flown directly over us. Our 40- and 20-mm shells made contact with engine nacelles and fuselages. Our automatic weapons gunners were terrific: Kelly, James, Keenum, and Grimm had nursed those guns, firing short bursts every day, and had sometimes slept by them, just waiting for a chance like this. The steady stream of tracers pouring out of those gun barrels was a beautiful sight.

An enemy plane approached our stern, and we watched with great admiration as a determined Marine Wildcat followed only a few yards above and behind it. The little Wildcat flew on through a wall of steel sent up by friend and foe alike, its guns planting a steady stream of hard-hitting 50-caliber bullets into the Japanese bomber until it seemed that the Betty should drop just from the weight of the metal it was absorbing. At last the bomber faltered and fell blazing into the water just fifty yards astern of us. The fighter veered sharply up and over on its way to another target, apparently undamaged. Every man on the *Sterett* who saw that performance let out a shout of admiration and delight. We later learned that the pilot was Maj. Joe Foss of the Marines, one of the highest scoring aces of the war.

Soon the attackers had all crossed our track. One crashed into the cruiser *San Francisco* near her after gun director and exploded in a huge ball of flame. It was apparent that the ship had suffered a number of personnel casualties. But twenty of the twenty-one bombers were in the water, most of them on fire and all of them destroyed. Not a single torpedo had reached its target. The wreckage of downed aircraft covered the water in every direction. We almost ran down a couple of their planes, coming so close we could have retrieved their rising sun emblems with a grappling hook. The *Sterett* had earned a taste of victory.

I called our "powder monkeys" up from the magazines for a look at what they had helped to accomplish. As soon as their eyes cleared the hatch and they realized that the burning planes were Japanese, they cheered loudly enough to be heard in Tokyo. The *Sterett's* morale was at an all-time high. We had finally been given a chance to demonstrate what we could do against enemy aircraft. The skipper used the public-address system to congratulate all hands; as he told them how proud he was of their performance, I could almost see their confidence and self-esteem build. A couple of our sailors had received shrapnel wounds but none were serious, and in the wardroom we sat around talking about the action—much like a bunch of kids after a ball game. We were elated. The transports returned to their anchorage to unload. That evening, the entire force moved south to avoid getting caught by the Tokyo Express.

CHAPTER 6

THIRD BATTLE OF SAVO ISLAND

WE WENT TO OUR BATTLE STATIONS AT SUNSET. J. D. Jeffrey and I were still talking about the air attack when a signaled message informed us that Task Group 67.4—the surface striking group that we were a part of—would soon be detached to return to the objective area. Our mission was to look for an enemy surface force reportedly en route to Guadalcanal. Once our transport group reached safe waters to the south, we left them and joined the strike force. The new group consisted of five cruisers and eight destroyers in a single column, with the ships in the following order from van to rear: the destroyers *Cushing, Laffey, Sterett,* and *O'Bannon;* the cruisers *Atlanta, Helena, San Francisco, Portland,* and *Juneau;* and the destroyers *Aaron Ward, Barton, Monssen,* and *Fletcher.* At high speed we headed north, swept quickly past the island's eastern tip, and then turned west into Lengo Channel. From my vantage point in the gun director I could see the dim shapes of the two destroyers ahead, their white wakes boiling back toward us in the darkness, and the almost indiscernible forms of the long column astern. It was a dark night with scattered rain squalls, but we could still recognize the vague silhouette of Guadalcanal on our left. From the flashes of gunfire and tracers flying back and forth along the beach, it appeared that our Marines and the Japanese were in a firefight. I was glad to be riding my comfortable little ship, where no one was shooting at me out of the darkness.

Jeff remarked on how difficult it must be for the skipper and Herb May on the bridge below to keep station in that tight formation. The interval between ships was only 500 yards, and we steamed at 20 knots—about 650 yards per minute. That interval had to be maintained by "seaman's eye," and the two of them were giving an excellent performance. We were mindful of the fact that the Tokyo Express had comprised a battleship or two during recent bombardments, but we had not been told what kind of enemy force we might expect to encounter on this run. Although our adrenaline was flowing, there was no particular apprehension about what lay ahead. The talk in the director focused on the events of the last day and reminiscences about our days at the Naval Academy. We steamed westward along the northern shore of Guadalcanal toward Savo Island. Soon we could see its vague outline ahead in the darkness—and then things began to happen.

J. D. clapped his hands to his radio headset and tilted his head to listen. A voice from the flagship calmly reported, "Enemy aircraft overhead." We stretched our necks and strained our eyes trying to see the planes in the inky night sky, but they were invisible. The next message was electrifying: "Seven enemy surface targets on the port bow. Bearing 312 true. Range 27,100 yards." It was Friday, 13 November 1942. The time was 0124.

The contact report had come from the *Helena*. (The *Juneau* and the *Helena* were the only cruisers equipped with surface-search radar.) The director and the guns swung around to the announced bearing. The men in the director concentrated on their assigned tasks as though this was just one of our morning drills, expertly turning the little knobs that generated estimates of the enemy's course and speed. Since the maximum effective range of our gun battery was a little over eighteen thousand yards, we had about ten minutes to wait before we would be in position to commence firing. We were there almost before we knew it. "Two large targets in that formation," Shelton reported. "They look like battleships." Battleships! And we had two heavy cruisers to match them. Fortunately, there was no time for that sort of thinking.

"Solution!" Chapman called out. "Enemy course 107—speed 23 knots." I relayed the solution to the bridge, where the skipper and Tom McWhorter needed all the information we could provide. Meanwhile, an unidentified voice on the TBS announced that there was a second enemy force to the right of the first one. We continued to head right for them, and I wondered why the first four destroyers did not break away from the cruisers to conduct a torpedo attack since we had the exclusive advantage of radar. Still there was no order from the OTC to do anything but move right down the middle, between the two Japanese forces. The range closed at an astonishing rate. When we were within four thousand yards I was able to see the enemy force for the first time. With my head stuck out of the director hatch, I could discern a battleship on our port side. By the time Shelton said, "Range three thousand yards," I recognized the gigantic superstructure of a *Kongo*-class battleship. She looked like the Empire State Building to me. We had chosen this ship (the *Heie*) as our target right from the start and had a perfect solution on her.

The tension in the gun director grew as we waited for orders. Chapman, normally very quiet and reserved, now turned to me and said, "Mr. Calhoun, if you smell anything bad, don't worry, it'll just be me." It was said loudly enough for everyone in the director to hear, and as we all laughed the icy tension melted away. We were still chuckling when a voice from the flagship announced, "Odd ships in column fire to starboard, even ships fire to port." We were the third ship in the column and so were obliged to forsake that perfect solution on the battleship. She was now clearly visible to the naked eye, and it seemed that at any moment she could blow us right out of the water. I muttered, "Oh, Christ!"—more a prayer of frustration than an oath—and ordered the director wheeled to starboard to search for a new target. I thought I had seen two battleships to port, and I assumed that they could see us as well. It was not easy to turn away and focus on the new targets that were supposed to be on our starboard side. But true to form, Shelton immediately detected one on his fire control radar. We started to track it, and within a few seconds we had the solution. Then, like a bolt of lightning, a searchlight from the battleship swept down our column. At that moment the voice from the flagship ordered, "Commence firing!" I repeated the command to the gun captains and the director crew. As our first salvo was fired, I watched the tracers arc toward their target. And in the next instant the world exploded.

The tactical situation became utterly confused; my observations during the rest of the engagement were oriented relative to the bearing on which our gun director was trained. Before long both the *Cushing* and the *Laffey* were out of action, putting the *Sterett* at the head of the formation. The *Atlanta* was on fire on our starboard quarter, but so were several Japanese ships—including our first target. Suddenly there came an impossibly bright flash, and shell fragments flooded the gun director. Once I ascertained that no one in the director was seriously hurt, I looked up and discovered that the steel mast above our heads had been hit— probably by two 5- or 6-inch shells. Our recognition lights and part of the rigging dangled there in a helpless mess. Had those shells struck just ten feet lower, no one in the gun director would have lived to describe the event.

The dim outline of a destroyer now appeared close on our starboard bow—a two-stacker, crossing from right to left. We prepared to let her have it with our two forward guns. I thought I recognized her as one of our own 1,630-ton class and reported that fact to the bridge telephone talker. But apparently my report was not received: the commence-fire order came up from the bridge. We were at murderously close range, and I concluded that the skipper knew what he was doing and that I was mistaken. There was no time to argue. I repeated the order. We were on a five-second salvo interval, and just in the nick of time Shelton yelled, "Sir, that's a friendly ship!" I knew from experience that Shelton's ship recognition skills were infallible. I yanked frantically at the handle of the cease-fire gong and shouted into my sound-powered telephone, "Cease firing! Cease firing!" The director pointer immediately elevated the guns so that if they went off the shells would fly harmlessly over the target. We did not fire. In a moment, the skipper backed full to avoid a collision with the target, which he now recognized as our companion the *Aaron Ward*. In the gun director we breathed a long sigh of relief and had just started to relax from that crisis when we spotted the prize. There, only two thousand yards away on our port bow, was a battleship.

She had absorbed all that our cruisers could dish out and was on fire from her bridge aft. She was making very little headway; I estimated her speed to be under 5 knots as she steamed in front of us. She was a perfect target. Beautifully illuminated by her own fires, her superstructure towered high above us, and I instructed Byers to train his sights on her "pagoda," or bridge structure. Before he had even trained around that far, the word came from the bridge to open fire. The instant that Byers reported, "On target," I repeated the commence-fire order to the gun and director crews. We poured nine salvoes (thirty-six projectiles) into that bridge structure, and I could see them explode against it. At that range every shot hit its mark, and those thirty-six 5-inch shells raised plenty of hell over there with any officers or men who were exposed. By this time we were less than a thousand yards away, and we could see several Japanese sailors dive overboard with their clothes on fire. I told the gun crews what their work had accomplished, and over my telephone I could hear their cheers as the news was relayed to them by their captains.

Tom McWhorter fired a full salvo of four torpedoes at the target. I saw two red explosions in the water a couple of minutes after hearing the "fish" leave their tubes; other *Sterett* observers also reported seeing them. It appeared that we had scored two hits in the engineering spaces (although subsequent assessments did not give the *Sterett* credit for them). The fires topside seemed to flare up, and once more I saw crew members running along her main deck and jumping overboard. She was dead in the water and burning fiercely when we left her. We crossed her bow no more than five hundred yards ahead of her—so close that she could not lower her guns far enough to hit us.

The action now reminded me of a no-holds-barred barroom brawl, in which someone turned out the lights and everyone started swinging in every direction—only this was ten thousand times worse. Shells continued to drop all around us, star shells and flares hung overhead, tracers whizzed past from various directions, and everywhere we looked ships burned and exploded against the backdrop of the night sky. I could not tell where our forces were. We seemed to be in the midst of about ten Japanese ships without a friend in sight. But we were the *Sterett*, and most of us believed that we were invincible. To my mind our skipper was the best in the fleet—I knew we would find a way out somehow. But my reverie was short-lived. I could not believe what I now saw. It was nearly a perfect setup.

Broad on the starboard bow and only about one thousand yards away was a large Japanese destroyer of the *Fubuki* class. With two twin gun mounts aft, the four guns on her stern were a match for all of ours. But both the ship and her guns were pointed away from us. She was on a heading almost opposite ours, and she still had not seen us. I estimated her target angle (our relative bearing from her) at about 150 degrees. She had her after guns trained on the centerline and was making very little headway.

With a single roar our four guns spoke together. Four tracers sped straight and true to the target and exploded in her bridge structure. Five seconds later we fired our second salvo, and four more tracers leapt across the intervening eight hundred yards. We could not miss, and we did not. I noted with admiration how beautifully the tracers, which were probably some three hundred feet apart when they started out from our gun muzzles, converged into a grouping no more than ten feet apart when they struck their target. Those four shells disappeared directly into the housings of the ship's after gun mounts. With a sudden, tremendous roar, she blew up. Her stern came completely out of the water, explosions obscured her after gun mounts, and a tremendous fireball burst skyward. As she settled back into the water, it looked as if the whole after section of her hull was cherry red. Involuntarily I cried out, "Oh, you poor son of a bitch!" The water around her seemed to boil, and her hull threw off steam with a hiss that we could hear aboard the *Sterett*. I described the scene to the gun captains and told them to send their powder monkeys up the ladder to the main deck so they could see what they had just done. A few seconds later I heard their shouts and cheers as they viewed their vanquished foe. She burned brilliantly for a few minutes while we steamed past her; then there was total darkness. Frank Gould remarked in a recent letter that he "saw our destroyer target with her well-deck awash after we fired torpedoes and steamed past her, distant about two hundred feet on our starboard hand." It appeared to many eyewitnesses that she had gone down. There was little doubt about that in my mind. I did not know until later that Tom had also fired two fish into her. They must have struck at the same moment as our second salvo of gunfire.

Soon I learned that the shell hits we had absorbed in the vicinity of the after gun mounts had done considerable damage. I heard confused background noises on my telephone, and someone who did not identify himself reported, "Sir, there's a bad fire in gun number four." I ordered him to use the sprinkling and flooding systems wherever necessary and received an acknowledgment; then I lost communication with both of the after guns. I looked aft and saw that there was indeed a bad fire back there. It appeared to be in both of the after guns and perhaps in the ammunition rooms as well. I called the bridge and repeated the report of fires in the two after gun mounts. As I spoke I saw two men dive overboard from the top of the after deckhouse, their clothes ablaze.

Still unaware of the magnitude of our damage and personnel losses, I took advantage of the lull to send Byers, Shelton, and J. D. down to the battle dressing station for treatment. They returned in only a few minutes, solemn and subdued. When I asked Byers if he had gotten his neck dressed, he said, "No, sir. There's guys down there with their legs off, and a lot of people are dead. Doc's got too much to do without us bothering him." That was the first indication we had of the heavy toll the men of the *Sterett* had already paid.

Tom McWhorter described our next encounter with an old Japanese three-stack cruiser on our port bow: "It was steaming at right angles to us and going from starboard to port. I have never been quite so furious as I was when I saw that ship for an instant and realized that I had no torpedoes that would bear on him. The captain asked me if I could give him one, but I had to tell him that I could not unless we changed our course about 100 degrees. By this time the cruiser had disappeared." We also saw this target in the director, but because we had only two 5-inch mounts in commission and no port torpedoes left I concluded that the skipper had thought it wisest not to fire on her. It appeared she had not seen us.

From my vantage point in the gun director I again looked aft, wondering how things were in the gun batteries. As I watched we were struck by a shell in the vicinity of the after deckhouse. In seconds an explosion ripped out of the top of gun number three. There appeared to be several fires in that vicinity now, all illuminating the Stars and Stripes as it waved defiantly twenty feet above the gun mount. Our brilliantly lighted colors, coupled with the fact that we were the only single-stack destroyer in the action, left little doubt as to our identity. And the Japanese had taken note of it.

LACKING A SUITABLE TARGET for their short-range 20-mm gun, Red Hammack, Peter Grimm, and Robert Priest stood near the centerline of the ship and watched the furious action. They could clearly see a battleship on the port side, seemingly on top of us. The explosion of the Japanese destroyer placed the *Sterett* in silhouette against a fiery background, and the huge enemy ship chose not to ignore the target. In Red Hammack's words:

> We were looking right down those 14-inch gun barrels. They fired a split second later, and at that same instant Peter dove head-first behind the trunnion of the starboard 20-mm and Priest ducked down in front of me, while I had turned my back to the battleship. I caught three pieces of shrapnel (in my left elbow, about a half-inch below my butt in my left leg, and in the right cheek of my fanny). I was really scared, and it occurred to me that I had just had my butt shot off. You can believe this or not, but suddenly I wasn't scared anymore. I was mad enough to whip the whole Jap Navy all by myself. Peter said, "You OK, Red?" and I said, "Hell, no. Those bastards just shot me in the ass!"

As we drew away from the battleship, there still appeared to be Japanese ships in every direction. Tracers continued to thunder over our heads, and every once in a while they hit us. We took two more shell hits in the vicinity of the after deckhouse, and the fires became more intense. In the gun director there was not much chitchat. I suppose all of us wanted to know what we could do to help.

Down in the engineering spaces Hugh Sanders and his outstanding team of senior petty officers, supported by a gang of nonrated firemen, performed flawlessly and courageously. Unable to see the action but aware that their ship was taking terrific punishment, they confronted one crisis after another: They maintained steam and fire-main pressure, coped with repeated electrical outages caused by severed wires, and expertly handled a succession of radical orders to the engines. By doing all these things they enabled the commanding officer to maneuver the ship and so to bring her safely through one of the fiercest surface actions ever fought by the U.S. Navy. Jess Coward took full advantage of the expert support rendered by his engineers. Throughout the battle he had called for radical speed changes to avoid collisions and to steer the ship when the rudder proved useless. When he retired from the melee he utilized the *Sterett's* best speed to get away, and on at least one occasion he had to call for "all back full" to avoid running aground. That dauntless "black gang" never failed to deliver what he requested.

When Tom McWhorter tried to communicate with his torpedomen after the encounter with the destroyer, he was unable to get any reply over the telephone. Now he asked the captain for permission to go below to ascertain the status of the torpedo battery. Permission was granted, and Tom climbed down to the main deck. He later wrote:

> When I got down to the tubes—on the main deck amidships—the first thing I noticed was a complete lack of activity. There was a pungent stench about the area; my feet slipped on the deck, and I almost lost my footing. As my eyes became accustomed to the darkness I could make out two or three bodies on the deck—prone and silent. Then I realized that the entire deck was slippery with human blood and pieces of human flesh.
>
> But no time for that now. They [the torpedo tubes] were not manned. I got up on the starboard tube, the one with the two remaining torpedoes, and trained it out. It trained out a few degrees and then grated to a stop; it was damaged and useless. Then I returned to the bridge and reported to the captain that the remaining torpedoes could not be fired. In addition to this, both of the after guns were disabled—leaving only the two forward guns as our total offensive armament and protection. I heard the captain say, "We will fight her until we sink!" This captain of ours was a fighter,

no mistake about it, and as long as we could contribute any appreciable amount of firepower to the melee, in which every gun counted, we would fight. Actually, it amounted to just that: the odds were so heavy against us that one torpedo or one gun was of unprecedented importance.

During Tom's absence Herb May asked the skipper if he planned to retire, and he had bristled at the suggestion. He replied, "Hell, no. We've still got two torpedoes left." But once Tom reported that those two fish were out of commission, he changed his mind. Turning to Frank Gould, he said, "OK, Frank, let's get out of here." That was a tall order. The gyro compass was out of whack, the steering cable was cut on one side (we were steering with the trick wheel and the engines), the ventilation system was damaged, the SC radar antenna was demolished, the emergency recognition lights were destroyed, the emergency power cable to the steering motor was severed, and the after magazines were flooded. Frank pointed us in a generally northerly direction. Our only armaments were the two forward 5-inch guns. There was nothing behind us but blazing ships, and nothing ahead but the dim outline of Florida Island. We had not seen an American ship for a long time, and I began to wonder if we were the only one left.

I called down to the bridge to ask to be put to use in some way during the lull in the fighting. Word came back that the captain wanted to see me. Turning over what was left of our gun battery to Jeff, I climbed over the side of the director and down the small ladder to the wing of the bridge. The skipper stood with Herb on the starboard side of the bridge, looking calm and unruffled. I walked over to him. "Did you want me to do something, captain?"

"Yes, Cal. I want you to go back aft. Do whatever you can to help them back there—but don't stay. Inspect our damage, and then come back up here and let me know what action is necessary to save the ship."

"Aye, aye, sir."

As I turned to go to the ladder, he put his hand on my shoulder. "Good luck."

THE FLAMES THAT HAD BEEN SHOOTING OUT THE TOP OF OUR NUMBER three mount had subsided, and the topside of the ship was dark. I groped my way down to the main deck and went aft along the starboard side. At the torpedo mount I encountered the first evidence of shell damage. The 5-inch hits near our torpedo tubes had done only superficial structural damage, but they had inflicted severe personnel casualties. I was able to recognize "Little Willie" Walker, one of our best-liked mess attendants, George Jackson, the veteran chief torpedoman, and "Smitty," one of his strikers, still lying where they fell. All were dead. Crossing over to the port side, I continued aft.

The upper handling room for 5-inch mount number three was a shambles. Three 14-inch shells had struck the port-side bulkhead and detonated on impact. Thousands of shrapnel fragments had made a sieve of the compartment, killing everyone inside; ignited bins of 5-inch ready service powder; and deflected upward through the gun mount itself, killing all but two of the gun's crew. Hodge and Keenum were removing the remaining cans of powder from the room when I arrived. Hodge entered through one of the holes gouged by the 14-inch projectiles (holes that measured twenty-two inches across and fifteen inches vertically), scooped up the hot powder cans in his arms, and hurried through the washroom door to dump them overboard. Keenum played a fire hose on him during the early part of this procedure but eventually gave this up and joined in the unloading process. Several cans of powder actually detonated in the air with low-order explosions after Hodge tossed them overboard. Keenum also operated the magazine's sprinkler system on his first trip into the compartment.

A single 5-inch hit had also penetrated the mount of gun number three without detonating. It mortally wounded V.R.E. Martin (GM 2/c), the gun captain, who insisted that the doctor attend to others because he was sure he would die anyway. I found what was left of this crew dead at their battle stations. Grann, the young first shellman of gun number four, had dived overboard with his clothing on fire; no doubt he was one of the two men I had seen from the gun director. He was never recovered.

Hodge and I moved aft on the main deck, leaving Keenum to fight the fire. Opening the hatch to the ladder, the two of us descended into the number four upper handling room. Here also casualties were heavy. The scene was similar to what we had encountered on the deck above. Shrapnel fragments had ignited ready service powder and started searing fires. The crew's quarters forward of the handling room were still ablaze. Ens. Perry Hall was single-handedly fighting the fire with a hose and appeared to have the situation under control. He exuded confidence and calmly assured me that he needed no assistance. Electrical, steering, and degaussing cables had been severed by shell hits. Gun mounts, ammunition hoists, bulkheads, and frames were twisted and distorted. But our watertight integrity was intact, and no machinery was damaged other than instruments and electrical steering-control devices. I marveled at the ship's ability to take punishment. I left Hodge to assist with the fire fighting and made my way back up to the bridge, to make my report to the skipper.

Perry Hall was the junior officer-of-the-deck when the engagement started. Sensing that he could be of greater help at his damage control station on the main deck, he asked for and was granted permission to go below. This is his account, written in 1977, of what transpired from the time he arrived on the main deck after our encounter with the battleship:

First I checked my 20-mm crew, who were watching intently the havoc around them. As we stood there, the starboard torpedo tubes released two torpedoes at a ship only a thousand yards away. The 5-inch battery commenced firing at the same ship. Then what had been a ghostly gray shape became a brilliant orange ship from stem to stern. It was as if a huge star shell had burst and illuminated the sea. It was like noon on a bright sunny day.

The next thing I knew, I was thrown to the deck violently, landing in a sitting position and momentarily blacking out. I got up, dazed but with no apparent physical damage, except cuts and bruises. I realized that we had been hit. There were fires aft of the torpedo tubes, the number three gun had been hit, and I could see men jumping over the side with their clothes ablaze.

I dashed forward to the wardroom . . . looking for the first lieutenant, Tiny Hanna. Tiny was assisting Doc Nyce with the wounded. I asked him what he wanted me to do. "Take charge of the after repair party," he ordered. As I turned to leave, he noticed that I had been cut and asked if I needed attention. It was only minor compared to the carnage around us, so I just left.

By the time I got out on deck the repair party had hoses playing on the fires. Unfortunately, shrapnel had pierced a number of the hoses topside, and pressure wasn't all it should be. The decks were slippery with blood, and potatoes were scattered about—plus the ship was turning to avoid gunfire and other ships—so maintaining footing was a problem. The screams of the wounded pierced the night and mingled with the orders directing the fire fighting. I continued aft.

The number four handling room was a near holocaust. Bits of burning bedding smoldered on the bunks, burnt bodies were scattered about the deck, and water poured into a shell hole just above the waterline whenever the ship heeled over. A 4- or 5-inch shell had passed through the ship and, miraculously, had not exploded. But the stench of burning flesh and powder made breathing difficult.

Men appeared, and we started to stuff mattresses into the holes and used shoring to hold them in place. A fire hose was put into action to extinguish the burning materials that had fallen into the powder room and to cool the 5-inch powder cans. By this time water was streaming over the hatch coaming and helping to flood the magazine. Bodies, mattresses, and other debris sloshed back and forth with the movement of the ship. Footing was difficult, and battle lanterns provided the only light. I had no idea what time it was or where the ship was. I knew we were maneuvering with the screws because I couldn't hear the rudder.

Finally the fires were out and the holes were plugged. I made my way topside. The sudden burst of fresh air into my lungs made me feel almost faint. I suddenly realized the battle was over and I was still alive. The horror of the last hour hit me like a punch in the stomach, and I retched. As the luminous water rushed along the side of the ship I glanced up and looked aft to the scene of the battle. Flaming hulks blazed like sacrificial altars to the gods of war. I felt strangely detached, as if I were on another planet surveying the earth in miniature. I stumbled forward to the bridge and made my report to the captain.

I arrived back in the pilothouse at 0345, in time to relieve Tom McWhorter as OOD (he had relieved Herb May shortly after we retired from the battle). We had made our way up to Florida Island, skirted its shoreline, steamed south toward Guadalcanal, and were about to turn to the east into Lengo Channel when I said, "I relieve you." Tom immediately went below. Ahead were the first faint streaks of dawn. To starboard was the dark outline of Guadalcanal, only a mile or so away. On our port side, in the dim distance, was Florida Island. With no gyro and a magnetic compass that was behaving erratically, navigating that narrow channel was no easy task. Somehow, Frank Gould managed to feel his way through to safety.

Until we entered Lengo Channel we had every reason to believe that we were the sole surviving ship of the task group. However, just as we turned east we intercepted voice radio broadcasts that revealed the existence of five companions somewhere ahead of us, still moving under their own power: the cruisers *Helena, Juneau,* and *San Francisco* and the destroyers *O'Bannon* and *Fletcher* were in Sealark Channel to our north and east. The *Sterett* was the last U.S. ship to steam away from the battle area. We reported our presence to the *Helena*—admirals Callaghan and Scott were both killed in the first few minutes of the action, and Capt. John Hoover of the *Helena* was now the senior officer present afloat (SOPA). We were directed to join up with the rest and take the screening station on the port bow of the formation. Captain Coward went to maximum speed, and we moved to our assigned station. As we steamed past the port side of the *San Francisco,* I counted twenty-six shell holes in her side. The *Helena* and the two destroyers in her screen, the *O'Bannon* and the *Fletcher,* appeared to be undamaged (we later discovered that the *Helena* had been hit but had suffered only superficial damage, while the two destroyers had not been hit). I could not help wondering about the fate of the other eight U.S. ships that had steamed into action with us just a few hours before.

Now we started to piece together a more comprehensive picture of our condition. Eleven shell hits had caused extensive material damage topside, but compared to our personnel losses it seemed negligible. We had lost a total of thirty-two men—twenty-eight killed and four missing. Fourteen more lay critically injured with severe shrapnel wounds and third-degree burns. Others (such as those in the director crew) were also hurt and in need of medical treatment and in some cases hospitalization, but they are not included in the casualty figures. The loss of shipmates who had become close friends over the past three years tempered any elation we might have felt over the damage we inflicted on the enemy. We were a somber crew.

AFTER RED HAMMACK WAS SHOT IN THE SEAT OF THE PANTS, he followed Peter Grimm's instructions and reported to the wardroom. He was the first of the wounded to arrive there. Doc Nyce asked, "Where are you hit, Red?" When Hammack told him, Harry responded, "Drop your pants."

As Red loosened his belt, someone—probably Tiny Hanna—came through the wardroom door carrying Hawkins, a young torpedoman 2/c, in his arms. One of his legs hung from his knee by a shred of flesh, and he was bleeding profusely. As soon as Red saw Hawkins, he pulled up his dungarees and decided he had better do something else, like help with the fire fighting. Harry Nyce sensed Red's reaction at once and said, "Hold it, Red. I need you here more than they do back aft. They have plenty of people to help with the fires, and I'm real shorthanded here." Red was one of the fifteen people who had received Harry's advanced first-aid training, and he stayed in the wardroom to help with the wounded. Recalling this experience, Hammack wrote:

> I have thought about Doc Nyce many times since then. . . . He was the calmest man I ever saw. I can see him now, quietly standing there as they brought the wounded in, some on stretchers, some in their arms. From time to time, Doc would point and say, "Take him out." These were the ones who had died, or were so far gone he knew he couldn't save them. I remember J. E. Robinson, from Dallas, lying in a wire stretcher. I said, "Robbie, what are you doing down there, goldbricking?" He smiled and said, "Yes, but don't tell Stu" (the chief commissary steward, who was his boss). I said, "OK, I'll give you just five minutes." Robbie smiled again. "That's about all it will take, Red." Just a little while later Doc nodded for him to be taken out. I helped carry him out on deck, in the dark, on the starboard side of the uptakes. As I put my end of the stretcher down

and straightened up, I looked aft over the midship deckhouse. I could see the reflection of the fires in the after part of the ship, and there in the light above gun number three, flying defiantly in the breeze, was Old Glory. The shadows danced back and forth as she waved, and the firelight showed the familiar red and white stripes, and the blue field with its forty-eight white stars. I was suddenly filled with thoughts of home, and a feeling of pride and exhilaration swept over me. Thrilled by the sight, I shouted, "She's still flying! We're not through yet, you bastards." And I thought, Francis Scott Key, you don't have anything on us. We know that feeling too.

Robbie died just a few moments later, as Red held his hand.

Hammack returned to the wardroom and found "a whole bunch of guys, in stretchers, on the deck, or just sitting and waiting until Doc Nyce could get to them. Some were full of shrapnel holes, some were gut-shot, and some were badly burned. They were a great bunch of patients. There wasn't a whimper from a single man in that wardroom, or for that matter from any man in the whole damn crew."

After I relieved Tom McWhorter on the bridge he made his way down to the wardroom. He was thinking about how good it would feel to get some sleep. Then he opened the wardroom door and saw the bloody assemblage of the wounded. Tom was aghast: in the stress of the moment he had forgotten the casualties. His gaze came to rest on three members of his torpedo gang who only minutes ago had performed so well in striking the enemy. All three were seriously wounded. They lay on the deck, seemingly in high spirits. Rhodes called out to him, "There's that man from Texas!" Shrieves said, "We sure gave 'em hell, didn't we? Did you see us get that tin can?" Rhodes added, "Yeah, and we sure knocked the hell out of that battleship!" But Hawkins was ominously silent. Tom replied, "You guys were wonderful." Then he asked Harry Nyce how he could help. Doc handed him a jar of sulfathiazol paste and told him to use it. Tom's first patient was a youngster with multiple shrapnel wounds. This is his description of what followed:

I managed to get him to my bunk by some means, laid him out, and started cleaning his wounds with warm water, spreading sulfathiazol over them and bandaging them up. A radioman came in to help me, a man named Janzen.

When we got that man fixed up we went back into the wardroom and got another. Some were suffering from shock, some from burns, and they had horrible wounds of all descriptions. There was not a whimper out of one of them.

While giving first aid, I told Harry Nyce that if he needed me I would be available and then went about my work. I met Solloway in the passageway, and he told me that Jackson, Smitty [M. E. Smith], V.R.E. Martin, and almost the entire crew of the after guns had been killed. This was the first indication I had of the extent of our casualties.

After a while Harry sent word for me to come back to sick bay. I finished up the man I was working on and hurried back. It was the first time I had been back near the heaviest damage, and because the sick bay was within ten feet of the number four handling room there was a putrid odor all about, the result of a combination of fire, burned flesh, blood, and death. It was unbearably hot. In sick bay, standing by the operating table, was the doctor, stripped down to his shorts for the heat. I followed suit.

Hawkins was brought in and laid out on the operating table. . . . His right leg had to be amputated. . . . Doc stuck a hypodermic needle into Hawkins's wrist, then gave it to me. "If he starts to pull out of it before we finish, give him another cc, Mac." Hawkins quickly passed out as the sodium pentathol entered his bloodstream. He also had been hit by a metal fragment in his left eye, which had seemingly pierced the cornea. He had a deep wound at his left cheekbone, and numerous other wounds all over his body. The doctor patched him up as best he could and called for the next patient. We were very apprehensive about Hawkins. He could well have died, but some spirit held him on.

Next came Shrieves, with a shattered leg but still in good humor. "You're not going to have to cut it off, are you, Doc?" he asked, anxiously. "I don't know, old man," Harry said. "I'll do all I can to save it." But this was just small talk, because the doctor knew it was hopeless. "I'll keep my fingers crossed, Doc." And as Shrieves passed out from the anesthesia, his fingers were still crossed in a futile little gesture. They remained crossed throughout the operation. . . . His leg had to be amputated.

Shrieves had just fired his torpedoes at the Jap destroyer when two 5-inch shells struck the port torpedo tube and exploded. Large fragments were thrown across to the starboard side, shattering the metal seats that he and Hawkins were sitting on. In danger of bleeding to death, Shrieves stayed on his seat until he saw the torpedoes strike home. Then, from out of nowhere, Chief Gunner's Mate Hodge appeared, applied tourniquets to Shrieves's and Hawkins's legs, and helped carry the two wounded men up to the wardroom.

The next man on the operating table was L. A. Martin. He was on a morphine jag, and in spite of his multiple wounds he was singing out that his name was "L-A-A-A Martin." He had a shattered left leg, injuries around his head and chest, and some ominous shrapnel holes in his abdomen. We got to work on his leg first. . . .

Doc and I were smoking one cigarette after another during all of this time. They helped enormously. The doc was doing a masterpiece of first-aid surgery—not a slack or hesitant motion throughout the ordeal. He was fighting hard for the lives of our shipmates. There was an incident . . . that did cause him to stop temporarily: he spilled some alcohol on the front of his shorts, and the stuff flowed down to his crotch. He howled with pain and danced around before he washed it off and cooled down with water. None of us could keep from laughing at him at the most unfunny time of our lives.

Red Spaulding was brought in next. He was in such bad shape that the doc held him until almost last. . . . Red was one of the most unforgettable men of my life. He was a red-headed, freckle-faced kid that I had known ever since he came aboard as an apprentice seaman; he was courteous and hard-working, with a personality that made me want to "run" him as I would a good plebe at the Academy. . . . But there was no doubt that I liked him and he liked me. I had personally given him his semaphore and blinker tests a couple of months before, when he was going up for his rate of coxswain. A little coaching and he made it in a breeze.

Back in the wardroom, when we began carrying men back to sick bay for surgery Red had remarked, "I wonder why they don't take me now?" Then he thought a little while and said, "Well, I guess those other fellows need it worse than I do." Though he was being given large amounts of blood plasma, he did not realize that the real reason was that his case was hopeless. . . . When he was carried in and stretched out on the operating table, he was still conscious and in good humor. Just then we dropped some depth charges in an embarrassing barrage on a submarine. The ship shook as the big charges blasted away. It was unexpected, and since we were jittery anyway from our recent surface action I was afraid that it would disturb Spaulding. To reassure him I remarked, "We're just kicking the hell out of their submarines now, Red. Just routine. Nothing to worry about." He might well have been trying to calm me down when he replied, "Sure, Mac. We'll get 'em the same way we did last night." Then we passed a few more remarks. When I was trying to get a morphine serrette through his skin, he said, "That arm is a tough one, Mac." I agreed—"Just like iron, Red"—and I wasn't just talking, either. "When old Doc Nyce gets through fixing you up, you will be like a new man, Red." "I hope so, Mac." Then the anesthetic took effect, and Red passed out with a faint smile on his lips. It was the last thing he ever said.

Harry Nyce began the hopeless task of doing what he could for Spaulding. . . . I was holding Red's hand with the hypodermic needle still in the vein of his wrist all through the short operation. Then I felt his pulse stop and told Nyce. He confirmed it; Red had bled to death internally.

During this time in the operating room, Red Spaulding had paid me the greatest compliment I have ever received; courteous to the letter and always respectful, . . . Red had repeatedly called me "Mac" while he was dying, with a naturalness in his voice as if he had always called me that. . . . Harry Nyce patted him on the arm and said solemnly, "You were a great boy, Red." And those were the sentiments of all of us.

WHILE TOM AND HARRY ENGAGED IN THEIR LIFE-AND-DEATH STRUGGLES in sick bay, the *Sterett* chased after the *Helena, San Francisco, O'Bannon,* and *Fletcher.* We caught up with them at 0600. It was comforting to be in the company of friends again, instead of being the lone American ship. As the day gradually dawned, we felt more secure. By this time we had a fair idea of the fates of our other companions who had not been able to retire under their own power. We already had surmised that the *Cushing* and the *Laffey* had been lost because we had seen the punishment they had taken. We were saddened to learn that the *Atlanta* was also gone, along with the *Barton* and the *Monssen,* and that the *Portland* was badly damaged and had to remain behind to lick her wounds in Tulagi. The *Aaron Ward* was also banged up and would have to be fixed in Tulagi (Watso would soon steam up there in the *Vestal* to repair both ships).

We also discovered that not only admirals Callaghan and Scott but also Capt. Cassin Young, skipper of the *San Francisco,* had been killed in the first few minutes of the engagement. Rank provided no protection: the battle had taken its toll of officers as well as enlisted men, mute confirmation of the fact that we were all in it together. As to Japanese casualties and losses, we knew that the battleship we had targeted was the *Heie,* that she was dead in the water at daybreak, and that our planes continued to work her over. We wrote her off as a kill. We were also certain that one destroyer had been sunk and one light cruiser damaged. Beyond that, we would have to wait for our intelligence reports. Most important, we knew that our task group had completely thwarted the mission of the Tokyo Express on 13 November 1942.

Daylight was accompanied by a growing awareness of the death and devastation the enemy had wrought upon our shipmates and our ship. The natural reaction to long hours of tension started to show in faces, and those men who had lost close friends were especially touching to see. One sailor in particular, who had known Jackson for many years, just sat and stared into space, saying over and over, "They got Jack." All of us looked the worse for wear, particularly Jeff: a shrapnel wound in his scalp had spilled blood all over his khaki shirt, and his left trouser leg was stiff with blood from the laceration in the seat of his pants.

I had climbed in and out of smoldering compartments strewn with debris, dead bodies, and soot and awash with seawater from the fire fighting. I needed a shower and clean clothes, but I said many prayers of thanksgiving. I was all in one piece. My main concern was over the welfare of Tiny Hanna. He was the only officer (with the exception of Harry Nyce, who I knew was all right) whom I had not seen since the action started. Viewing the two after gun mounts from the bridge, I recalled how they had looked up close when I inspected them earlier. I knew that Tiny's battle station was in that general vicinity, and I did not see how he could have escaped injury. Yet I could not bring myself to ask specifically about him; I was afraid the reply would be that he had been killed. So I just kept quiet and waited.

At about 0930 I heard someone climbing the ladder to the bridge, and when I turned around there was Tiny, big as life—which was plenty big. He smiled and took my hand in his big paw. "Damn glad you made it, Cal." I responded in kind and said another silent prayer of thanks. Later I learned that Tiny had almost single-handedly removed the wounded from gun number three after it had been hit. He had been standing alongside a stack of potato crates, and when the shells landed on the other side of the crates the hundreds of shrapnel fragments that would otherwise have hit him lodged harmlessly in the potatoes instead. After helping to remove the wounded from the gun mount, he stood down on the main deck and, without assistance, took each stretcher as it was passed down to him and lowered it to the deck. Others then joined him to carry their wounded shipmates to the battle dressing stations for first aid. When I saw Tiny that morning his uniform was torn and covered with blood, and he was still working at the most gruesome task of all—removing dead bodies from the gun handling rooms. Some of our sailors had started the grim work of sewing the remains of their lost comrades into canvas sacks, readying them for burial.

Harry Nyce had performed his duties in superb fashion. His foresighted preparations were a blessing. He had distributed well-selected first-aid equipment to each of several subdressing posts and outfitted the wardroom as the main battle dressing station in a thorough manner. As the wounded began to arrive he received, evaluated, and administered emergency first-aid treatment to them in the wardroom. Then, when it became apparent that he was going to be overwhelmed by the number of casualties, he transferred his base to the little sick bay. Had he begun surgery too soon, the fate of many of the wounded would have rested on judgments made by the pharmacist's mates as to which man was in greatest need of a skilled surgeon's services. (I am confident that their judgments would have been sound, but they could not have compared to those of a veteran of several thousand operations.) His first anesthetist was Coleman Conn, signalman 1/c, who, although inexperienced and thoroughly sickened by what he observed, deserved the highest praise for his work. He stayed with Harry until relieved by Tom McWhorter at about 0400. It was 0930 when the doc finished with Red Spaulding and proceeded to the officer's staterooms. The *Sterett's* builders had not provided beds for the care of critically wounded men, so we put them in the officers' bunks. Thank heaven there were exactly enough bunks to handle them! Harry continued his treatment of those in critical condition in the staterooms until we were able to transfer them to a hospital ship on the fourteenth.

IT MUST HAVE BEEN 0930 WHEN I LEFT THE BRIDGE. I went below to the galley and fixed myself a sandwich. Then I walked through the wardroom to the stateroom I shared with Doc Nyce. In Harry's bunk was a young machinist's mate 1/c named Parkis with nasty shrapnel wounds in his right leg. Below him in my bunk was Hawkins, who had lost one eye and had had his leg amputated. Parkis was cheerful and talkative, but Hawkins was only semiconscious and was barely able to ask for water. I had just walked across the passageway to look in on some of the others when the general alarm rang again. "Oh, God," I thought. "Not now!" Then I raced back to the gun director.

As I passed the bridge Herb May told me that one of the cruisers had reported an unidentified plane astern of us. We all remembered that two Japanese carriers were reported to be somewhere in the vicinity, and enemy aircraft were especially unwelcome at that point—we had no fighter cover and would barely be able to defend ourselves with our damaged guns. The director crew all reported at their stations despite their wounds, and there we waited. I perched on top of the director and scanned the northern sky for approaching aircraft. Through my binoculars I could see the crews of the three cruisers at their gun stations. The *Helena* was two thousand yards away on our starboard quarter, and behind her were the *San Francisco* and the *Juneau*, each about seven hundred yards apart. A few scattered clouds did little to block the hot sun. On our port side some twenty miles away (but looking much closer) was the large island of San Cristobal. Behind us and still clearly visible was Guadalcanal, some fifty or sixty miles distant.

I noted that the *O'Bannon* was absent from the screen and remembered that she had been dispatched to take a position sufficiently removed from the formation so that she could send a summary of the previous night's action without the Japanese plotting her location (and thus ours) by radio direction finder. That left only the *Fletcher* and *Sterett* to provide antisubmarine protection, and the *Sterett* was little help because our sonar control circuits had been damaged. But we were making good speed, and it occurred to me that a Japanese sub would have to be sitting right on our projected track to get a shot at us.

I examined the cruisers again. The *San Francisco* looked like the battle-scarred veteran she was. She was badly damaged near her bridge, where she had absorbed heavy shell hits, and in the vicinity of her after conning station, where she had been hit by the Japanese plane the day before. Also plainly visible were the twenty-six holes I had seen earlier in her port side. The *Helena* had reported being hit in the area around her aircraft crane, but I could not see any sign of damage and wondered how she could have sailed through the thick of it (and I knew she had—I had seen her) without an apparent scratch. Then I turned my glasses to look at the *Juneau*. I knew that she had reported being hit with a torpedo just a few hours before. Again, I could discern no visible sign of the damage. She kept up with formation speed, and I watched admiringly as she steamed along with a bone in her teeth, looking very much like an overgrown destroyer. I examined her bristling armament, her multitude of 5-inch guns, and thought, She's beautiful. One of her signalmen started to send a message. I put my binoculars down and continued to stare her way.

Without the slightest warning, she exploded—disintegrated—in a tremendously violent blast. I watched with horror as whole 5-inch gun barrels flew hundreds of feet into the air. Huge pieces of the ship's superstructure were hurled sky-high in lazy parabolic curves. A gigantic column of black and gray smoke went up for thousands of feet. Yellow and orange flames flashed at the center of the explosion for the first few seconds, but soon there was only an immense cloud of smoke, which seemed to hang motionless for minutes. Slowly, the bottom of the cloud started to rise off the water's surface. I put my binoculars to my eyes, anxious to see what was left.

Nothing appeared in the space the *Juneau* had occupied only a few minutes before. There was not a stick, or a spar, or a boat, or a life buoy; nor was a single man visible. I strained to see a head, or a body; but as the smoke cleared, I could see absolutely nothing. Only then did I look at Jeff, and both of us mouthed the words simultaneously—"Jesus Christ." No words, then or now, could possibly express the shock and the despair that we felt over the loss of the gallant *Juneau*. It was the most horrendous tragedy I have ever witnessed.

Still utterly incapable of comprehending what we had just seen, those of us in the director simply looked at one another, speechless, for several minutes. The *Juneau* was gone—completely and entirely—within the space of a few seconds. As far as we could determine, she had taken every one of her heroic sailors with her when she went.

A submarine attack seemed like the most logical explanation. But I began to wonder if the cause of the explosion could have been aboard the ship. I knew that she had been torpedoed during the night engagement, and I thought of our own damage and our many severed electrical lines. I wondered if the *Juneau* had suffered similar damage to a magazine, which then exploded due to a short circuit. I turned the director over to J. D. and (after a stop on the bridge to get Jess Coward's concurrence) went below to order our shipfitter to reflood the magazine. I had told him to pump it out an hour or two earlier, but now I countermanded that order. I did not want the *Sterett* to risk a similar explosion.

By the time I returned to the director our lookouts had seen two explosions on the starboard horizon. We concluded that they were the self-destruct detonations of two or more fish from the same submarine that had fired on the *Juneau*. Obviously that sub had been at the right place at the right time (or the wrong time, from our perspective). We had probably gone right over her. Still, we left the after magazine flooded. The formation was zigzagging radically now, and a B-17 showed up to cover us. Even that one Flying Fortress provided a much-needed sense of protection.

We secured from general quarters, and I went below once more to visit the wounded. All were in critical condition, but their spirit and determination were inspiring to us all. In the stateroom next to ours were three casualties. As I walked through the doorway the first one I encountered was Shrieves, who had lost a leg. He turned his head to see who had come in. "Hello, Shrieves," I said. "How do you feel?" His face was pale, the result of shock and loss of blood. He smiled and said, "Pretty good now. The only trouble is that damned fly that keeps walking around on my foot [pointing to his stump] and tickling me—chase him away, will you?" I patted his shoulder and walked over to the lower bunk to check on Richard Skutely (seaman 1/c), who had suffered severe burns on his face, shoulders, arms, and hands. "Skute" was one of the most likable youngsters on the ship, and one of the most capable seamen. I leaned over and spoke to him, and although he could not see through his swollen eyes he recognized my voice and said, "Mr. Calhoun? Oh, I feel swell. We sure did give those bastards hell, didn't we?" I assured him we had and went on to look at the others. Many were still unconscious, but without exception those who could speak voiced concern over nothing but the ship, their shipmates, and how much damage we had inflicted on the enemy. I knew that the *Sterett* could not take full credit for anything but the destroyer, but I vowed that when these kids went over the side in their stretchers they would see the painted silhouettes of a battleship and a cruiser on our bridge as well as the destroyer that had already been put up there as our legitimate "kill." We could erase the other two later.

The *Sterett* had only two pharmacist's mates and would have experienced a sad shortage of trained first-aid personnel if not for the far-sighted program started by Doc Scharbius while we were in the Atlantic. Harry Nyce kept it going, not only giving general instructions to the entire crew but also conducting the special, advanced course for fifteen particularly well qualified men that was mentioned earlier. Their long months of training paid handsome dividends. In addition to their invaluable first-aid work during the battle, these men administered continuously to the needs of the critically wounded for the seventy-two hours when their lives hung in the balance. One of these specialists was a youngster named Seymour.

Stationed in the number four 5-inch gun mount, Seymour received severe burns on his hands and arms when ready service ammunition caught fire. Despite this, he was able to train a hose on the fire, minimizing the damage. Not satisfied with that performance, he devoted himself to the care of his wounded shipmates. For three days, with little if any sleep, he helped to feed them, brought them water, and in general rendered the most valuable sort of assistance without any thought to his own painful injuries. Others in the special advanced program included Hiram Hodge (who saved the lives of Hawkins and Shrieves by applying tourniquets to their injured legs), C. E. Conn, W. R. Hammack, C. R. Lovas, and F. A. Boudreaux. All of these men were officially cited for their outstanding performance in the captain's action report of 20 December 1942. There must have been ten more who deserved special commendation, but unfortunately I do not know who they were.

AFTER THE LOSS of the *Juneau* we noted that the SOPA, Captain Hoover of the *Helena,* did not detach a ship to return to the scene and search for possible survivors. From Captain Coward on down the line, we all felt that Hoover's decision was sound. In fact, it seemed like the only logical course: most of us were sure that there were no survivors and that any ship sent back for rescue purposes would also be lost. The Japanese sub that got the *Juneau* was no doubt waiting there, hoping to get a shot at the rescue destroyer.

After lunch Captain Coward, Frank Gould, and I gathered in the wardroom to begin the task of compiling a meaningful action report. The first thing we discovered—though it came as no surprise to us—was that no member of the bridge watch had recorded the times of events as they occurred. If one imagines for a moment what the *Sterett* bridge was like during the battle—shells flying in every direction, the ship darkened, our own guns firing just a few feet in front of the bridge windows, and the torpedo gang scurrying from one side to the other to reach first one target and then another—it becomes apparent that keeping an accurate log was an impossibility. As a result, the log and the action report were constructed later. We tried to make reasonable estimates of precisely when things happened, but I am certain that we achieved only a modicum of accuracy and completeness.

The three of us agreed on the sequence of events that is laid out in this narrative. We were also in agreement on what we saw when we encountered the battleship, the cruiser, and the *Fubuki*-class destroyer. All of us were absolutely sure that we had observed the *Sterett's* 5-inch gun shells hit the cruiser, the battleship, and the destroyer with telling effect; the many fires in the *Heie's* superstructure; enemy shells strike the *Cushing, Laffey, Atlanta,* and *San Francisco;* sailors dive overboard from the battleship; the violent explosion of the enemy destroyer; and two huge, red underwater explosions in the vicinity of the battleship's after and midship areas at the time when we expected our torpedoes to hit.

Our action report reflected the careful consideration that took place in that post-mortem session. I assume it was the best summary Captain Coward could put together in the time that was available to him. But I should point out for the benefit of historians who seek to document specific details (and especially to reconstruct the movements of each participant in the Third Battle of Savo Island) that the accuracy of at least some of the written official records is doubtful. Given the circumstances that prevailed on all but one of the ships of Task Group 67.4 (the *Fletcher,* which was the last ship in the column and thus may have avoided the center of the melee), I question whether any of them was able to record events with sufficient accuracy to provide the requisite data for such an analysis.

Although we first conferred on the preparation of the report on 13 November, it took the skipper a full week to write it, have it typed, and sign it. Even then, it contained many typographical errors. I note this not as a criticism but as an indication of how hectic a period this was for him. I did not see the report until after it was delivered, but I was given a chance to contribute recommendations for awards based on my own observations. I made such recommendations for six people:

- Jeffrey, J. D., Lt., USN: For his cool and efficient performance of duty as assistant gunnery officer, when, after being struck in the back and head by shrapnel, he remained at his post until relieved by the gunnery officer during a lull in the action. Silver Star.
- Hall, Perry, Ens., USN: For his courage in personally supervising and engaging in the fire fighting below decks. Silver Star.
- Hodge, H. J., CGM: For his immediate, courageous, and efficient action after the ship was hit by enemy shells. He assessed the damage, took charge in the vicinity of the number three and number

four handling rooms, fought the fire, removed the wounded, and personally removed ready service ammunition that was on the point of exploding. Navy Cross.

- Keenum, L. G., CTM: For his assistance in fighting the fire on gun number three and in the number three handling room, and for his heroic action in entering the flames from this handling room in order to operate the magazine flooding valves, an action that may well have saved the ship. Navy Cross.
- Shelton, J. W., FC 1/c: For his cool and efficient performance of duty as rangefinder operator, when, after being painfully wounded by shrapnel, he calmly identified silhouettes as they appeared, gave target angles and speeds, and ranged under the most trying conditions. Silver Star.
- Byers, R. O., BM 1/c: For his cool and efficient performance of duty as director trainer, when, after being wounded by shrapnel, he stuck to his post until ordered by the gunnery officer to leave during a lull in the action. Silver Star.

Captain Coward did not initially recommend specific awards for any of those cited. We were unaware of these details until many months later—but it did not really matter. Our own knowledge of the *Sterett's* performance, coupled with the comments made by the Navy's most admired combat leaders, was enough to make us all proud.

After the meeting with the skipper and Frank Gould, Harry Nyce asked me to accompany him to survey the remains of our dead shipmates and make positive identifications. It was a request that I could not refuse, especially since I knew our crew as well as anyone aboard: I was a "plank owner" (someone who has been aboard since a ship's commissioning) and had become acquainted with most of them from the day they reported on board. Even so, I found it very hard to recognize six or seven of these men, who only a few hours earlier had been the picture of healthy young manhood. At the same time, the task was not as bad as I had anticipated, because I found that even those bodies with terribly disfiguring wounds held a quiet dignity. They had been transformed, I thought, into impersonal symbols of courage and patriotism. I was not looking at Chief Torpedoman Jackson, for example, but at the hallowed shell of a warrior who had given his life for our cause and who now expected us to prove ourselves worthy of his sacrifice. Of course, there was a gruesome side to the task. Each of the bodies had to be sewn into a canvas bag weighted at the foot with a 5-inch projectile, in preparation for burial at sea. Perry Hall was one of those assigned to this detail, and he later commented on the problems he and his helpers encountered when they had to straighten limbs that had become fixed in distorted positions by rigor mortis. It was not a pleasant job.

Late in the afternoon, all was finally ready. The bodies of twenty-eight of our shipmates were laid out on the main deck aft in one long row. All hands in the ship's company (except those on watch) were formed in solemn and silent ranks on the fantail. Off to one side a squad of bluejackets stood at attention with rifles at the "order arms" position. An hour or so earlier as I watched the preparations, I was convinced that this would be little more than a mechanical operation—an unpleasant job that had to be done. The scene had not softened or improved since then. The bodies had been lifeless for more than twelve hours; unembalmed, they generated the unmistakable stench of death. Blood soaked through the canvas shrouds and collected in little puddles on our gray steel decks. Behind us were our two damaged 5-inch guns, looking almost like skeletons with their blackened shell holes and twisted metal shields. On either side were the unshaven, worn, and sad faces of men who had just fought desperately for their very lives and experienced the loss of a good number of their comrades. It was not a pretty picture. But I suspect that, in our private reflections, each of us had come to accept the fact that our lost shipmates were no longer in those canvas bundles.

With bowed heads, we waited for Jess Coward to speak. He began to read the burial-at-sea service from the Book of Common Prayer:

> Unto Almighty God we commend the souls of our brothers departed, and we commit their bodies to the deep; in sure and certain hope of the Resurrection unto eternal life, through our Lord Jesus Christ; at whose coming in glorious majesty to judge the world, the sea shall give up her dead; and the corruptible bodies of those who sleep in him shall be changed, and made like unto his glorious body; according to the mighty working whereby he is able to subdue all things unto himself.

Then, in a quiet voice, he spoke with pride and admiration of the way our shipmates had served their country and given their lives so that others might be free. In a low tone that was only slightly unsteady, he said, "We will never forget our departed shipmates." I could not hold back the tears that welled up in my eyes, and I was aware that most of us were having the same reaction. Tom McWhorter described the ceremony in these words:

> The guard of riflemen fired three volleys, and as the names were called out, one by one, the mute bags of canvas were lifted and slid over the stern, disappearing in the wake of the ship. "Jackson . . . Walker . . . Kula . . . Klepacki . . . Perry . . . Martin . . . Smith, M. E. . . . Robinson . . ."—the names droned on. "Smith, Joseph . . . Kreilick . . . Stapleton . . . Spaulding . . . Tynan. . . ." Each name meant a great deal to us. It seemed that the ceremony would never

end. When the last of our departed shipmates had slid into the blue waters of the Coral Sea, the crew slowly and silently walked away. Darkness soon set in; we were safe from air attacks for the day. The *Sterett* had paid a terrible price for victory.

Finally, there is this poignant recollection by J. D. Jeffrey:

All action finally over, the scene shifts to afternoon. The final, climactic event of the *Sterett*'s most heroic, bittersweet day occurs with burial at sea. I vaguely recall Captain Coward reading the service. But my vivid, lasting memory is of Seaman George Burris, a Georgia boy and probably the youngest sailor on the ship. He stands next to the wooden slide down which the canvas-encased bodies will leave the ship on their final journey. In one of Burris's hands is a pot of grease; in the other is a paintbrush. The captain's words are completed. Burris looks questioningly at the veteran chief Hodge standing next to him, in effect asking, "Shall I grease the slide now?" Hodge nods. Burris has the honor of performing the final rite for our twenty-eight fallen shipmates. He does it with dignity. Somehow, his simple act seems the appropriate ultimate tribute, a valorous deed in itself, on a day when so many valorous deeds were performed.

We arrived at Espíritu Santo on the morning of 14 November. As soon as we came within signaling range, Adm. Kelly Turner flashed the following message from his flagship:

In dissolving Task Force 67 I express the wish that the number sixty-seven in the future be reserved for groups of ships ready for as high a patriotic endeavor as you have been. Although well aware of the odds which might be against you, I felt that the impending Jap night attack on 12–13 November was the time when fine ships and brave men should be called upon to do their utmost. For your magnificent support of the project of reinforcing our brave troops on Guadalcanal, and your eagerness to be the keen edge of the sword that is cutting the throat of the enemy, I thank you. In taking from the enemy a toll of strength far greater than that which you have expended, you have more than justified my expectations. For our lost ships, whose names will be enshrined in history, and for cherished comrades who will be with us no more, I grieve with you. No medals, however high, can ever possibly give you the reward you deserve. With all my heart, I say, God bless the courage of our men, dead or alive, of Task Force 67. —Turner

CHAPTER 7

BATTLE REPAIRS

ONCE WE ARRIVED AT ESPIRITU SANTO we had little time to reflect on the battle. Our first priority was to get the critically wounded to the hospital. Hawkins and L. A. Martin in particular needed immediate care. Before we even dropped the hook our whaleboat was in the water, and we transferred Hawkins and Martin to Mobile Base Hospital (MOB) Three. Because that facility was relatively small we kept the rest of our wounded shipmates on board until the hospital ship *Solace* arrived that afternoon. She had received word of the *Sterett's* casualties by radio, and soon her motor launch—staffed by a team of doctors and nurses—was at our accommodation ladder, taking our shipmates aboard with great care and affection. As we had planned, the torpedomen were able to look up at the bridge as they left the *Sterett* and see the painted silhouettes of the enemy battleship, cruiser, and destroyer; they noticed them and were cheered by those symbols of their outstanding performance. All hands gathered at the rail to see them off and convey our wishes for a speedy recovery.

Harry Nyce was greatly distressed by the knowledge that, had he had access to the trained personnel and the facilities of a hospital surgery, he would not have had to amputate in at least two instances. I noticed that he seemed depressed, and when I asked him why he responded that what he had done was more like butchery than the expert surgery of which he was capable. I reassured him that without his courage as well as his skill as a doctor and a surgeon, many of our wounded would not have survived. But it was many weeks before he seemed to come to terms with himself. Finally he accepted the fact that aboard a destroyer the lack of medical facilities was unavoidable. His frustration with this aspect of his role was probably the real reason he applied for a transfer to Pensacola for a course in aviation medicine.

After we had transferred our patients to the *Solace* we pulled up to a tanker to fuel. As soon as we moored to her, she caught fire. For a little while we wondered if we were jinxed, but the fire proved to be only a superficial one topside and was soon extinguished. Finally we relaxed, and all hands got some much-needed sleep.

The morning of 15 November dawned bright and clear, and we were ordered to move alongside a small seaplane tender, the *Tangier*, for temporary repairs. That done, we discovered that our old friend Watso was in port. He was now the commanding officer of the USS *Vestal*, a heavy repair ship, and had relieved Capt. Cassin Young of that command only a few days before the engagement in Iron Bottom Sound. With Jess Coward's blessing, I went aboard the *Vestal* for a visit. My host knew a great deal about our night action. He told me how proud he was that his old ship had distinguished herself. He also noted that he was about to send special equipment and expert personnel to Tulagi to assess the damage and to assist with the repairs of the *Portland* and the *Aaron Ward*. He spoke of Captain Young with the highest praise and obviously felt his loss personally. After a long talk about the old days aboard the *Sterett* I departed, inviting him to come aboard for lunch the next day.

Watso arrived for lunch as scheduled and seemed to enjoy his visit as much as we did. We took him on a tour of our damage, and he was visibly moved. As he left, he promised that when we returned after our repairs he would join us ashore for a drink. He was certain that we would be sent to the States, and of course we hoped that he would be right. Also on the sixteenth we received word of the magnificent performance of our new battleships, the *South Dakota* and the *Washington*, in another engagement the night before. It appeared certain that a last-ditch effort by the Japanese to retake "Cactus" had been crushed. We felt that at last the Navy had rendered to the Marines the kind of support we would have liked to provide months before but could not because we lacked the necessary resources. It certainly gave boost to our morale, and I am sure it was greatly appreciated by General Vandegrift's 1st Marine Division.

We had been busy since our arrival, making temporary repairs and cleaning up the mess that the enemy's shells had created. The overhead, bulkheads, and decks of the handling rooms and adjacent compartments all had to be scrubbed down with soap and fresh water to remove the bits of humanity that had been deposited there. The waterlogged ammunition had to be off-loaded; debris, wreckage, and dirt had to be cleaned out. I will skip the gruesome details of how we disposed of the pieces of our dead comrades, but daily reminders of their loss only served to make us more determined than ever to beat the hell out of the hated enemy.

The actions of 12–15 November seemed to settle the issue of Guadalcanal. Now the heavens opened with a flood of congratulatory messages, many of them addressed specifically to the *Sterett*. When the cruiser *Pensacola* arrived, she sent this greeting to the *San Francisco, Helena, Sterett, O'Bannon,* and *Fletcher:* "The officers and crew of the *Pensacola* wish to express to you their heartfelt admiration for your heroic action." We were surprised and pleased to receive the *Pensacola's* message, but shortly thereafter came the one that touched all of us more deeply than any other. It was from the commanding general of our Marines on Guadalcanal. Addressed to Task Force 67, it read: "It is our belief that the enemy has suffered a crushing defeat. Our thanks for the sturdy efforts of Lee last night, and to Kinkaid, for his pounding of the foe by our aircraft has been grand. We appreciate all of these efforts, but to Scott and Callaghan and their men, who against seemingly hopeless odds—with magnificent courage—made success possible by driving back the first hostile attack, goes our greatest homage. In deepest admiration, the men of Cactus lift their battered helmets in proud salute. Vandegrift." This expression of gratitude by our hard-pressed Marines, who demonstrated their valor on a daily basis, said it all. Yet more were to come. From Rear Admiral Tisdale, the administrative commander of all destroyers in the Pacific Fleet: "If words could add to the tribute paid you by the men of Cactus, my staff and I would join all Americans in saying this: We are proud to belong to the same service with you." And from Admiral Halsey, at his headquarters in Nouméa: "To the superb officers and men on land, on sea, in the air, and under sea, who have performed such magnificent feats for our country in the past few days: You have written your names in gold letters on the pages of history and won the undying gratitude of your countrymen. My pride in you is beyond expression. No honor for you could be too great. Magnificently done. God bless each and everyone of you. To the glorious dead, Hail heroes, rest with God."

A few days later we were ordered to proceed to Nouméa. As soon as we arrived we were overrun by a squad of repair experts who came aboard to determine whether our damage could be repaired by a base facility somewhere in the forward area. Destroyers were in short supply, and the fleet commanders wanted to keep as many of them as possible. Those that were damaged were returned to the rear areas with great reluctance. However (as any *Sterett* sailor could have told them), the experts quickly decided that we needed the services of a shipyard to have two 5-inch gun mounts and at least one quadruple torpedo tube mount replaced plus considerable structural work done. So we were to be sent back, at least as far as the naval shipyard at Pearl Harbor. Of course, we all hoped that our ultimate destination would be the good old U.S.A.

No sooner had the repair team left than we were told that Admiral Halsey himself was coming aboard to inspect our damage. Captain Coward asked Frank Gould and me to join him on the quarterdeck to greet the admiral. He wore his four-star insignia for the first time, having just been notified of his promotion to the rank of admiral—a fitting reward for his outstanding leadership. We had a personal stake in the fight that he led, and his promotion was proof of its importance. I had never met him before but I had seen his picture, and no one could have failed to recognize the bushy eyebrows, the strong chin, or the direct gaze that bespoke confidence and strength. He shook hands with each of us and asked to be shown all of our battle damage.

As we made our way through the gunnery department the skipper described the damage. He told the admiral what each shell hit had done.

Here, the gun captain was mortally wounded and insisted that the doctor take the other wounded first, because he knew he was beyond help; in these two major-caliber hits the whole handling crew and most of the gun crew above were killed instantly, and four members of the gun crew dove overboard with their clothing ablaze—they had not been recovered, as far as we knew (later we learned that all but one had been saved). The admiral was quiet and pensive throughout the tour, as though trying to imagine what it must have been like to be a *Sterett* sailor during the battle. From time to time he simply shook his head as we described events.

When he had completed his visit and was about to leave he turned to face us. I was surprised to see that there were tears in his eyes. For perhaps two or three minutes he told us in a low voice, one that was steady but charged with emotion, how proud he was of our performance. I wish I could recall his exact words, but I do remember some of his thoughts— he regretted that he had to send destroyers against battleships but was sure that the small ships would do their utmost; he was amazed that any destroyer could absorb eleven shell hits (three of which were 14-inch projectiles) and still steam away from the action under her own power; he was profoundly moved by the many stories of heroism, and by the mute but eloquent evidence of punishment and sacrifice that was apparent at every turn as he toured the ship. Finally he thanked us, with a sincerity that added a special quality to his words, and said, "God bless you!" We stood there filled with admiration, respect, and pride and watched him climb into a waiting jeep and drive off. It was an unforgettable, once-in-a-lifetime occasion. To those of us who witnessed it, Admiral Halsey's name will always lead the list of inspirational combat leaders of World War II.

Later that day an awards ceremony was held aboard the *San Francisco* at which some twenty officers and men received the Navy's highest award for heroism, the Navy Cross. Our captain was among those so honored. As soon as he returned to the *Sterett*, he called all hands to the forecastle and read us this memorandum, a copy of which I still possess:

Thanks to the heroic efforts of our departed shipmates, the splendid battle efficiency and cool-headed determination of all hands, every last officer and man, I was awarded the Navy Cross.

That honor belongs to the *Sterett* as a fighting unit; to the toughest, sharpest-shooting ship that sails the seas—not to me as an individual.

Admiral Halsey has not yet had time to read the *Sterett's* action report. When he does, I'm sure there will be more medals handed out. The entire ship's company deserves special commendation. I'm sure we'll hear more about that.

But the greatest honor of all for me was to have had the privilege to lead the scrappy *Sterett* into battle, to watch and admire the punishment you dished out to our enemy, and then to bring the ship safely out of battle when there was nothing else to shoot at, while all hands coolly and efficiently tended our wounded shipmates, put out severe fires, and repaired damage.

The Japs will be most unhappy when they learn that the *Sterett* is after them again.

We are now headed for Pearl Harbor. Expect to arrive there 4 December. What we do after that I do not know. I hope and pray we'll head for the coast. All hands are entitled to a few good liberties.

We departed that afternoon, in company with the cruiser *San Francisco*—but not before the Communications Office delivered the following telegram, sent on 29 September and mailed on 3 October: "From Winston-Salem, N.C., to Lt. C. R. Calhoun, USS *Sterett*, care of Bureau of Navigation, Navy Dept., Washington, D.C. Your son arrived today. Congratulations. All's well. Virginia sends love. Dad."

THE LONG VOYAGE ACROSS THE PACIFIC was uneventful and gave us all time to reflect. Harry Nyce and I had long talks about life's values and where we fit in the scheme of things. He seemed to have come to terms with his performance in battle; I found myself in possession of a renewed faith in God and a sense of inner peace. Ginny and I had been blessed by the arrival of a new life entrusted to our care. I was convinced that nothing could be worse than the ordeal I had just gone through. If I could make it through that, I could make it through anything. A certain feeling of indestructibility came over me, and I knew I was not alone in that feeling. For some reason I had emerged without a scratch, while all around me others had been injured or killed. I had accumulated a huge debt of gratitude, one I could never repay in full.

As we approached the entrance to the channel at Pearl Harbor on 4 December, I recalled that the last time we had looked on that scene the *Mississippi* was heading out to sea and signaling for us to follow her. That was June 1941. A lot had happened in that year and a half. But here I was on the bridge once more, about to get my first look at the site of Japan's act of treachery. I peered through my binoculars, trying to locate signs of damage from the attack. There were many ships in the harbor, and it was obvious that something unusual was taking place. A remarkably large number of sailors were out on the decks of those ships; as we drew closer it dawned on me that they were manning the rail. "Captain," I asked, "do you know if the president is making a surprise visit to Pearl Harbor?"

He turned to me with a puzzled look. "No, Cal, why do you ask?"

"Because it looks as if all these ships are manning the rail."

He looked with his own binoculars and said, "Well, I agree with you, but I can't offer any explanation. Maybe the president is coming as you suggest."

By this time we were well into the harbor. We could see the sailors of every ship arrayed along the lifelines in immaculate white uniforms, and the bands of the larger ships with their instruments in hand. We were ahead of the *San Francisco*, and as we drew abreast of the first ship in the harbor a bugler blew "Attention." All hands jumped into position. At a single note from the same bugler, they rendered a hand salute. Then we heard, "Hip hip hooray! Hip hip hooray! Hip hip hooray!" All of those white hats were raised to us at each cheer. There was no presidential visit. They had manned the rail to honor the *Sterett* and the *San Francisco*. Even the men of the huge air station on Ford Island were formed along the cement seaplane ramps.

Each of the ships present repeated the procedure as we drew abreast of it. They gave three cheers in turn to the cruiser as she followed in our wake. As we steamed past the larger ships their bands played the "Victory March," "Anchors Aweigh," or one of John Philip Sousa's marches. It was a welcome beyond description—one that I am sure none of us has forgotten. I have never felt prouder, or more humble, than I did on that day. We also received the following message from Admiral Nimitz: "No words can express my admiration for the *San Francisco* and *Sterett* and the officers and men who man them, but to you I give what no others have more fully merited—the Navy 'Well done'—[and] my wish for you is that your repairs may be fast and effective and your personnel losses made good by men as willing as the shipmates you have lost to give their lives for their country and their Navy's honor."

The admiral came aboard two or three days later, after his staff had thoroughly inspected our damage. We met him in the wardroom, and he extended his hand to each of us. Turning to the skipper, he explained that he had proclaimed his admiration for the men of the *Sterett* in his official message, but that in the meantime he had come aboard to express to us in person his great appreciation for the ship's outstanding performance. He made a quick tour of our damage and listened carefully as the skipper explained the scope of it. Once he had seen it all he turned to Jess Coward and said, "Well, captain, how long will it take you to be ready to go back to the States?" Without a moment's hesitation, the skipper said, "We're ready right now, admiral." Admiral Nimitz just smiled and said that he was ordering us to accompany the *San Francisco* back to Mare Island for repairs, adding that he suspected we would consider that to be the most important news he could give us. Concerning the welcome we had received when we entered the harbor, he told the skipper that it was an indication of how the entire U.S. Navy felt about the *Sterett's* conduct in the night action of 13 November. I was impressed with the admiral as a man of exceptionally fine character. He seemed to exude kindness—a quality one would not normally expect to find so visible in a great military leader. His business completed, he asked that we dispense with any side honors for him and left the ship, pausing to shake hands with several crewmen who were standing at attention as he passed. I am sure all of us felt that the Pacific Fleet was in the best possible hands after that visit.

We broadcast word of our return to the States over the public-address system at once, and a great cheer went up from our crew, who had been hoping for such news ever since our departure from Guadalcanal. We left for the last leg of our return journey on 7 December—it seemed an appropriate way to mark Pearl Harbor Day.

As we approached the Golden Gate on the eleventh the weather thickened, and we found ourselves in a pea-soup fog. Captain Coward anchored until it cleared. Meanwhile, the radio blared out all sorts of jubilant greetings to the hero of the Third Battle of Savo Island, the USS *San Francisco*, as she returned in triumph to the great city for which she was named. Every able-bodied citizen was urged to participate in the gigantic waterfront welcome that had been planned. The cruiser dutifully entered the harbor and, despite the fog, slowly steamed up and down in the vicinity of the piers to let herself be seen, finally mooring at her assigned pier where she was instantly overwhelmed with a crowd of well-wishers. We felt sorry for her men, who would be delayed in departing on leave to see the loved ones from whom they had been separated for many months.

While the city of San Francisco turned itself inside out to welcome its cruiser, the *Sterett* proceeded quietly to the Mare Island Navy Yard, where we moored and promptly sent our leave and liberty parties ashore. My request for twenty-three days of leave had been approved. Herb May, H. E. Jervey (our assistant engineer, from Columbia, South Carolina), and I went directly to the office of the captain of the yard and arranged for a free ride to Washington, D.C., the next morning aboard a Navy transport plane. It was a miserable trip insofar as comfort was concerned. The plane did not have heat, so we ran up and down the center aisle to keep warm and had a member of the aircrew wake us up whenever we fell asleep. But we were homeward bound, and nothing could diminish our joy over that fact. We would have made the trip by oxcart or dogsled if necessary.

Herb May left us in Pittsburgh. From there on we encountered exceptionally rough weather—but even this had amusing consequences.

With the exception of one Navy nurse and two sailors, "Jerv" and I were the only Navy passengers. All of the others were Army officers, and most of them were ferry pilots. Every last one of them got airsick, while not a single Navy representative so much as looked pale. Our nurse especially seemed to appreciate the humor of the situation.

In Washington I boarded a Piedmont Airlines flight to Winston-Salem and soon arrived home. My three weeks of leave were, as always, wonderful. But there was bad news along with the good. Our little boy was not well: something was seriously wrong with his kidneys, and he also experienced projectile vomiting. Preliminary examinations in Winston-Salem were inconclusive, so we decided to take him to San Francisco—in that way we could utilize the facilities at the University of California hospital and still be together during the weeks the *Sterett* remained at Mare Island before departing for the western Pacific. The next two months were enjoyable but also very worrisome. As is so often the case for service wives, the brunt of the anxiety and responsibility fell on Ginny's shoulders.

ONE SATURDAY NIGHT IN EARLY JANUARY the *Sterett* was asked to provide a senior lieutenant, a chief petty officer, and ten additional petty officers for shore patrol duty in the town of Vallejo. I went, together with Hodge and ten petty officers handpicked for their leadership abilities and physical toughness. During the weeks of liberty in San Francisco our sailors and those of the cruiser *San Francisco* frequently got into altercations over which ship had single-handedly won the war. For the most part these fights were harmless, seldom involving damage or injury to civilians and usually resulting in only black eyes or fat lips. During the early hours of our shore patrol duty we were called to break up three fights of that kind and had very little trouble reestablishing order once we separated the combatants and returned them to their ships under escort.

At 0100 we were called to a reported riot at a bar in Vallejo. I took Hodge and five men in the patrol van; what we saw when we arrived was a scene from a Mack Sennett comedy. Four sailors with their backs to the bar were slugging it out with seven or eight other sailors in what seemed to be the central event of the disturbance. The local police had responded with about six officers, who were all involved in scattered individual fights. Hodge and I agreed that the ringleader of the eight aggressors was a small sailor whose pugilistic style suggested that he may have been a Golden Gloves champ. When he saw Hodge and his team move in, he broke off the neck of a bottle and thrust it toward the chief's face.

Hodge cracked the sailor's knuckles with his nightstick, and he immediately dropped the bottle. Then the chief grabbed him by the collar and, holding him at arm's length, started for the paddy wagon. The culprit continued to yell at the top of his lungs and swing wildly at Hodge. A quick glance at his companions showed them to be in the firm grip of our other shore patrolmen. The police got their assailants under control, and we all made our way into the street, where we lined up the prisoners to load them in the patrol wagon. Hodge's prisoner had not stopped shouting and struggling, but fortunately the chief's reach was long enough to keep this wildcat at a safe distance.

As we waited in line, Hodge remarked, "Mr. Calhoun, I think I should let this guy have one."

"No, Hodge, he's drunk," I said. "Don't hit him if you don't have to."

A few seconds later the sailor grabbed Hodge's nightstick from his belt and brought it down on the side of his head. The blow would have knocked out most men, but Hodge just shook his head and looked at me.

"Now?" he asked.

I nodded. "Yes. Now."

Hodge's right fist caught the sailor on the point of his jaw. The young man's feet left the ground, and he sailed headfirst through the open door of the paddy wagon. That ended the riot. All of our prisoners suddenly became very cooperative; we had no trouble returning them to their ships, complete with written shore patrol reports that detailed the behavior for which they had been apprehended. All of them faced captain's mast the next day, with appropriate disciplinary measures. I was secretly pleased to note that only three were *Sterett* men. Against eight from the cruiser *San Francisco* and other ships, it appeared that the *Sterett's* sailors had acquitted themselves well. Hodge had a sprained thumb and a lump on his head but otherwise suffered no ill effects. I am sure he remembered for a long time the coup de grace that he had administered so effectively. We referred to the incident as the Battle of Vallejo. No battle star was awarded for it, but it was woven into the fabric of the *Sterett's* reputation and became a favorite topic of conversation.

On 18 January 1943 Lt. Comdr. F. G. Gould relieved Comdr. J. G. Coward as the commanding officer of the USS *Sterett*. We were all very sorry to lose Jess Coward, but we had expected it, and we liked Frank Gould. We vowed that we would give him our complete loyalty and work closely with him to help keep the *Sterett* a happy and efficient ship. Frank was delighted with his new assignment. He threw himself into the job of supervising our repairs with typical painstaking thoroughness.

We were fascinated with some of the new equipment and armament that was put aboard. New torpedo mounts replaced the damaged ones, and new 5-inch gun mounts were installed aft. We were fitted with new 40-mm antiaircraft guns and a beautiful surface-search radar with a PPI scope that enabled us to see every contact on a large visual display. It placed our ship at the center of the picture and showed every other ship

The "Scrappy *Sterett*," as Jesse Coward described her, departs Mare Island Navy Yard, 6 February 1943. Her battle damage repaired, she deployed on 10 February to rejoin the South Pacific Force in the Guadalcanal area. Note that her damaged 5-inch gun shields aft have been removed and not replaced. (U.S. Navy Photo)

within range in the appropriate position relative to us. It left little to the imagination and made me wonder how any task force commander could select a ship that did not have SG radar as his flagship.

Like every other veteran ship that returned to the States for overhaul, the *Sterett* was vulnerable to the personnel rearrangers in Washington. Before we could leave Mare Island we also lost Hugh Sanders and Tom McWhorter. I was especially sorry to see Tom go, because he had given so much of himself to the men of the *Sterett*. Losses by transfer were also costly in the enlisted ratings. The list of those transferred to new construction or shore duty included Ed Coppola and C. C. Landers, both chief machinist's mates; Hilbert Jenson, chief torpedoman; C. R. Reese, chief boatswain's mate; Harry Stenslie and W. W. Talbot, chief electrician's mates; and twelve other petty officers. Still we counted ourselves lucky, for we retained people like Byers, Chapman, Keenum, Hodge, Plecker, and Shelton. In my view, the *Sterett* still had the best crew of any destroyer in the Navy.

On 10 February 1943 we left Mare Island, passed under the Golden Gate Bridge, and headed west for Pearl Harbor. The old routine of drills and practices started over again, but this time we had a veteran crew—one that had seen it all—and it was relatively easy to break in the new arrivals. By the time we reached Pearl we were running pretty smoothly and became anxious to get back under the Southern Cross, where we knew we were needed.

We played musical chairs on the bridge after the skipper left. I moved up to the post of executive officer, and J. D. Jeffrey took my place as gunnery officer. Each of us welcomed our new assignments, and the business of the ship continued on an even keel. I had some concerns about my ability to locate the stars well enough to carry out my new responsibilities as navigator. But after a few days of practice I was able to take my sights and work them out with no difficulty. We arrived in Pearl Harbor on 16 February, and for the next week we took advantage of the many target services available there. By the time we left on the twenty-first we felt pretty good about our battle-readiness. It seemed that we had managed to fill the holes in our roster with well-motivated and intelligent people. As to Admiral Nimitz's question—whether they would be willing to give their lives for their country and their Navy's honor—we would have to await the ultimate test. But there was little doubt in my mind that they would answer the call.

CHAPTER 8

RUSSEL ISLANDS SHUTTLE

WE CROSSED THE EQUATOR ON 24 FEBRUARY 1943 and had just started to wonder if we would ever see land again when we arrived at Espíritu Santo. Frank Gould and I had always maintained a cordial relationship. Now he appeared to have confidence in me as his exec, and I respected him as a highly competent professional. At sea, he gave me all the authority I needed to do my job. In port, I was his negotiator and intelligence-gathering agent. It was a great arrangement, and I thoroughly enjoyed my new role.

Our new assignment kept us almost exclusively in the Guadalcanal area, and we frequently anchored in Tulagi or in Purvis Bay, on the coast of Florida Island. One rainy night in Tulagi a merchant ship called on the voice radio to say that she was trying to negotiate the channel to her anchorage but that she was without radar and absolutely blind. Frank plotted her on our navigational chart and, by taking continuous ranges and bearings on her with our new surface-search radar, directed her to her exact anchorage location. This was an early demonstration of the innovative possibilities of radar.

At this time ComSoPac decided to augment the existing airstrip facilities at Guadalcanal by building a new landing field in the Russel Islands, sixty miles west of Tulagi. Transport of the necessary materials and equipment was to take place under the cover of darkness. The job was assigned to several small to medium-sized amphibious craft, and our task was to shepherd them to their destination over a period of several weeks. When we were first ordered to perform this mission I discovered that one of our old four-stack destroyers had already visited the small harbor where the new base was to be established. Her commanding officer was Lt. Comdr. "Punchy" Shea, a 1936 graduate of Annapolis who (like me) had been a member of the 4th Battalion.

I went to see him aboard his ship, the *Trever* (DMS 16), a converted World War I destroyer. It was an inspiration to go aboard a truly heroic element of the Navy. The ship was ancient and, like her sisters, was barely holding together. Ships such as the *Trever* and the *Reuben James* performed some of the most hazardous tasks of the war. I had observed the *Southard* carrying aviation gas to Guadalcanal in fifty-gallon drums stored on deck and unloading them onto the beach in the face of an imminent air attack. Many difficult escort duties were performed quietly and efficiently by these four-pipers. They were pitifully ill equipped to oppose any Japanese force—surface, air, or submarine—yet they accepted every assignment without complaint and in most cases delivered the goods. They deserved our admiration, and Punchy Shea seemed to exemplify their spirit.

Asked how to enter the Russel Islands base at night, he sat down at his wardroom table and explained how he had done it. There were no navigational aids on which to obtain a fix, but he mapped out how we could proceed on a westerly course until the higher of two small peaks was on a specific northwesterly bearing, and then turn to that course and proceed until we were within a certain distance of the beach. At that point we could safely anchor and wait for our amphibious craft to unload. With luck they would complete their unloading before daybreak, and we could be well on our way back to Florida Island by sunrise.

We made our first run to the Russel Islands on the basis of Punchy Shea's advice, and it worked like a charm. We formed our small charges in a column astern of us at twilight and were a few miles east of Savo Island by dark. We traveled with all units darkened, and as we drew near our destination we could see the twin peaks. We lined up the pelorus on the higher of the two, and when it reached the prescribed bearing we changed to that course. Within half an hour we were at anchor waiting for the transports to unload. These short trips were usually without incident, and we derived a measure of satisfaction from the knowledge that we were helping to expand our air defense capabilities.

One evening shortly after we had cleared the harbor with our little convoy, our sonar operator obtained a contact. Captain Gould immediately developed an approach strategy, and within minutes we were on our way to conduct a depth-charge attack. Out on the starboard wing of the bridge as we closed on the contact, I heard the sound of an airplane; looking up and aft, I saw a twin-engine aircraft flying directly up our wake. I stepped into the pilothouse and told the skipper in a quiet voice that there was a low-flying enemy plane overtaking us. The words were hardly out of my mouth when we heard the aircraft pass overhead. The captain fired his depth-charge barrage, and seconds later a stick of bombs fell harmlessly in our wake about a hundred yards astern. We had been lucky—it is hard to understand how the pilot could have missed at that altitude, but somehow he did. I was chagrined that neither the air-search nor the surface-search radar had picked up the attacker, and from that night on we routinely went to general quarters as soon as we started out. The incident was never repeated, but it served to demonstrate that although Guadalcanal was presumed to be relatively secure the enemy could still strike without warning.

On several occasions we witnessed dogfights directly over our heads as we returned from these trips in the early morning. Once we saw the pilot of a Japanese plane bail out. Tiny Hanna and I were about to propose to pick him up in a whaleboat when three more Japanese planes appeared. We gave up on the project, concluding that it would make us vulnerable to strafing.

Frequently we carried Army personnel over to the Russels, or back to Guadalcanal on our return trip. On one occasion a young Army major rode back with us, and he elected to remain on the bridge and chat. I was happy to have the company. We had a box seat for a dogfight that morning, and it apparently raised the possibility in his mind that the *Sterett* might become the target of one of those planes. He looked around apprehensively.

"How thick is that metal?" he asked, pointing to the pilothouse bulkhead.

"About a quarter of an inch."

"And how thick is the hull?"

"It's about the same."

He looked at me in disbelief. "A quarter of an inch? Where the hell do you take cover when they shoot at you?"

"There is no cover."

He pondered that for a few seconds. Then he said, "I'll take the Army any day. At least we have a foxhole."

"Well, every man to his own taste," I replied. "At least we have three good meals a day, and clean sheets to sleep on every night." I would not have traded places for all the money in the world.

THE COMSOPAC STAFF must have felt that the *Sterett* deserved a break from its routine, because in early April 1943 we were diverted to make a few escort runs from Espíritu Santo to Guadalcanal. The *Aaron Ward*, our companion from the Third Battle of Savo Island, took over our Russel Islands resupply duties. We steamed south from Tulagi to pick up several transports loaded with supplies for the troops of Cactus and arrived at the objective area by 7 April. The transports unloaded all morning while we patrolled the periphery of their anchorage, providing antisubmarine cover. The *Aaron Ward* had traveled to and from the Russels that morning; she herded her three LCTs as far as Savo Island, then broke away to pick up the LST 449 off Lunga Roads and escort her out of the area.

Intelligence reports indicated that the Japanese planned a big aerial offensive against Guadalcanal. That morning we received a message telling us to expect a heavy air attack of at least a hundred planes. It was a warm and sunny day, and I was on the bridge with the skipper discussing the warning. We passed the word to the crew over the public-address system. At about noon Rear Adm. "Pug" Ainsworth's cruiser/destroyer force departed on its way to bombard Munda. A few minutes later we received a Red Alert and went to general quarters. The transports immediately got under way and headed east, and because we were northeast of them we turned to a southeasterly course to close.

We were just north of the eastern tip of Guadalcanal and pretty well in the clear when the enemy planes first came into sight. At first they were behind us, diving on unidentified ships that had apparently been caught close to the anchorage. Using the public-address system, I gave the crew a blow-by-blow account. The microphone was on the starboard side of the pilothouse, and by standing just inside the door to the bridge I could watch the attack as it took shape. The planes dove on their targets and scored at least one hit. Black smoke billowed skyward from the damaged ship—I could not tell which one it was.

From Guadalcanal we received word that some sixty enemy planes were directly over the eastern tip of the island. It was clear that they had seen and were about to attack the formation of merchant ships we were escorting. I walked onto the starboard wing of the bridge in time to see the first Val dive-bomber break through a cloud, headed toward the lead merchantman in the starboard column of the formation. My battle station was at the secondary conn atop the after deckhouse, where I could take control of the ship in the event of a casualty to the bridge. I decided that I had better get back there and went down the ladder two steps at a time. Before I reached the bottom the first bomb fell with a loud "crump" close to its target, and the plane that had delivered it flew slowly up our starboard side only a hundred yards away and very close to the surface. The pilot obviously wanted to draw our fire away from his squadron-mates. We obliged him with all our starboard-side automatic weapons. Many of our tracers slammed into the after portion of his fuselage, but none did serious damage. He flew merrily on his way despite the added efforts of Chief Torpedoman Keenum, who stood on the main deck and determinedly fired a tommy gun at the plane in hopes of scoring a lucky hit.

At the starboard midship 20-mm gun, Red Hammack was having a difficult time. His loader seemed to be so fascinated by the attacking planes that he was slow to replace the magazines. Hammack solved that problem by shouting a string of expletives and directed his fire at those planes that had not yet released their bombs. The port-side gunner also focused on such high-priority targets, but at the moment they were all on the starboard side. Red opened fire on a plane that was just starting its dive, and I watched as his tracers arched toward their target and were joined by another stream of tracers coming from somewhere behind me. My first instinct was that these were from Japanese planes that were now on our port side, but soon it was clear that this line of bullets was directed at the same target that Red Hammack had selected: as the target descended, so did the tracers. They had to be from our own port-side gun. I had the sudden feeling that if I did not duck at once they were going to hit me in the back. I ducked down and to the left, and within a fraction of a second something walloped me in the right arm. It felt like a hard-hit baseball, and it knocked me off my feet. I landed on the deck in a sitting position.

The telephone talker at the midship 20-mm guns was Ron Giffen, yeoman 2/c and the captain's writer. He was at my side in an instant, tearing off my shirtsleeve for use as a tourniquet. The air raid continued for perhaps five more minutes, with our gunners shooting at one target after another until at last the Japanese aircraft retired. Our Marine fighters gave chase and scored several kills. At this point I got back on my feet and found Harry Nyce at my side. He took me by the arm and led me forward to the wardroom. I reclined on the starboard transom while he examined my wound.

He assured me that there was no bone damage but said that there was a hole about the size of a 45-caliber slug in the underside of my right upper arm. I felt no pain and asked him to dress the wound so that I could get back out on deck. He told me to wait until he had taken care of three other wounded men, and said that when he returned he would take me to sick bay and try to remove the bullet. Then he poured me a tumbler of his best medicinal whiskey and told me to "work on it" until he returned. The tumbler was empty by the time he reappeared about half an hour later.

In sick bay he opened the wound and probed with his scalpel for another thirty minutes, searching for the slug. Finally, he said, "Cal, I'm doing more harm than good. I haven't been able to find any fragments"— he thought there were as many as three—"so I'm going to close this up and wait until we can get you to a hospital." He walked me back to the wardroom and examined my hand and the surface of my arm with a pin to determine the extent of any loss of feeling. It was quickly apparent that I was insensitive to pain from the tips of the fingers on my right hand all the way up to the site of the wound.

"Well, old man," Doc said, "how would you like to go home?"

I thought he was kidding. "Come on, Harry, for a little thing like this?"

"It isn't just a little thing. You've severed the radial nerve, and unless you can get to a neurosurgeon very quickly you could lose the use of your right hand. I'm going to transfer you to MOB Three. They have an excellent neurosurgeon there. They can repair the nerve, and then they'll send you home, because this will take at least a year to regenerate."

It was hard to believe that I would be sent home. While I was pleased with the prospect of being reunited with my family again, the thought of leaving the *Sterett* and my shipmates really distressed me. That afternoon we learned that the air attack had caught and sunk the old oiler USS *Kanahwa* and our friend the USS *Aaron Ward*. The *Kanahwa* had to be abandoned almost immediately, while the *Aaron Ward* stayed afloat for several hours. Both ships suffered heavy casualties, and we were all concerned about the welfare of our friends aboard.

The *Sterett* returned to Tulagi that night and made another run to the Russel Islands base, again witnessing a dogfight on the way back. On 9 April we left for Espíritu. I had tried to collect and organize my belongings in preparation for my transfer, and when I left the ship the next afternoon Harry Nyce, Tiny Hanna, and Harold Jervey accompanied me and helped to carry my seabag, which contained all of my worldly possessions. Tiny delivered it to the hospital's master-at-arms; I never saw it again.

It was hard to say good-bye, and as I watched their boat pull away from the landing I silently prayed that they would survive the war. (They all did.) Now I was on my own. I walked back into MOB Three's receiving ward and down the road to recovery.

CHAPTER 9

VELLA GULF

JUST BEFORE I LEFT the *Sterett* I told Frank Gould that I thought Herb May could do a good job as executive officer. He was next in line in seniority, extremely popular, a natural leader, mature, and industrious, and I knew Frank Gould liked him. Within the hour he moved into my now-vacant stateroom. When Harry Nyce, Tiny Hanna, and Harold Jervey returned to the ship after dropping me off at MOB Three, they found the new Gould/May leadership team in charge. It was apparent that the operational style and routine administration of the ship would not change much because of my departure.

J. D. Jeffrey was by this time quite comfortable in his role as gunnery officer, and since the *Sterett's* departure from the States he had shared a room with Doc Nyce. They saw eye to eye on most aspects of shipboard life and were a positive force on wardroom morale. J. D. counted on the same nucleus of star performers that had rendered such outstanding support in the past. Chiefs Hodge and Chapman, Byers, Gibson, and the other veterans of the Guadalcanal Campaign all continued to turn in the kind of sterling performances that had become their trademark. The *Sterett's* crew did not deviate from the routine of drills and practices that had kept the ship in the "expert" category in gunnery. Ever since the attack on Pearl Harbor, training was the number-one priority aboard the *Sterett*. Meanwhile, she took on some of the least glamorous assignments in the theater, escorting the logistic supply line to our troops on Guadalcanal and the Russels. The crew watched with envy as the new "cans" (*Fletcher*-class destroyers) dashed up the slot to Munda, Rendova, and New Georgia, where the action was now furious.

The *Sterett* toiled away the summer months, aware that Rear Adm. "Pug" Ainsworth's cruiser/destroyer force, Task Group 36.1, was intercepting and doing battle with just about every Japanese force that attempted to reinforce their garrisons in the central Solomons. These actions included the Battle of Kolombangara, in which we lost the cruiser *Helena* and the destroyer *Gwin* and suffered damage to the cruisers *Honolulu*, *St. Louis*, and *Leander* (a New Zealand ship). In exchange for these losses the Japanese cruiser *Jintsu* was sunk, sending Admiral Izaki and some 483 of his shipmates to join their ancestors. Four facts were clear to Frank Gould and his crew of veterans: Japan's desperate efforts to bolster its strength in the Solomon chain continued without pause; they were parried successfully by Ainsworth's cruisers and destroyers; the cost in lost and damaged ships (and American lives) mounted steadily; and there was still plenty of fighting to be done. The crew of the *Sterett* wanted badly to get into the game. Everyone on board believed that she could take whatever the enemy could throw at her. Consequently, no one put in for transfers to newer ships. J. D. questioned several of his petty officers on that point, and they made it clear that they did not want to transfer anywhere. They felt that their ship was special—and because they felt that way, their conviction became a reality. But it seemed that the high command had relegated them to the second team. The men of the *Sterett* wanted a shot at real surface action—the kind they proved they could handle in November 1942.

On the morning of 6 August 1943 the *Sterett* completed an uneventful escort mission to Rendova. As she rounded Savo Island and headed toward Tulagi, where her crew could relax (even the slow convoy escort assignments required them to remain at battle stations all night), five U.S. destroyers appeared several miles to the east, steaming westward at high speed. One broke off from the formation and headed directly for the *Sterett* to deliver a secret, priority message from the commander of Task Force 31, Rear Admiral Wilkinson:

> Comdr. Moosbrugger in *Dunlap* with division Able One and Able Two less *Gridley* and *Wilson* depart Tulagi at twelve-thirty [on the] sixth and proceed Vella Gulf via route south of Russels and Rendova Island to arrive Gizo Strait at twenty-two hundred same date. Make sweeps of Vella Gulf. Avoid minefields on line Vanga Vanga to Makutu Island. If no enemy contact is made by zero two hours [on the] seventh return down slot at maximum speed to Purvis. Warfield's Peter Tares will remain in port. All times love. *Sterett* acknowledge.

This was exactly what the crew of the *Sterett* had wanted. Frank Gould and his officers pieced together the context of the sally: Army and Marine troops on New Georgia Island had almost captured Munda after weeks of fierce combat, and the Japanese must have realized that they were about to lose their airfield there as well as the island of Kolombangara. So they probably planned either to evacuate or to reinforce their garrison that very night, and our intelligence unit had learned of their intentions (perhaps from coast-watcher reports). The after-action report by the commander of Task Force 31 attests to the accuracy of this ship-level analysis:

> From contact reports of vessels in the Rabaul area and from other indications, it appeared that a "Tokyo Express" might run on the night of 6 August, presumably to reinforce the Kolombangara garrison with men and supplies. These indications became apparent on 5 August. At that time there were eight destroyers available to

Commander Task Force 31 in the Guadalcanal area. Of these, two were obligated on escort duty, but the remaining six were free for use to intercept the suspected enemy. There was not adequate time for a cruiser task force to reach the area and no request for additional forces was therefore made by CTF 31, particularly since, unless the enemy appeared in great strength, six destroyers were believed adequate for the purpose.

In other words, only six ships were available in the Guadalcanal area to counter the Japanese threat, they were all destroyers, and the good old *Sterett* was one of them. Now that the chips were down it did not matter that she was not brand-new, that she had only one stack and four 5-inch guns, that she was slightly smaller than the more modern *Fletcher*-class ships. She was there. More important, she was commanded by a highly competent naval officer—and he and his executive officer, gunnery officer, first lieutenant, chief engineer, communications officer, medical officer, key chief petty officers, their principal assistants, and at least half of the seamen and firemen in the crew were veterans of the Third Battle of Savo Island. They were anxious to prove that they were up to any challenge. The *Sterett* could still be counted on to take her place in the first-team lineup and to perform like a pro.

American ground forces actually took Munda on 5 August. In the terse language of the secret message quoted earlier, Rear Adm. T. S. Wilkinson (who had relieved Rear Adm. Kelly Turner as commander of amphibious forces in the South Pacific on 15 July 1943) handed a tough task to Comdr. Frederick Moosbrugger, commander of Destroyer Division 12 and a new arrival in the Tulagi area: stop the Tokyo Express in the Vella Gulf. But tough tasks were routine for Freddie Moosbrugger. A former destroyer skipper (the *McCall*) who had seen plenty of action against the enemy and had performed with distinction, he was soon to write his name in the pages of naval history as a brilliant and heroic tactician. Moosbrugger was told what to do, but how to do it was left entirely up to him. Daylight fighter cover would be provided, and the small force of American PT boats ("Warfield's Peter Tares") in the Blackett Strait area had been ordered to remain in port so as to stay out of the way of Moosbrugger's six destroyers. These included his own division, consisting of the *Dunlap*, *Craven*, and *Maury*, plus Destroyer Division 15 (less the *Wilson*): the *Lang* (flying the pennant of Comdr. R. W. Simpson), *Sterett*, and *Stack*.

Moosbrugger's division had operated as a unit since May 1941 and had made night torpedo attacks (using radar control) its specialty. Simpson's ships were very well acquainted with each other and had often worked together in peacetime and in the Atlantic, but for the most part they had pursued independent assignments in the Pacific. Moosbrugger informed his skippers that he intended to steam up the gulf with his two divisions in separate columns four thousand yards apart, Destroyer Division 12 slightly in the lead, and that his three ships would open fire first using only torpedoes. If they encountered personnel barges, Destroyer Division 15 was to train its guns on them. Aboard the *Sterett* J. D. explained the battle plan to his officers, the director crew, and the gun captains. It was understood that, if all went well, they would open fire once the torpedoes of their companion division exploded. If by some quirk of fate Destroyer Division 12 failed to hit anything, then the *Sterett* and her cohorts would let loose with all their weapons.

I asked Comdr. J. D. Jeffrey (now retired and living in Chevy Chase, Maryland) to write about the Battle of Vella Gulf so as to include a first-hand account of the engagement in this book. I have edited his narrative only slightly and consider it one of the best chronicles ever written about this particular action.

With little trepidation I told Captain Gould that the gunnery department was as ready as it ever would be. He looked at me knowingly; training drills never gave one practice at dodging enemy shells. Half our crew had only the haziest notion of what went on in a night engagement.

The ship took position on the left flank of the close formation as it headed west past Savo. It always gave me a queasy feeling to pass Savo going west. In November 1942 the waters between Savo and Guadalcanal marked the gateway to hell, and even to get within sight of them could mean a shooting match like the one the *Sterett* encountered on 13 November 1942. Referring to the ship after that engagement, one of our sailors told an anonymous reporter, "She's some baby." And with wartime censorship, her name became the "Baby." As we steamed past Savo nine months later, everyone on the "Baby" felt akin to Columbus starting west on an unknown ocean with uncharted dangers waiting to strike.

The six ships were a beautiful sight in their high-speed formation. The bow waves leaped up and out like bleached streamers on a blue background, while astern the frothy wakes were gradually disintegrating threads that separated us from the safety of well-established bases. To the north we could see the Russel Islands, over which floated lazy, golden cream-puff clouds set in a bright blue sky. Ahead to the west and low on the horizon was an ominous line of storm clouds.

Dinner was served at 6:00 as usual in the wardroom on 6 August. Very little uneasiness could be felt, but anticipation ran high. The new officers fervently hoped we would run into the whole Japanese Navy; the older and more experienced quietly prayed that any engagement would be short, with a minimum of casualties to our forces.

After dinner, a shower, and a change into clean clothes, Doc Harry Nyce and I sat in our room talking about everything except what might happen during the coming night. Harry always had a knack for expressing pleasant thoughts at crucial times, a gift that stood him in good stead. Destroyer doctors had an unenviable position. They either died a thousand deaths from the boredom of professional disuse or had so much business that one medico could cope with it only through superhuman effort. Come to think of it, Harry's middle name was Cope. Aptly named, he was well acquainted with both extremes and handled them with near perfection.

After Doc left to inspect sick bay and first-aid equipment around the ship for the hundredth time since noon, I picked up a book with the vague feeling that something remained to be done. Naturally, an all-night session meant that food on station would be in order along toward midnight. Varner, the wardroom steward's mate who was always ready, willing, and able to provide a short-notice snack, soon produced a cheese sandwich and an apple, which with my one remaining candy bar would take care of that need.

At 8:30 (2030 Navy time) the general alarm startled me right out of my chair. To me, and I suspect to most of the crew as well, it was the most fearfully respected sound in the Navy: an angry tocsin reaching every remote corner of the ship, an incessant and ominous clanging announcing that anything (or maybe everything) was about to happen. All men were being summoned to come forth and do battle. Strapping on my .45 and my life jacket, I stepped out on deck and into the blackest night I ever saw. Through the opaque void I groped upward—more by familiarity than by sight—to the gun director, the highest battle station on the ship, located directly over the bridge. The director was a metal shell, a cube of perhaps fifteen feet, that swiveled in a complete circle and housed the computers, radar, optical rangefinder, communication circuits, and controls that were the electrical-mechanical brain directing the fire of the 5-inch main battery.

It took perhaps thirty minutes for our eyes to adapt to that gloom—there was no way of marking precisely the passage of time. After thirty minutes it was just as black as when we had first come out. The feeling of claustrophobia that settled on us became understandable when we realized the clouds were not much higher than the mast.

On schedule at about 10 o'clock, we cleared Gizo Strait (the narrow opening between Vella Lavella and Kolombangara islands) and entered Vella Gulf on a northeasterly course. The charts showed that the gulf did not provide much more operating room than its restrictive entrances. The director crew settled down to the indeterminate wait with which they were so familiar. I speculated for a brief moment, as I had many times before, on the ship's good fortune in having this crew. There was not one man I would have wanted to replace.

Chapman, chief fire controlman, was the mainstay in the director. His fire control gear generated the many computations that automatically aimed the guns with precisely the right amount of lead space to compensate for the target's motion. Chapman alone could spell the difference between defeat and victory. Gibson was Chapman's first assistant, a highly competent technician in his own right. He operated the radar, which on a night like this would make a target as obvious as if it were in noonday sunlight.

The optical rangefinder operator waited as a standby. Even though radar served as our eyes at night, the optical operator asked for no more than a candle anywhere on our side of the horizon to get a distance. Our previous operator, Shelton, had phenomenal eye-ranging abilities, proven in battle. When radar first arrived aboard ship, there were serious discussions in the gunnery department about whether unproven radar or proven optics would be the primary ranging device.

Lt. Max Dolson, assistant gunnery officer (who had reported aboard less than a month before), wore the headphones connected to the intership TBS radio to keep us current on the tactical situation and orders from the flagship. He was prepared to step into any job in the event of a casualty or to lend a hand to any of the men operating special equipment.

Crouched underneath my feet sat Conn, the inscrutable. As the phone talker between bridge and director, all information and orders from the captain to the gunnery officer passed over his circuit. Tucked away in his corner, he had sat through every engagement the ship had had. I don't think he had ever seen the enemy or, for that matter, any target we had ever fired at. After many months of observation I decided that Conn was the least curious and most fatalistic man on the ship—but the personification of quiet capability in battle.

As gunnery officer, with my head stuck through a hole in the top of the metal cube that housed the director, I had the best view on the ship in all directions. My telephone headset connected me to the four gun captains. To correct the gunfire calculations, I shouted instructions to Dolson or Chapman below. To my left (with his head also poked through the top of the director cage) sat Byers, a chief bos'n's mate and for two and a half years the director trainer. He had trained the director sights (as well as the whole director housing) left or right onto the target through every antiaircraft action as well as the night surface engagement at Savo Island. There could not have been a better man for the job in the entire U.S. Navy. Starr was stationed next to Byers, and with his head also stuck through the top of the director cage (irreverently referred to by some as our three-holer). As director pointer, he had been through the same battles as Byers and was equally expert in his job. Tonight he would ensure that the sights remained on target in the vertical plane.

These were the men within my immediate sight and hearing. I could hear the voices and the occasional laughs of the other men whose secondary positions made them no less important to the crew. Everyone had his job, and one man's failure to perform his well could render useless the efforts of all. This crew had worked together for so long that its teamwork was flawless.

After an hour, talk became very desultory. Chapman, usually quiet, chose to remain so. Max and Conn were waiting for information over their headphones and could not risk missing it the first time it was sent. Gibson figured that if he kept his attention riveted on the radar it would not act up. Starr eyeballed the surrounding gloom, ever on the alert. Only Byers seemed to be in a talkative mood, and his endless supply of sea stories helped to keep down our rising apprehension.

Once we cleared the strait the three destroyers of the first division (the *Dunlap, Craven,* and *Maury*) pulled ahead. They were poised to deliver a torpedo attack as soon as they spotted their quarry. The second division (the *Lang, Sterett,* and *Stack*) was on the starboard quarter of Moosbrugger's division. Of course, all ships were at general quarters, with guns manned and ready. A heavy mist started to fall. I was barely able to make out the phosphorescent wakes of the first division before; now they were swallowed up by that wall of nothingness into which they had disappeared.

Shortly after 2330, the thought of the cheese sandwich became overpowering. What was the sense of waiting? I carefully unwrapped it and bit into it—once. That must have been the signal. The news that came over all the phone circuits almost simultaneously made food extraneous: "Four targets appearing around point of land. Range twenty-two thousand yards." I tossed the remainder of the sandwich over the side.

All eyes strained into the night. The rain and mist made binoculars useless, but without them the wind and moisture lashed our eyes with just as detrimental an effect. We were blind in that inky blackness—blind physically but not electronically, thanks to radar. With our guns trained out, we could open fire with every assurance of hitting our target as soon as Chapman reported, "Ready."

The rapidity with which two groups of ships can close on each other head-on at 30 knots is phenomenal. "First division preparing to fire torpedoes," Dolson reported. And then in the next breath, "First division has fired torpedoes."

No one could describe how slowly time elapsed after those fish were fired. How much longer must it have seemed to the men who fired them? After what was probably only a minute I was sure they had missed. But still we waited. Why didn't the captain give the word to open fire? Finally, our guns ready and locked on target, I requested permission to open fire. The request was not answered— it did not have to be. After what we later learned was only four minutes, the torpedoes struck home. Two simultaneous red flashes tore into the night. The lead enemy ship, a destroyer, sank almost immediately. The second was a cruiser that burst into brilliant flame.

How to describe the feeling? It was not a feeling at all, but rather a lack of feeling. I stood there paralyzed, unable to move or speak or even to think. My eyes were hypnotized by the sight. Time had lost all meaning. How many seconds the paralysis lasted made no difference. Everyone was affected in the same way. Then reality asserted itself, and we awoke completely. It seemed as if we had all been injected with some stimulant that gave us unlimited energy and confidence. Our guns roared.

At fairly close range, we poured perhaps fifteen salvos into the hulk of that second ship. Each salvo caused further damage and started new fires. When it seemed that the target could no longer stay afloat, we checked fire to catch our breath. Two targets were accounted for. Byers and I spotted the third at the same time, but he coupled perception with action and swung the director sights around. It was a destroyer, very foolishly hugging the flames of the burning target. Obviously, there was never a more bewildered or confused destroyer in any navy at any time. She was traveling at about 5 knots with all guns still trained in and no signs of damage. She was not just silhouetted: she was lit up like a Christmas tree under a dozen spotlights.

Our first ranging salvo, fired in seconds, fell slightly ahead of the target, but the second caught her squarely amidships. I gasped. The ship virtually disintegrated before our eyes as a gigantic column of flame rose into the air. There was only one explosion. A part of her stern, the last visible trace of the ship, went under as a subsequent salvo exploded above it.

We checked fire. An exultant feeling pervaded the ship. In not more than fifteen seconds the remotest snipe buried in the depths of the engine spaces heard about "our destroyer." The engineers went through hell submerged in their small hot spaces, hearing the reverberation of guns high above but never seeing where the shots landed, never watching the shots aimed at us, and never knowing when a shell would burst upon them and scatter its steel fragments, break deadly steam pipes, or let in a rush of seawater that might trap them inescapably. Now it all seemed worthwhile.

Dolson started to chuckle—obviously some amusing messages were coming in over the intership radio. He relayed them in snatches. "The division commander (Commander Simpson, aboard the *Lang*) compliments us on the shooting. . . . Now he's telling the *Stack* to get hot and start shooting at something. . . . The *Stack* says that they were getting ready to shoot at that can, but before they could get their sights on it we'd sunk it!" Even Chapman loosened up after that one.

Throughout the action the ship had been making high-speed turns. "How's the water on gun four?" I asked, knowing that every turn resulted in waves that practically washed the number four gun crew over the side. Number four was the gun closest to the water and unprotected by any shield. "Not bad on the gun," replied Keefe, the gun captain, "but the boys in the lower handling room report no bottom at twenty-five." His absurdity, couched in the phraseology of the leadsman, brought a laugh but was also high praise for his men below, who battled cascades of water while continuing to send up ammunition.

The lull in the battle stretched on. The information coming over the intership radio was vague, but we gathered that the first division had accounted for the fourth ship, another destroyer. [The fourth ship, the Japanese destroyer *Shigure*, turned tail and outran her pursuers to Bougainville.] Standing precariously on an exposed exterior ladder, Chief Gunner's Mate Hodge stuck his head over the side of the gun director to report that the number one gun had jammed and would be out of action indefinitely. The number three gun had also jammed during the shooting, but it was now operable.

Scarcely had Hodge disappeared down the ladder when an unrecognizable target appeared. Silhouetted against the burning oil, it looked like a barge with a barn-like structure on it. This target was never explained or identified, but it was clearly an enemy craft. We opened fire, and it exploded almost instantly; perhaps it had carried ammunition.

Burning oil floated on the water and cast a flickering orange glow through the drizzle onto our companion ships. As we edged toward the flames, an uneasy feeling slowly invaded my consciousness. Almost inaudible at first, there came a sound that soon grew louder. The cries of what must have been hundreds of men in the water will always haunt me and everyone who heard them. We passed through a large group before we were ordered to stop. But as we cautiously backed down to where they were, silence prevailed. Undoubtedly they had recognized our ships as enemies. Their silence may have been an act of fanatical hara-kiri or just common sense, but clearly they had no wish to be picked up.

The division commander issued orders to take prisoners no matter how long it might take. Not one was taken. We were all uncomfortable about lying dead in the water, an easy target for any lurking sub. After about twenty minutes he realized the futility of attempting to take prisoners, and we rejoined the first division. The story ran rampant that while we were dead in the water some men had thrown over lines to which they attached flashlights for luring the Japanese. After subsequent research, I was able to discount completely the rumor that any such atrocities were committed.

The six ships retired in column at 30 knots. Turning southward after we rounded the northern tip of Kolombangara Island, we secured from general quarters. For seven hours we had been at battle stations, but no one seemed tired. Smiles of jubilation lit the faces of all—men slapped each other on the back. I descended to the bridge, where Captain Gould and I congratulated each other briefly. It was surely one of the most satisfying moments of his naval career.

A few minutes later I sat in the wardroom with the best-tasting cup of coffee ever poured when Harry Nyce came in, wearing the original mile-wide grin. "Well, Jay, you did it!" Anytime he congratulated the gunnery department it was high praise indeed. I laughed, remembering a less than successful target-practice session the previous spring when Harry, with great tact, referred to our inability "to hit the side of a barn."

The next morning under gray skies six destroyers entered Tulagi harbor. They seemed a little wet and bedraggled, but on every masthead was two-blocked a broom—symbol of a clean sweep of Vella Gulf.

Thus ended the *Sterett's* second nighttime surface battle—but what a difference there was between the two. At the Third Battle of Savo Island, the ship was hit by eleven shells (including three 14-inch projectiles) and suffered fifty-five casualties: twenty-eight crew members were killed, four were reported missing, thirteen were critically wounded, and ten received minor injuries. At Vella Gulf, the *Sterett* was not even scratched. In the first engagement, the U.S. force lost four destroyers and two cruisers, and another three destroyers and two cruisers took severe punishment. In the second, no harm came to any U.S. ship. In both cases, significant damage was inflicted on the enemy, and the main objectives of our forces were achieved. While the two battles took place in radically different military contexts, the single factor that appears to have played a critical role in the Vella Gulf victory was the existence of a well-conceived plan of action—one that, according to E. B. Potter's excellent biography, *Admiral Arleigh Burke,* was drawn up days in advance and made available to Commander Moosbrugger. Like Rear Admiral Callaghan in the Third Battle of Savo Island, Moosbrugger had just arrived and assumed command on the eve of the action. If there was a plan at Savo, it certainly was not apparent to us in the critical opening stages of the battle—and I have seen no evidence in the fifty years since to indicate that one did in fact exist. On the other hand, at Vella Gulf Capt. Arleigh Burke was the commander of Destroyer Division 12 until 3 August, when he was relieved by Commander Moosbrugger and departed by air to take the helm of Destroyer Squadron 12. Burke developed the two-pronged attack plan and left it behind for the new commander to use when the appropriate time came. Moosbrugger used it, and it worked brilliantly— how unfortunate that no one thought to prepare for the night action of 13 November 1942 in a similar fashion.

THE STERETT RETURNED TO PURVIS BAY across from Guadalcanal on 7 August. On the ninth she entered Vella Gulf again on another offensive sweep with five other destroyers. On this run, she encountered several personnel barges. Because they were made of wood they did not appear on radar, and their presence was not disclosed until they chose to open fire on the *Sterett* with heavy machine guns. That was certainly a mistake from the Japanese point of view. The *Sterett* responded in typical fashion, lashing out with every weapon that would bear on the targets. Our ships made short work of these unfortunates, sinking two and setting four others on fire (they probably sank later).

Two days later, Lt. Perry Hall was transferred to submarine school in New London, Connecticut. Perry received his orders several days before the Vella Gulf action but delayed his departure in order to get in on the fight. He was frustrated by the fact that Destroyer Division 12 got to fire its torpedoes first, but even so he managed to fire one of his fish into a burning enemy vessel, helping to finish it off. He had made a significant contribution to the *Sterett* legend and would be missed by everyone on board.

After the Vella Gulf engagement the men of the *Sterett* enjoyed a brief period of justifiable pride and satisfaction, but it lasted for only a few short weeks. In that time they became more aware of the influx of new *Fletcher*-class destroyers. The production pipeline delivered these new ships to the South Pacific at a steady pace. The *Sterett*'s sailors welcomed the evidence of America's industrial strength because it confirmed what they had always believed: if they held the line against the Japanese Navy during the critical phase, reinforcements would arrive and make victory inevitable. The downside of this scenario was that the most challenging assignments went to the new destroyers—they were bigger, more heavily armed, and better equipped to do the job. As a result the *Sterett* and her prewar sisters, veterans who had won the right to play on the first team, were assigned to less glamorous, less exciting roles. Life became a routine series of escort duties between the Solomons, Espíritu Santo, and Nouméa, and morale started to erode.

Then the high command demonstrated that, contrary to popular view, someone on the staff (perhaps Admiral Halsey himself) understood the needs and concerns of its sailors. In early October the *Sterett* was ordered to Sydney, Australia, along with the *Cleveland* (CL 55) for ten days of rest and rehabilitation. The news came as a wonderful surprise. With the exception of the three months spent at Mare Island in early 1943, the war had occupied practically every minute of the *Sterett*'s time since her departure from San Diego in June 1942.

The reaction of her crew members was predictable: the mood of boredom and frustration quickly became one of anticipation and excitement. Sydney was world-famous as a liberty port, and the *Sterett*'s sailors planned to make the most of their opportunity. Some planned sightseeing excursions to various places of interest, while others imagined new conquests in the arena of romance. (Doc Lea repeatedly warned the men about the risks of the latter activity.) During a brief stop in Nouméa, a few high rollers purloined a 50-gallon drum of gasoline—in case a car materialized for their use in Sydney. This was optimism at its highest level, and it suggests the kind of imaginative planning that went on in some sailors' minds.

The executive officer at this time was Lt. Comdr. David C. Miller, USNR, a Naval Academy graduate (class of '34). Dave had gone into the Merchant Marine after graduation and returned to the Navy after the attack on Pearl Harbor. He relieved Herb May (who was the "acting" exec after my detachment in June). Seeking to improve his professional skills, Dave took the opportunity offered by the *Sterett*'s trip to Sydney to attend a special training course somewhere in the area. J. D. Jeffrey recalls that

> Dave's temporary absence left an interesting situation aboard ship. Herb May and I were the next senior officers, very close in rank. Under existing rules it was not precisely clear who was senior,

although it seemed Herb had the edge. Some months earlier, when the exec's job was vacant for a short time because of Cal's departure, Herb had very ably filled in. Now, in Dave's absence, Herb insisted that I have the opportunity. Of course, it was not Herb's decision, or mine. Very obligingly, Captain Frank decided it was time I got my feet wet, figuratively, and I was delighted. Navigation with its precision had always interested me; and although I had previously worked out navigation problems alongside the exec and chief quartermaster, I now got the job for real, temporary though it was.

But the new navigator found the heavens to be uncooperative. Australia's barrier reef demands special navigational care, but the sky remained cloudy day after day—celestial navigation was simply impossible. The *Cleveland* was no better off than her escort in this respect, and each day she asked the *Sterett* for her best estimated position.

J. D. was worried. He knew that Frank Gould, who had done so much of the *Sterett's* navigating while he was exec, was concerned about their inability to obtain a fix. But on the last day of the voyage the sun broke through the overcast for a few minutes. J. D. was ready for it, and he was able to get a sight. That single sun line indicated that the *Sterett's* dead-reckoning position was accurate, and landfall occurred precisely as planned. A day or two later J. D. learned that the *Cleveland's* navigator had missed the sight and used the *Sterett's* data for his entry. Frank Gould must have been pleased.

Once in Sydney J. D. had to shift gears and concentrate on his role as executive officer—specifically, his responsibility for maintaining discipline and order. He knew that his sailors had been under stress for many months, with no chance to relax or blow off steam. Now they had arrived in one of the most sophisticated liberty ports in the world, and he waited for some sort of explosion. But it never came. Only relatively minor infractions were reported. There was one instance of a *Sterett* sailor really losing his self-control, getting into a fight, and returning to the ship late. J. D. figured that a hard-line response would send the right signal to the rest of the crew. So the sailor was deprived of his liberty for the remainder of the visit—a punishment that (as J. D. put it) "would seem the substantial equivalent of a year in jail ashore." But the acting exec's hard line came unglued when Doc "Tex" Lea took an interest in the case.

Lt. Austin W. Lea, USNR, reported aboard the *Sterett* a month before her visit to Sydney. He took a broad view of his responsibility for the welfare of the crew, playing the combined role of physician, chaplain, and defender of the helpless with a prevailing philosophy of fairness and compassion. Now he interceded on behalf of the sailor who had fallen from grace. He pleaded his case in the privacy of the acting exec's stateroom, pointing out that forgiveness in this case would have a salutary effect not only on the culprit but on the entire crew. J. D. bought Doc's argument and allowed the accused to go ashore during the rest of the visit. He behaved himself, and the impact of the decision on the crew appeared to be positive. The leadership of the *Sterett* had demonstrated that in return for their dedicated service they would receive fair and compassionate treatment.

When the ship left Sydney on 18 October, the men of the *Sterett* were relaxed, refreshed, and ready to get back to the grim business of the war. They returned in time for the landing on Bougainville and the first raids on Rabaul and were soon back in the cycle of escort duties, at-sea fuelings, air raids, dawn alerts, submarine contacts, and shore bombardments. From an unidentified *Sterett* history—marked only as "Enclosure B"—comes the following account:

> On 1 November 1943 the *Sterett* escorted the *Saratoga* on her memorable raid when her air group stopped the Japanese from making a counterattack on our beachhead at Bougainville. The *Sterett* returned from this raid in time to fuel and go back up in company with the *Essex* and *Bunker Hill*. On 11 November, while making the second raid on Rabaul and Bougainville, the formation was attacked by at least fifteen torpedo planes and dive-bombers of a reported sixty-plane raid. The *Sterett* shot down one of those unassisted and another aided by another destroyer.

It was at this juncture that Lt. J. D. Jeffrey decided it was time to move on. He had experienced just about everything one could expect to face on a destroyer, and he wanted to go to Pensacola and earn his wings as a naval aviator—and of course he wanted to get back to his bride. All of us shared the desire to get home; we missed the warmth and companionship of our loved ones and wondered how they managed to cope with the problems of parenting, rationing, budgeting the money we were able to send home only at irregular intervals, and worrying about our safety. But J. D. wanted to become a naval aviator, something he certainly could not do as long as he remained aboard the *Sterett*. (I spent three years and eight months on the ship and did not want to leave her, but in my case that was consistent with my objective: I cherished the earnest hope that by some fluke I could become her skipper.) In his two years aboard the *Sterett* J. D. gave of himself in large measure, and his contributions to the efficiency and morale of the ship were worthy of special commendation.

In the hectic scramble from place to place Ens. Roy B. Cowdrey, under orders to join the *Sterett*, somehow managed to catch up with her.

He reported aboard on 24 October 1943 after trying unsuccessfully to join her in Sydney (so for the next two years he had to hear, "Remember when we were in Sydney?"). He promptly took up his duties as torpedo officer and soon was sent ashore to attend gunnery school at Espíritu Santo, a move that had the full support of the incumbent gunnery officer. J. D. was laying the groundwork for his eventual departure by ensuring that there was a qualified replacement on board. Then came the news he had been waiting for—an Alnav (a message addressed to all ships and stations in the Navy) requesting applications for flight training from officers of his class. To apply, one had to offer proof that one was physically qualified for aviation duty. Understandably, Dave Miller was not enthusiastic about losing J. D. and was not about to expedite his departure. However, during a brief stop in Espíritu a few days later Jeffrey noticed a seaplane tender in port on which he could get the necessary flight physical. This is what he remembers: "It was unfortunate that at the exact time of my scheduled physical exam, a ceremony was also scheduled at which Frank Gould was to receive his Navy Cross and Chief Hodge, Harrington, Burris, and myself commendations for the Vella Gulf action. Dave was militantly insistent that I attend the ceremony, but I was not to be denied. Frank and I had been through Vella Gulf. This ceremony, though important and impressive, was the pale aftermath." So it is clear that Jeffrey's battle performance, as well as that of Hodge and the others, was duly noted by Frank Gould.

To quote again from the *Sterett* history:

> Shortly after the Rabaul raids came the invasion of the Gilberts, which was relatively uneventful from a naval point of view despite bloody Tarawa. The *Sterett* operated with Task Force 58 during this invasion and for the next ten months continued to screen Task Force 58, picking up pilots, driving off air attacks, and doing the various jobs that come a destroyer's way.
>
> On 9 December the *Sterett* participated in the first neutralization of Nauru, one of many to come.
>
> During the Marshall campaign the *Sterett* continued to operate with Task Force 58. Preliminary to the main bombardment of Roi Island, the *Sterett*, *Lang*, and *North Carolina* were directed to conduct intermittent bombardment the night before the landing in order to harass personnel and to prevent repair of damage inflicted on the airfield by air strikes conducted the previous day. This bombardment was most effective and accomplished the purpose intended. The next day the *Sterett* supported the landings with a bombardment, along with the battleships of Task Force 58.
>
> The *Sterett* spent Christmas anchored in Efate, where there was a large mansion set on a hill and surrounded by lush tropical foliage. It

looked like the planter's plantation in *South Pacific,* and the Navy (with its typical good sense) had converted it into a very nice officer's club. It was here that Jeffrey and Max Dolson, the assistant gunnery officer, chose to spend Christmas Day. Max was a former college tennis star, and J. D. was a tennis enthusiast who had never had much time to play. Despite the disparity in their skills they spent an enjoyable day on the court that adjoined the club. Although away from home and their loved ones, they counted their blessings: they were alive and healthy, they were on solid ground, and for that day at least no one was trying to kill them.

In the weeks afterward J. D. settled back to await his orders. Frank Gould had endorsed Jeffrey's request for flight training shortly before he was relieved of his command in early January 1944. J. D. was truly sorry to see him go. He and Frank had shared many hair-raising days of deadly combat, and each had acquired a high degree of respect for the courage and professional competence of the other. J. D. was also apprehensive about having to weather the initiation period of a new commanding officer. The *Sterett* had her unique qualities and her idiosyncrasies, and not every skipper would find them compatible with his own precepts and expectations.

As it turned out, the personnel detailers achieved a new standard of excellence when they selected Frank Gould's replacement. Lt. Comdr. Francis J. ("Champ") Blouin hit the deck running when he assumed command of the *Sterett,* and J. D.'s reaction to him—as well as a description of his own detachment a few weeks later—is summarized in these comments from a recent letter:

> In the short time I served under him, I concluded that the *Sterett* was indeed in good hands and would continue to be a happy and efficient ship. The only action I recall while Champ was skipper was a shore bombardment in which the *Sterett* was one of a number of ships participating. Riding the *Sterett* was yet another Destroyer Division 15 commander, one Charlie Stuart. This particular action involved saturation bombardment of an island (its name now forgotten), and the *Sterett* was assigned a certain square of beach as its target. During the course of the bombardment, a large explosion occurred in the enemy-held interior well away from the *Sterett's* assigned area. Commodore Stuart, seeing our area quiet and hoping maybe for a home run, ordered the *Sterett* to shift fire. Alas, to our knowledge we caused no havoc ashore. This, probably my last action as the gunnery officer of one of the now-numerous ships of the fleet, showed how far our Pacific fighting power had come. The United States had overwhelming ship superiority, able literally to pound enemy-held islands at will. That the amassed ships could not wipe out all enemy shore resistance prior to beachhead landings did

not detract from the magnitude of their numbers and the enormity of their firepower.

Orders to flight training came in due course, with detachment in March 1944. The detachment location was appropriate, reflecting some form of progress in the twenty-five months I had been aboard. I joined the ship while she was in the frigid waters of Casco Bay, Maine; I was to leave it halfway around the world in the tropical port (not tropical paradise) of Espíritu Santo, New Hebrides, South Pacific. The details of my departure also seemed appropriate. I was to fly out on 15 March. I thought I would spend one last night on board and take a boat to the air terminal the next morning. But on the afternoon of 14 March the ship received sudden orders to get under way. With unceremonious dispatch, my possessions were hurriedly assembled, dumped into a whaleboat, and deposited (along with myself) ashore. The next morning, as I was about to board the big Mariner seaplane transport for takeoff, I scanned the ships in the harbor. The *Sterett*, of course, was not there—she was off for yet another mission.

CHAPTER 10

THE BLOUIN ERA

L T. COMDR. FRANCIS J. "CHAMP" BLOUIN reported aboard the *Sterett* in Pearl Harbor on 13 January 1944, a Sunday. He relieved Frank Gould as commanding officer the very next morning, a fact that spoke volumes about his innate sense of trust and his self-confidence. There was no time for an inventory of classified publications or an inspection of the ship's physical condition. Frank Gould had assured him that all of the publications were accounted for, that the *Sterett* was in excellent shape, and that there were no critical personnel deficiencies. Those assurances from a brother officer were enough for Champ. He said, "I relieve you, sir," and assumed the heavy responsibilities of command. The ship was scheduled to get under way that very day, and he was determined to take her out as his ship.

Francis J. Blouin, USNA '33, graduated in the upper half of his class. He had five years of destroyer experience aboard the *Overton, Monaghan,* and *Cole.* In 1941 he was posted as a Navy Department communications watch officer in Washington, D.C. It was the last place in the world he wanted to be when the nation found itself at war on 7 December of that fateful year. It was late 1943 before he could extricate himself from shore duty: it was next to impossible for such a valued member of that communications team to leave, but somehow Champ managed to do it. The *Sterett* was the beneficiary of his efforts.

On 14 January 1944 the *Sterett* was moored directly ahead of an aircraft carrier, and there was a strong wind blowing against the pier. Scheduled to get under way to join in the Marshall Islands campaign at noon that day, the new skipper called for a tug to assist in holding the *Sterett* clear of the flattop. Given the demand for such services by many major combatant ships that morning, it is not surprising that no tug ever materialized to assist the destroyer. Champ confronted his first challenge as a new commanding officer. He now admits to having had butterflies in his stomach, but nevertheless he determined that it was essential for him to go, tug or no tug. He moved the ship like a veteran and got clear with a beautiful display of expert ship-handling skills, using more power in the process than anyone on board had previously witnessed. It was a great way to begin the "Blouin era." The new captain had shown the crew that he was highly competent and unflappable. The *Sterett*'s officers warmed to the new captain's enthusiasm and his obvious charisma. He roamed the ship alone to observe the crew at work and inspected the armament, engineering plant, and communications and radar equipment closely. He

Somewhere in the western Pacific the *Sterett* makes her approach to fuel from an unidentified carrier. The clusters of men "topside" are waiting to handle fuel hoses and rig the high line for transfer of stores and personnel. (U.S. Navy Photo)

was a careful observer, and he asked the right questions. It was not long before he fully appreciated the *Sterett*'s capabilities.

Escorting the new battleship *Alabama*, the *Sterett* reached Funafuti in the Ellice Islands on 21 January. Two days later she departed as a unit of Task Force 58 with the carriers *Bunker Hill* and *Monterey*. This was the kind of duty that the destroyer's officers had cut their teeth on. Acting as escort and plane guard for a fast-attack carrier was a demanding role that required heads-up performance, and the *Sterett*'s men were proud of their skill in that capacity. Commenting about this period in a recent letter, Champ Blouin (now retired Vice Admiral Blouin) said this: "We were part of a carrier group, with lots of attendant screen orientation and plane-guarding duties. When a plane went down on launch or land, if the pilot survived we retrieved him and got ice cream for our efforts. Wee Willie Williams was usually the star of these episodes—wearing a harness and line he would go over the side, swim to the pilot, and bring him back. This, plus refueling and carrying mail, all made for exciting days, but there was little action for the *Sterett* during these first weeks except for shore bombardments."

From 29 January until 7 March 1944 the *Sterett* toiled in the Marianas and the Marshalls. When the *Bunker Hill* and the *Monterey*, along with other Fifth Fleet carriers, struck Roi and Namur islands in Kwajalein

Atoll, the *Sterett* was there. When the carriers attacked the great Japanese base at Truk on 12 February, she was there also. She was still in the line-up when they raided Tinian and Saipan five days later. These were busy times, and the pace of operations never slackened. Often these carrier strikes were conducted over periods of a week or more and were inter-rupted only to refuel and replenish at sea every third or fourth day. Fre-quently there were enemy air attacks to counter. "The attacks on Truk and the Marianas were filled with action," Admiral Blouin recalled. "Again we were with a carrier task group. There was no surface engage-ment, but there were gigantic air battles, with ships firing at aircraft, many aircraft dog fights, and the spectacular sight of both U.S. and Jap planes falling from the sky."

There was no time to relax, and the skipper lived on the bridge so as to be immediately available in case of emergency. The ship made it back to Espíritu Santo on 13 March but left a few days later as part of the inva-sion force headed for Emirau Island. While the official history offers few details, typically on such missions the ship engaged in shore bombard-ment for a day or two before the landings; was subjected to air attacks while in the objective area; was menaced by the threat of Japanese sub-marines; and took part in offensive air operations launched from the car-riers (screening the flattops from submarine attack and plane-guarding to rescue downed aviators). It was a hectic pace, but the men of the *Sterett* loved it. Following the Emirau invasion, the ship was ordered back to the Puget Sound Navy Yard. She stopped at Purvis Bay on 4 April, Efate on the seventh, and Pearl Harbor on the sixteenth, reaching Puget Sound on the twenty-fourth.

No wartime visit to the States was ever long enough to suit the offi-cers and the crew, and this visit was exceptionally short. Only the most urgent repairs were completed before the *Sterett* was sent back to the war zone. By 30 May she was back in Majuro anchorage in the Marshall Islands. (On the way there the crew underwent two weeks of concentrat-ed training exercises in the Hawaii area. These exercises included gun-nery drills against a target towed by the USS *Lamberton* [DMS 2], whose skipper was Lt. "Cal" Calhoun.) The *Sterett*'s battle-readiness was excel-lent. On 6 June she sortied with Task Force 58 to prepare for the inva-sion of the Marianas. From 11 to 25 June she screened and plane-guarded for the carriers as they launched strikes against Saipan, Iwo Jima, Guam, and Rota. During this period she was frequently called upon to help repel enemy air attacks. Admiral Blouin remarked, "At Saipan—once more with a fast carrier task group—we did some shore bombardment, but my most significant recollection from that period is of the hundreds of Japan-ese bodies floating in the ocean after their suicidal jumps into the sea." The *Sterett*'s log contains the following entry for 23 June 1944:

1015—Proceeded to investigate raft in water. Captain at the conn. Steaming on various courses at various speeds. 1020—Recovered two Japanese survivors from raft. Rank not determined. Both malnourished, condition weak. Were fed and bathed. Placed under guard. 1115—Alongside *Essex*. 1120—Commenced transfer of prisoners. 1145—Completed transfer of prisoners. Received twelve Japanese prisoners of war. Placed under guard. 1633—Transferred fourteen prisoners of war to *Indianapolis* [at Saipan Island in the Marianas].

From 25 June to 7 July the *Sterett* concentrated on antisubmarine patrol duties around Rota and Guam; shore bombardment assignments on Guam were added for good measure. Next came carrier escort work during the attacks on Yap, Palau, and Ulithi, which occupied the rest of July and the first week of August. Then it was back to the States again, arriving at the Puget Sound Navy Yard on 20 August. This time the Navy brass was more reasonable: for eight glorious weeks, the officers and crew enjoyed all the comforts and pleasures that were available only on the mainland. There could hardly have been a more appreciative group of sailors.

The *Sterett* left the West Coast once more on 13 October for the Hawaiian Islands and arrived there five days later for one of the most concentrated periods of training she had ever witnessed. For a month her guns were fired at every conceivable target, surface and air alike. She also launched torpedoes, conducted antisubmarine exercises with live submarines, and engaged in close-order tactical drills, escort duties, and task force maneuvers. By the time she left on 19 November, her crew had attained their highest-ever level of readiness. Her next stop was Manus in the Admiralty Islands; more escort duties followed. She returned to Lunga Point, Guadalcanal, on 29 November, and was back in Manus three days later. On 11 December she entered Leyte Gulf, in the Philippines, for patrol and convoy duty. The following excerpt is from the official ship's history prepared by the Office of Public Information, Navy Department:

> On 27 December the *Sterett* left Leyte for a run to Mindoro that was to prove one of her most grueling tasks of the war. On this trip, the *Sterett* screened the third resupply echelon to Mindoro. Commencing early on the morning of the twenty-eighth, the convoy was subjected to repeated air attacks of varying intensity, particularly vicious over the next three days. The number of planes in a raid varied from one to twenty-five. The formation was under actual air attack for a total of six and one-half hours and was subjected to five major attacks during that period. Only one of these, on the morning

of the twenty-eighth, could be considered successful from the enemy's viewpoint. On this one the planes were able to come in on the formation with a very short approach [with a land background, and emerging out of heavy clouds] and make four successful suicide dives.

The *Sterett* splashed her first plane out of this series of raids with the assistance of another destroyer at 2000 on 28 December, during the second large attack. On the morning of the twenty-ninth, the *Sterett* assisted in shooting down another enemy suicider. At 1706 and 1717 that afternoon she assisted in shooting down two more. At 1925 the *Sterett* splashed one with full radar control. No other ship had the target under fire, and he was seen to burst into flame and hit the drink. The *Sterett* also participated in repulsing the large raid on the afternoon of the thirtieth, in Managrin Bay, Mindoro, during which several of our ships were hit. During this run to resupply Mindoro it is estimated that the enemy lost at least twenty-five planes from ships' antiaircraft fire. Of these, the *Sterett* knocked down one unassisted and aided in shooting down three more. She returned to San Pedro to fuel and replenish ammunition in time for the next operation, the invasion of Luzon. She was in the screen of the San Fabian attack force and helped beat off air attacks en route to Lingayen. At Lingayen Gulf the *Sterett* carried out her assigned shore bombardment mission and put a shore battery (then firing on our landing craft) out of commission with counter battery fire.

In a recent letter, Neale T. Fugate of Dallas, Texas, who as Ensign Fugate was the torpedo officer at the time of these air actions, said this:

My main memory of the *Sterett* was that it was a happy, tight, and efficient ship. I can't remember how many times I was told that the ship was made out of Texas horseshoes. There was a lot of kidding and banter across the wardroom table and on watch, all of which came across as promoting a sense of ease and competence. Very few personality feuds seemed to occur. The crew was very proud of the ship's gunnery and of the ship. The tale was often told of the *Sterett*'s exploits and tough times in and around the Solomons, and those who hadn't been there still took pride in the ship's fine service. It's wonderful how an action like that can pass through time, and later glue men together.

I remember being very scared on occasion. The main reaction always seemed to hit me after the event. And it seemed to hit the crew that way too. The first suicide planes didn't bother us too much, but after the first attack had time to soak in for a week or so we got pretty uptight with the idea. I think our first experience was at night on the Mindoro resupply run, as we sailed up the Sulu Sea. A kamikaze hit an ammunition ship a couple or three thousand yards from us. The water-hammer concussion was so heavy that many of us thought we had taken a torpedo. The first impression was gut-wrenching, and the later reaction was even stronger. As to being scared, the worst was to have to stand still and watch the attacking planes come in. I was on the bridge to man the torpedo director and would have given anything to have a 50-caliber machine gun to use. Too much topside weight, they said.

The *Sterett* showed some fancy gunnery on that run. It was a dark night with low clouds, and the Jap planes hopped over the hills to the east, stayed just above the clouds, and then dropped down on us. We picked one up on radar, got a solution, and began firing the 5-inch gun. We could follow the trajectories by the tracers, and we saw the first two rounds pass into the clouds. The third seemed to stop, hang for a minute, and then drift down. There were still two rounds in the air when the plane was hit.

On that same trip, on a dark, dark night with a heavy overcast, a plane came at us from starboard on a skip-bombing run. The lookout near me and I agreed that we saw the bomb skip clear over the ship. Then when the plane went over us we could see the "meatballs" on his wings. We could have knocked him out of the air by throwing potatoes, if we had had any. The moving cones of fire that followed the planes as they passed over the convoy were awe-inspiring.

It wasn't all grim. Once we were patrolling (weren't we always?) just outside of Los Negros Harbor, where we were staging for the Marianas operation. An island just off the harbor entrance held some of us spellbound. There was a clear, blue sky, a bright sun, and a pretty good surf running. Above the blue water was a white cloud of spume and spray around the base of the island. A rich red-brown band showed above the spray, and above that appeared the glittering emerald green of foliage. The island looked as if it were floating above the ocean on a white, fluffy cloud. After so many dull, colorless days at sea, it was witchery!

Admiral Blouin adds:

At Leyte, I remember that one of our sailors went to the beach, AWOL. The mud was a foot deep. He was picked up by the Army, and they wanted a sack of potatoes as a reward for apprehending him—we offered two sacks if they'd hold him an extra day. We also learned a good morale lesson here. A former shipmate of mine now had his own squadron, and under his tutelage for several afternoons (if all was quiet) we'd put twelve enlisted men in a boat with one case of beer. It was amazing—some of them came back buzzing! After the men had all gone through this process we put the officers into the "cocktail boat," and they had their libation as well.

One night at Leyte we had to escort a ship out of the gulf. An air attack took place after the *Sterett*'s departure. When we returned to our anchorage, a very irate commanding officer came over from an adjacent destroyer to complain that our 40- and 20-mm guns had hit his ship. Fortunately, I was able to convince him that we were not guilty—we hadn't even been there.

Later, when we were ordered on a run to Mindoro, we had to trade beer to a merchantman to get supplies and ammunition from him; our crew did all the labor. There was a lot of action on that run, with frequent air attacks. One of our accompanying destroyers was hit and had to be beached. The *Sterett* was credited with a couple of aircraft kills during that raid.

Fate deprived Champ Blouin of an award for his conduct during the action at Mindoro. The senior commander (who was the screen commander during the initial phase of the action) later lost his flagship, with all of his records, and was temporarily out of action. Champ was second in seniority and thus became the new screen commander. More air attacks followed. Consistent with his inspirational style of leadership, he always rewarded his juniors for outstanding performance of duty. In this case he took it upon himself to recommend the skipper of the *Wilson*, the *Sterett*'s companion ship during the engagement, for a Navy Cross. No recommendation was made for an award for Champ because no senior officer was present during the later phases of the action (and he certainly could not put in for one himself). His officers and crew all felt that he was entitled to some sort of reward—but such are the vagaries of life in the Navy.

IT WILL BE OBVIOUS TO THE READER that this author has had a difficult time doing justice to the human aspects of the *Sterett* story during the months after his departure from the ship. But the many letters and conversations from which this book was compiled make it clear that during the Blouin era the *Sterett* was in her highest state of combat-readiness. It is also apparent that veterans of the period still possess the same enthusiastic respect and admiration for their skipper, their shipmates, and their ship that also characterized the "plank owners" (the original crew). Some of their comments convey the esprit de corps that prevailed during Admiral Blouin's command. From William H. Deuel, former watertender 1/c and now a resident of Deming, New Mexico:

On the lighter side, the men in the fire room were an especially close-knit group. I always have to chuckle when I look back at some of the stunts we pulled. We were a group of young, hungry men, standing the twelve-to-four watch in the hot fire room. I suppose every watch had one man who was a superior food thief. We had a little fellow by the name of Rip Kelly who, when sent out to scout for food, would generally come back with something. One night when the bakers were baking pies and a line of men were helping to relay the pies from the oven to the shelf, Rip just happened to be in the galley. He took up the last position in line. Suddenly the door opened, and because we were at darkened ship the lights automatically went out. The door shut, the lights came back on, and Rip was missing—and so was one pie. We advised Rip to hide for a while. We were sure that the cook would be after him. And so he was. He came down to the fire room, really mad. Of course no one knew anything about a pie, or about Rip. The cook didn't find either of them, but we all certainly enjoyed that pie when the coast was clear. It was just amazing what we were able to cook with steam; we could of course boil coffee, or cook delicious hams that somehow always managed to fall through the hatch into our fire room when provisions were taken aboard.

Many of those who wrote to contribute observations about the men of the *Sterett* mentioned the impact of the ship's doctor on their lives and their welfare. Admiral Blouin has gone to considerable lengths to acquaint me with the expanded role of Doc Lea's ministry, which went far beyond the boundaries of medical science. He was chaplain, counselor, father-confessor, friend, ombudsman, and co-conspirator to officers and men alike. J. D. Jeffrey has already described how the doctor persuaded him to take a more compassionate stance with a wayward sailor in Sydney. Other shipmates cited many similar cases in outlining the tremendous contribution he made to the morale of the ship.

Roy Cowdrey (now a retired Navy captain living in Annapolis) has related many anecdotes about Doc Lea. One day the doctor went ashore in Efate with Roy, his pharmacist's mate, two other individuals, and five shotguns to bag a few wild chickens. Not only did the group fail in its primary mission, but they managed to get lost in the jungle on the way back. Fortunately, they encountered a native (complete with dyed hair) and for a few shotgun shells hired him as their guide back to the harbor. "Fuzzy Wan"—as Roy identified him—proceeded to demonstrate his superior marksmanship by hitting a chicken with every shot, a feat rendered all the more impressive by the fact that Fuzzy had a rusty French gun with no trigger. Roy now admits that the medicinal alcohol that Doc had taken along in case of snakebite may have had an effect on the *Sterett* hunting party's aim. No battle stars were awarded for this engagement.

Doc Lea's reputation as a doctor was good from the start, but it was greatly enhanced when he performed an emergency appendectomy on the wardroom table in very rough weather. Champ conned the *Sterett* out of formation and took a slower, more comfortable course while his medical officer did the surgery. The patient recovered nicely, and the crew's confidence in both the doctor and the captain skyrocketed. Doc Lea was also a perennial wardroom treasurer—an important job, but one that few people ever wanted.

On several occasions Doc observed that one of the mess attendants was habitually belligerent, surly, uncooperative, and abusive in language as well as manner. Doc's solution was to speak to "Big Willie," who by that time had become the chief mess attendant. He told Willie that his subordinate was a troublemaker and that his reputation as a leader was hurt by his apparent inability to discipline him effectively. The next day the doctor confronted a new problem—Willie had broken the "undisciplined" mess attendant's jaw. Doc had to take the man to a dental surgeon aboard the battleship *Massachusetts* to patch him up. Apparently the culprit made the mistake of reacting to Willie's reprimand with his fists. From that day forward the troublemaker's attitude improved markedly. Doc would never have countenanced the use of violence to enforce discipline, but when he learned that the chief had acted only in self-defense he supported Willie's response. He had solved a troublesome problem, and his messmates appreciated his efforts.

In April 1944 the *Sterett* escorted the *Mississippi* and a couple of cruisers to a Seattle shipyard, and Herb May (who was the doctor's roommate) was sent ahead to arrange the repair schedule. Herb called Ellie—Doc's "one and only"—from San Francisco and urged her (without telling her why) to take the train to Seattle on the twenty-fourth. The ship would be in port for only five days, and without advance notice she could not have arrived in time. Champ convinced the local authorities to waive the waiting period usually required for a marriage license, enabling Doc and Ellie to get married in the Bremerton Navy Yard chapel. Herb May was the best man, and "Pete" Cowdrey (Roy's wife) was the matron of honor. The Leas held a reception for the officers in their hotel room. Doc recalled, "I had brandy, a quart of Three Feathers, and a quart of Schenley Black Label, all from my medical supplies." The tiny brandy bottles were clearly marked "U.S. Navy Medical Corps"; if Champ noticed, he maintained a discreet silence.

To judge from the comments made by his *Sterett* shipmates, Champ never slowed down. His era was marked by repeated volunteer actions:

"Unless otherwise directed, I am leaving the screen to investigate and identify surface radar contact." It turned out to be two downed, wounded Japanese pilots.

"Unless otherwise directed, I am leaving formation to take safe course and speed to permit the doctor to perform emergency surgery." As we already know, the appendectomy was successful.

"Unless otherwise directed, I am proceeding to search for and recover survivors." Frequently, the *Sterett* was successful on such missions. Champ had promised when he relieved Frank Gould that he would maintain the ship's reputation as a superb fighting unit. There can be no doubt that he did. The *Sterett* was in action of some kind almost without pause during every operational assignment while he had command. Many of the air attacks that her crew fought off during this period were fiercely fought multiplane raids. The *Sterett* always seemed to have her rabbit's foot at work—but in reality, her secret was a combination of relentless training schedules and dedicated men.

Nearly everyone who wrote about his memories of this ship mentioned the contributions of "Big Willie," "Wee Willie," or "Sylvester," as he was variously called. Champ told of the many times he went into the water, harness and line over his shoulder, to bring a pilot or some other helpless survivor back to the ship's side, where by reason of his great physical strength he was able to lift the man on board. His performance as the first loader of gun number two was already legendary when I served on board, and he continued to perform in that capacity with increased skill and grace for the remainder of the *Sterett*'s actions. Willie was also a talented musician, and on afternoons when we were not at general quarters he would bring his saxophone back on the fantail and (together with Pomerance, who played the clarinet) entertain his shipmates. Sometimes he also acted as the ship's barber. I have been unable to locate Willie. He should be honored at some future *Sterett* reunion; in Doc Lea's words, "He was enormously well liked and respected by both officers and crew." Admiral Blouin recently echoed those words and added his own commendations of Willie's outstanding performance.

I would be remiss if, in summarizing the *Sterett*'s history during World War II, I failed to mention those individuals who were specifically cited by Champ Blouin in his letters on personal actions and the performance of duty while he was in command. One such individual was Dan Poor, who came aboard on 25 January 1943 as an ensign and was detached on 14 June 1944 as a lieutenant. Admiral Blouin wrote, "I would like to make some complimentary comment about Dan Poor, who, as communications officer, was officer-of-the-deck at general quarters and did a magnificent job backing me up. A Harvard grad, with the broad accent of Boston's prewar days, he adapted wonderfully to destroyer life in crumpled dungarees." He continued: "Doc Lea was a tower of strength, both medically and in the critical area of morale. He must have been the crew's most loved officer. And Herb May grew up on that ship; the *Sterett* gave him his first responsibilities, and he served the ship with distinction through just about the entire war. As my executive officer and navigator, he was just what I needed, and he kept it a happy ship."

Other comments made by *Sterett* veterans about the Blouin era, while they do not amount to anecdotes, provide brief snatches of color and style. Leonard D. Woods, a graduate of the Merchant Marine Academy, reported aboard on 11 October 1943 and was the last crewman detached from the *Sterett*, on 2 November 1945. An ensign when he arrived and a lieutenant when he left, Woods was chief engineer for most of the Blouin era. He made the following remarks in a 1988 letter:

> Sherman Pomerance was a close friend, and along with Big Willie he played the sax and the clarinet. They were very good and very entertaining. Sherm was transferred to the destroyer *Bush*, which was sunk at Okinawa. He was killed in an attempt to get some of his shipmates out of the water onto an LCI. The LCI was under attack; Sherm was last seen going into the ship's screws.

> One interesting experience came when we were nested with another group of "cans," and Herman Wouk came over and visited us. If memory serves, we ended up in a poker game together.

> Christmas of 1943 was spent in Efate (we were there to refuel and resupply), but for Christmas of 1944 we were in Leyte Gulf. It was one hell of a difference. I recall that 1944 Christmas, because we agreed to put the captain's gig over the side and let each man enjoy two cans of beer. While the gig was away from the ship, we came under kamikaze attack. The beer was finished despite the Japs. The *Sterett*'s men knew what was important.

> One of the strangest events occurred when we transferred the staff and belongings of an admiral from one carrier to another. Somehow his liquor supply turned up missing. Because of hangovers, a few members of the black gang had to find alternates for the watch. The black gang was also famous for the excellent turkeys they somehow managed to obtain and cook in the fire rooms.

At the *Sterett* reunion in Philadelphia in 1989, I met Leonard Woods for the first time. He shared many of his recollections of the ship and its people:

> We had an excellent group in engineering. Any time there was an emergency they were always there, always equal to the situation. You just could not have assembled a finer bunch of people. I always appreciated the fact that the captain bent over backward for them when it came to leave and liberty. That really helped, because it was a rough life "down in that black hole," as Cowdrey used to put it.

The reinforcement of Mindoro was one hell of an operation. Champ was the commander of the screen, and we had a number of ships hit by kamikazes. Then that ammunition ship was hit, and the blast caused a tidal wave you could hardly believe. That was a very traumatic time, and as always Champ did a superb job. He ran the ship right up to the beach as far as he could go—any closer and we'd have run aground. The *Sterett* took out those gun emplacements on the ridge with deadly accuracy. I'd never seen the guns fired so fast for so long—they were red-hot. Once at Mindoro when we were alongside a destroyer that had been hit by a kamikaze another plane dove at us; the other ship took a second hit.

Woods asked if I knew Gordon S. Husby, who reported to the *Sterett* on 12 December 1943 as an ensign and was detached on 24 July 1945 as a lieutenant. Husby served as first lieutenant during his tour. His nickname was "the Bruiser": he was a lineman at the University of Washington before the war and had played in the Rose Bowl. Shortly after he arrived on board he persuaded Woods to spar with him on the fo'c'sle one afternoon, "just for exercise." Woods landed what he thought was a light blow to Husby's face. In a split second, Husby reflexively connected with a right to the jaw; Woods suddenly found himself airborne and nearly sailed overboard. That ended Woodie's availability as a sparring partner. The incident typifies the caliber and character of the men of the *Sterett*. They were tough, and capable.

For 27 January 1945 the *Sterett*'s log entry states: "1127—Pursuant to BuPers dispatch 201239, dated 19 October 1944, Comdr. Francis J. Blouin, 72447, USN, was relieved as commanding officer of USS *Sterett* (DD 407) by Lt. Comdr. Gordon B. Williams, 81170, USN." The transfer was completed by high line from the USS *Morris* (DD 414) in Lingayen Gulf during the early phase of the invasion of Luzon. Troops were headed ashore; carrier aircraft patrolled the skies above; battleships, cruisers, and destroyers bombarded Japanese positions; and a multitude of landing craft, ship's boats, and other vessels moved across the water's surface at a hectic pace. It was a busy scene, and an appropriate setting for the *Sterett*'s change of command.

The Blouin era had come to an end. I wish I could have had a part in it. The *Sterett* performed with great distinction in one of the most dangerous periods of her career: a full year of almost continuous combat operations. As was always the case, the commanding officer had imbued the men of the *Sterett* with the essence of his character. His achievement showed in the crew's cheerful, enthusiastic, and aggressive performance, and it added another chapter of bold and courageous action to the ship's proud history.

CHAPTER 11

THE FINAL ACT

"**GORDY" WILLIAMS AND I BECAME FRIENDS AT THE NAVAL ACADEMY,** where we were classmates. Watching him perform as a "B" squad stalwart on the gridiron, I admired his guts and his sincerity. In 1944 Lt. Comdr. Gordon B. Williams was the executive officer of the destroyer USS *Wedderburn* (DD 684) in the western Pacific. In early December he received orders to take command of the *Sterett*. He was detached from the *Wedderburn* and spent the next several weeks engaged in a common activity in those days—chasing around the Pacific on whatever transportation was available in an effort to catch up with the ship to which one had been assigned. Gordy hitched a ride aboard the *Morris* from Hollandia, New Guinea, and learned that both the *Morris* and the *Sterett* were slated to participate in the invasion of the Philippines, with landings scheduled to take place on Mindoro on 15 December and on Luzon on 9 January. Gordy busied himself on the *Morris*, acting as the squadron commander's chief of staff, until the two ships finally met on 27 January. He transferred to his new command by high line on that date. Champ Blouin then crossed to the *Morris* by the same method for the first leg of his journey to his new command, the destroyer *Ingersoll* (DD 652).

The *Sterett's* new skipper found that he had inherited a well-trained ship's company, with a core of veterans from many engagements in the southern and central Pacific. He spent his first several days at the helm on shore bombardment missions in support of our ground forces, now fighting desperately to gain control of their objectives, and on screening assignments for our transports, which were so vulnerable to attack by either submarines or aircraft. The invasion plan proceeded on schedule, and on 30 January the *Sterett* was ordered to escort a fifty-ship convoy (a mix of merchant and navy craft that had already off-loaded their cargoes of troops and supplies) safely out of Lingayen Gulf. As soon as they reached the Philippine Sea the convoy was dispersed, and the *Sterett* was sent into an area she was very familiar with—the bays and sounds of the Solomon chain from Guadalcanal to New Georgia. There a concentrated period of training and rehearsals had begun for the huge force that would soon invade the Ryukyus.

Captain Williams proved to be a stern and uncompromising teacher. He refused to allow the men of the *Sterett* to rest on their laurels. He was well aware of their skills and of their outstanding record in past actions. But he was also keenly aware of the tendency of championship teams to become so enamored of their own prowess that they lost their focus and thus their hard-won titles. He was not about to allow that to happen to the *Sterett*. For the next several weeks the ship engaged in all sorts of training exercises—not only those intended for the individual ship, such as damage control, fire-fighting, man overboard, gunnery, torpedo, and antisubmarine drills, but also those involving the entire amphibious strike force, with practice landings and naval gunfire support of ground forces.

By 27 March 1945, when she sailed from Ulithi as part of the Fifth Fleet's amphibious task force to participate in the Operation Iceberg invasion of Okinawa, the *Sterett* was again at peak combat-readiness. The task force arrived in the vicinity of Naha before daylight on 1 April. It was Easter Sunday: Okinawa's D day. The *Sterett* was relieved of her escort duties and assigned to patrol the transport area. She was also made available for shore bombardment missions on call.

It quickly became apparent that the Japanese had abandoned their beach defenses and concentrated their troops along the Shuri Line, which ran across the island from the Hagushi beaches to Naha. Gen. Simon B. Buckner's ground forces exerted heavy pressure against the defenders. For the first five days the situation remained relatively quiet, but aboard the *Sterett* Gordy Williams and his shipmates were under no illusions. They were aware that Okinawa was uncomfortably close to the Japanese home islands, that it was strongly fortified, and that it would be defended with courage and determination. But they did not know that in planning Operation Iceberg Adm. Kelly Turner had thought it prudent to station destroyer pickets at about twenty designated geographic points around the island to provide early warning of approaching enemy aircraft. The preliminary design was submitted for review and coordination to Adm. Marc A. Mitscher, then the commander of Task Force 58. Mitscher's chief of staff at this juncture was Capt. Arleigh Burke, who had drawn up the blueprint for the Vella Gulf engagement. Burke saw that Turner's plan called for single destroyers at the picket stations around Okinawa. He pointed out to Mitscher that these ships would inevitably become prime targets for the kamikazes and that no one destroyer could defend itself successfully against simultaneous attacks by as many as four or five planes. (As it turned out, this was a conservative estimate: the picket destroyers *Evans* and *Hadley* were attacked by as many as twenty-three aircraft.) Burke suggested that the destroyers be stationed in clusters of up to four ships so that they could render mutual gunfire support to one another; Turner apparently considered the idea incompatible with his order of priorities for destroyer operations. Soon, however, the wisdom of Arleigh Burke's recommendation would become abundantly clear.

A preview of what was to come occurred on 6 April at radar picket station number one, located fifty miles north of Okinawa and occupied by the destroyer *Bush* (DD 529). She had been subjected to several kamikaze attacks over the previous two days and had repelled them. But her luck was about to run out. By noon on the sixth she had downed one attacker and avoided three more. Then they literally swarmed all over her. For another three hours she was able to avoid a direct hit and even scored another kill, but shortly after 1500 a single plane came in low, penetrated a hail of antiaircraft fire, and struck the starboard side between the stacks. The explosion it caused in her forward engine room was devastating. The destroyer-transport *Colhoun* (APD 17) moved over from her picket station to protect the crippled destroyer. The struggle to keep the *Bush* afloat continued until 1700, when a fresh wave of thirteen Japanese aircraft attacked both ships. The *Colhoun* was struck first. About fifteen minutes later the *Bush* absorbed a second hit that almost cut her in two. At 1745 she received a third hit. It was too much. She sank about forty-five minutes later, with eighty-seven sailors on board. The *Colhoun* also went down some six and one-half hours after she was hit, taking thirty-five men with her.

Down in the objective area sixty miles away, the *Sterett* was on patrol. What had started as a calm, peaceful morning turned tense as radio reports of the attack on radar picket station number one made all hands aware that combat was not far off. At about 1000 a large number of enemy aircraft were reported to be approaching from the north. The entire combat air patrol (CAP) was sent out to intercept them. Despite many confirmed kills CAP simply could not contain all of them, and more than two hundred kamikazes penetrated the transport area. The lumbering transports got under way as quickly as they could, while the *Sterett* and her companion escorts opened fire on the attackers.

Gordy Williams had gone to general quarters as soon as the approaching raid was reported. He increased speed to 25 knots while the bogies were still ten miles away and started shooting as soon as they were within effective range. First the 5-inch and then the 40-mm and the 20-mm guns joined the harsh and deafening battle-chorus. The sky was filled with tracers, exploding shells, Japanese planes (some falling in flames, others homing in on their targets), and the smoke ascending from our damaged ships. The *Sterett*'s skipper conned his ship with extra care and skill. He had experienced a similar melee during the Battle of Kolombangara in July 1943, while he was engineering officer of the destroyer *Woodworth* (DD 460). She had collided with one of her companions, and Gordy was determined at least to spare the *Sterett* from that fate.

The transports were the planes' main targets. They carried vital supplies and ammunition, and they were slow and vulnerable. The destroyers formed a loose protective ring around their charges. One enemy plane almost scored a hit on the *Sterett*, but her veteran gunners shot it down. It missed by no more than thirty yards off the starboard beam. The pilot's body and parts of his plane were recovered by the *Sterett* after the fight.

Many ships were hit. On top of the loss of the *Bush* and the *Colhoun*, the destroyers *Mullany* (DD 528), *Newcomb* (DD 586), *Leutze* (DD 481), *Howorth* (DD 592), *Hyman* (DD 732), *Morris* (DD 417), and *Haynsworth* (DD 700) and the destroyer-escort *Fieberling* (DE 640) were all damaged and sent to the protected anchorage of Kerama Retto (about eighteen miles south of Naha) to be patched up by our tenders and repair ships. Despite the toll they had inflicted on our ships the Japanese failed to reduce the capabilities of U.S. forces in any significant way, and they lost about two hundred planes in the process. The conquest of Okinawa continued on schedule.

Aboard the *Sterett* pride and satisfaction were the dominant emotions. She had scored one positive kill and had at least participated in the downing of five more Japanese aircraft, at a cost of 250 rounds of 5-inch ammunition and innumerable 40- and 20-mm rounds. Gordy Williams took to the public-address system to tell the crew what a good job they had done and to give them the Navy's highest accolade—"Well done."

That first day served to indicate exactly how ferocious the enemy's attacks would be for the duration of the Okinawa campaign. It was clear that the occupants of the radar picket stations were in for a fight. If you had asked any sailor on the *Sterett* on 6 April 1945 what he thought would be next on the ship's agenda, chances are he would have replied, "We'll probably be assigned to radar picket station number one." And that is exactly what happened. On the morning of 7 April the *Sterett* was ordered to that station along with the *Bennett* (DD 473) to provide early warning of the approach of Japanese aircraft. Since station number one was on a direct line between Japan and Okinawa, it was certain to attract the attention of every enemy raid southward. The men of the *Sterett* knew all about the *Bush* and the *Colhoun*, but they adopted their characteristic attitude: "Well, what the hell, somebody has to do it—and besides, who can do it better?"

A protective CAP of between four and six fighters from one of the fast carriers was assigned to picket station number one from one-half hour after sunrise to one-half hour before sunset. Of course, the Japanese were aware of this schedule. They concentrated their attacks at dawn and at dusk, although skirmishes went on all day too. Without the protection of our fighters, the picket force (which included destroyer-escorts as well as minecraft, landing craft, and patrol boats that had been assigned for rescue purposes) were at a distinct disadvantage. Gordy Williams gave this account of the events of 7–9 April 1945:

Each destroyer division usually had one ship equipped with extra electronic gear that enhanced its capacity for early detection and control of the CAP. The destroyer so equipped was then designated as a DDR, for radar picket. The *Sterett*, in Squadron One,

Division Twelve, did not actually have extra electronic gear due to weight limitations, but she had been labeled as a DDR anyway. Following our orders, we joined the *Bennett* in radar picket station one at about noon. The scuttlebutt took on a new tone, and the ship buzzed with excitement. "How long before we get creamed? Can this old can take a kamikaze? Is our shooting good enough? What are our chances?" The *Sterett* had swapped shots with a Japanese battleship at Savo Island and had the 14-inch scars in the superstructure to prove it. We were well trained, the ship was fast, and we had proved we could shoot straight. Morale was high. I had been through eight campaigns and engagements, and had held every job on a destroyer from "George" to captain in my six straight years on this type of ship. I felt confident of my own and the ship's ability to meet any challenge.

Early in the evening of the seventh as we patrolled stations with the *Bennett*, two low-flying planes came in and attacked her. She was about three miles north of the *Sterett*. The *Bennett* was able to shoot down one of the planes, but the second crashed into the forward fire room, killing and wounding many personnel and incapacitating the ship. Because the planes came in on the far side of the *Bennett*, the *Sterett* was unable to render gunfire support without shooting over her and running the risk of hitting her. The risk was magnified by the fact that kamikaze tactics usually involved at least some very low-level approaches; and even when the aircraft dove from above, the stream of gunfire had to follow the plane in its descent and then stop before it got so low as to hit the structure of the target ship. An appropriate damage report was sent, and the *Bennett* was ordered to proceed to Kerama Retto. The *Sterett* was directed to remain on radar picket station one. Two small ships (LCSs) were directed to join us for limited gun support or, as some members of the crew observed, to pick up survivors.

The dawning of 8 April had special meaning for me—it was my thirtieth birthday. I wondered, perhaps a bit morbidly, if this was to be my last day on earth. We were directly in line for the next kamikaze attack, and the odds were against us. The carrier group would provide CAP for us for most of the day, but we would be on our own at the most dangerous periods of half-light—dawn and dusk—when the fuel limitations of our planes and the distances involved necessitated leaving the picket destroyers unprotected. To my relief, we received no attack at dawn, and shortly thereafter the friendly fighters arrived overhead.

The day passed with the condition watch alert and the air controller in the *Sterett's* combat information center in constant conversation with the carrier's CAP. I listened to these conversations and read the messages that the decoding watch constantly brought to the bridge for my perusal and information. Our ground forces were advancing inland on Okinawa in heavy fighting, aided by heavy bombardment from ship batteries and carrier aircraft. Throughout the day none of the anticipated attacks occurred, but as sunset was not until 1930 there was plenty of time before the inevitable dusk general quarters. The steward, James Bailey, had remembered my birthday and provided a nice birthday cake at dinner. The wardroom was fairly relaxed and there was considerable kidding, although the tension could be felt under the calm exterior. After dinner I returned to the bridge and called the ship to general quarters about a half-hour before sunset, which was about ten minutes before the CAP would depart to return to the carrier. Dusk came, and then night, and I felt reasonably sure that I would not meet my maker on this date.

The morning of 9 April was strictly routine on the *Sterett*. Dawn general quarters, with gun drills, were held as usual. After daylight, with the arrival of the CAP, the condition watch was set and the ship proceeded with normal advanced-area routine. Emergency drills were held in the afternoon (collision, damage control, man overboard, and so on) and were efficiently carried out. I had formed the habit of timing all drills with a stopwatch and was satisfied insofar as speed, thoroughness, attention to detail in battle dress, and general procedures were concerned. . . .

As evening approached and the CAP prepared to leave, the *Sterett* went to general quarters as usual. This was at about 1850, with sunset due at about 1930. About five minutes after the departure of the CAP, the combat information center reported many bogies approaching from the northwest at a distance of forty miles. I took the conn and ordered all engines ahead flank speed—25 knots. Then I went to the loudspeaker system and made the following announcement: "We have Jap planes en route heading directly for us—if you characters ever want to sleep with a blonde again, you had better shoot down these bastards as soon as they come up." I sensed that it eased the strain a little bit. My plan was to fishtail (make rapid changes of course to port and starboard) at high speed to become as elusive a target as possible, and at the same time to keep all my guns firing.

In a few minutes the gun director was locked on the enemy plane formation, which now began to break up into five segments. I gave the order to the gunnery officer to open fire as soon as the Japs were within range. We had clear weather and good visibility, and in a few minutes five planes identified as Vals came at us. . . . Four of these planes headed for the *Sterett*. The fifth peeled off and went after the two small craft now several miles from us. This plane dove over one LCS and overshot the hull, but knocked off the mainmast. In accordance with his suicide pact, the pilot had flown to his death.

Up in the gun director, Roy Cowdrey had a good solution and was doing a superb job. One Val zeroing in on us was shot down by the 5-inch guns when it was still about four miles away. Now Roy shifted to a second Val, and it was hit shortly thereafter. Once it hit the water, the odds were cut in half. The two remaining planes were heading directly for the bridge structure, their machine guns blazing to strafe the gun crews and other exposed people. I ordered the bridge personnel to take cover on the port side—the kamikazes were coming at us on the starboard beam. All of the quartermasters and signalmen scrambled to the opposite side except Signalman 1/c Conn, a rather laconic individual from Tennessee who stated flatly, "If you stay, captain, I'm staying also." I appreciated his attitude, and the starboard wing of the bridge was not quite so lonely in those memorable few seconds of ultimate peril. Below us on the 01 level, Steward's Mate 3/c James Bailey and his gun crew fired their 20-mm gun at its maximum rate while bullets struck all around them and hit the ship's side. This gun crew literally sawed off one wing of the attacker, and it hit the water no more than fifty yards away on the starboard beam. One wheel of the plane ricocheted and wedged under the starboard anchor chain.

The fourth Val was headed directly for the bridge structure. The kamikazes liked aiming at this point, which obviously was the most likely location at which to score lucky hits on critical ship-control personnel. If the plane was hit and lost altitude while aiming at the bridge, it could still damage the ship at the waterline or in vital engineering spaces. This Val was hit by gunfire, but it struck the *Sterett* just above the waterline and directly below the bridge, exploding into the mess hall. It made a ten-foot hole in the ship's side, bashed in the diesel generator, and did some damage to the fuel oil tanks directly below. The damage control parties worked quickly to ascertain the extent of our wounds and whether there was any loss of vital ship services. I slowed to 15 knots as we lost steering control on the starboard cables. Dusk was descending as I called for casualty reports and further damage evaluations. It was with the utmost relief and satisfaction that I received the report of none dead, and only minor injuries. In fact the number-one personnel casualty appeared to be our own favorite medical officer, Doc Lea, who was thrown off balance during our radical maneuvering. Fortunately, he had no broken bones, but he did suffer some painful contusions. We had been through and survived a full-fledged kamikaze attack by four simultaneous attackers without the loss of a single man.

Our communications were intact, and we were able to get action and damage reports off immediately. A relief destroyer was ordered out to relieve us of our picket station duties, and the *Sterett* was ordered back to Kerama Retto for emergency repairs of battle damage.

Chief Engineer Leonard Woods offered this account of the kamikaze hit:

> I was in the forward engine room, at engine control. At first the 5-inch started firing, then the 40-mm, and finally the 20-mm. The hit by the plane created quite an explosion, and in engine control we were in complete darkness. The point of impact was just forward of the forward fire room. The plane severed all of the electrical cables on the starboard side, went through the emergency diesel generator room (putting that out of commission), and then cut all the cables on the port side of the ship. All of our circuits were out, and repeated efforts to reset the breakers were futile. The chief electrician's mate suggested we abandon the engine room, but I wasn't ready to do that yet. Then the hatch opened, and I was handed a sound-powered telephone from the bridge. Captain Williams instructed me to try to restore power with our emergency jump system, and then to try to trim the ship with ballast. We were able to do so. Speed was restricted then to about 3 knots. How we escaped without serious injuries to our people I'll never know. Much credit must be given to Captain Williams for his leadership in directing total command of all the steps necessary to save the ship.

Again the *Sterett* had been tested to her utmost, and again she had passed the test. For his performance during and after the kamikaze attack Gordy Williams was awarded the Navy Cross, the third *Sterett* skipper to be so honored.

The *Sterett* made it to Kerama Retto under her own power—no small accomplishment under the circumstances. Once there she went alongside a repair ship, whose crew welded a steel plate over the huge hole made by the kamikaze and removed what was left of the Japanese plane and its pilot. In little more than a week the *Sterett* left the vicinity of Okinawa for Bremerton, Washington (stopping at Guam and Pearl Harbor), and permanent repairs at the Puget Sound Naval Shipyard.

Her repairs completed in early July, the *Sterett* steamed down the coast to San Diego for refresher training. After a couple of weeks of concentrated drills and practices she was ready for combat again, despite a large turnover in personnel and the loss of many old-timers. In late July she moved to Pearl Harbor to take part in more training exercises, including shore bombardments of Kahoolawe Island. Gordy Williams reported that his ship was ready to return to the conflict—but her fighting days were over. President Truman authorized the use of atomic bombs, and soon after they were dropped on Hiroshima and Nagasaki the Japanese capitulated. Surrender ceremonies were conducted aboard the USS *Missouri*, and the *Sterett* was on her way home.

THERE IS NO SINGLE EYEWITNESS ACCOUNT of the *Sterett*'s last days, but the following remembrances capture the sense of loyalty and comradeship that developed in those who served on her. From Roy Cowdrey—

Gibson carried me while I learned—bless him and the other chiefs. I remember him telling me to pick the target, and he'd get the solution and tell me when to shoot.

I remember a request from Signalman 1/c Conn—who had been our director/bridge telephone talker—to move him out of the director and assign him to the bridge for general quarters. I granted his request.

Lastra, the director pointer, was the boatswain's mate assigned with me to the after fueling station, which more often than not was underwater during our refuelings. The bridge would repeatedly call down to us to ask how much longer it was going to take before we had received our capacity intake. Our response was always, "How in the hell would we know? We're just trying to keep from going overboard with these solid seas back here!"

I remember all those dawn and dusk general quarters, straining to see a periscope or spot a bogie, when we were always required to hold various and sundry casualty drills and were often so tired that we could barely stay awake.

I remember "Big John" Kosalko—gun captain of the number two 5-inch mount—hanging out of the door instead of the hatch and firing more rounds than the other three guns because of "Big Willie" and Varner (two terrific black sailors, both in and out of that gun). John knocked someone out when the sailor panicked during one action. Hodge and I tried every which way (short of making the checks on the exam paper) to get John rated up to second class.

I remember Herb May scheduling loading drills every day, regardless of the fact that we may have fired umpteen rounds in anger the day before.

I remember Okinawa and hearing Herb in combat, during dusk alert and just before we were hit, saying, "Here they come, low on the horizon." Lastra tapped me on the shoulder as he pointed to the planes at about thirty degrees.

I remember Montenegro (FC 3/c), the rangefinder operator, being blinded by Jap searchlights at Guam when we tried to shoot them out.

I remember the stroke that Gordy Williams almost had when he was brought to the *Sterett* for the first time by the regular gig crew—they sported Mohawk hair cuts, no shoes, and cutoff jeans. The *Sterett* crew knew it was good.

I remember Fink, the chief boatswain's mate, and his dog who only had one pup—lack of space, you know.

Then there was "Your Typhoon"—green water over the gun director.

We chipped paint, weighed it, and tried to determine how much excess weight we'd removed. The result was that I had red, green, and yellow guns for a while—different chromatic colors.

From Neale Fugate—

Fairly early in my stint, the *Sterett*'s torpedo tubes were removed and replaced with two 40s. Then later, just before Okinawa, a radio transmitter/receiver outlet was set up on the gun director platform; we had become a picket ship. The radio hookup gave lookouts direct communication with the combat air patrol. Jap planes had begun to come down the chain of islands to Okinawa, mostly on suicide missions. Against shipping, they would come in below air search radar effectiveness but high enough so that it was difficult for the surface search radar to pick them up. The lookouts were supposed to spot these incoming planes early and coach the CAP over to them. It worked.

On the evening of 9 April 1945, after the CAP had to head back to base, a squad of Jap planes showed up. I was on the gun director deck for this surface search routine with two exceptionally good lookouts. One of them spotted the planes (five of them) ten to twelve thousand yards out. As I remember, he climbed up the gun director ladder, reached down to guide the gunnery officer's head up out of the top hatch, and pointed out the incoming planes to him. The director trained on them, got a solution at around eight thousand yards, and began firing at about five thousand yards. The 5-inch got two of the planes at around three thousand yards away. One of the remaining three turned south and went after two small landing craft that were with us. The landing craft were fitted with 40s and 20s, and they shot down their attacker. By then our 40s and 20s had come into action. One plane was hit and exploded no more than fifty yards off our starboard beam, showering our decks with debris. The remaining plane, now heading straight for our bridge and strafing us from murderously close range, absorbed a hail of 40- and 20-mm shells from our superbly courageous gunners, who never flinched. They were still firing when the plane hit us amidships, at the waterline. As one of our Brooklynites put it, "You could of drove a Mack truck tru duh hole." Evidently the plane was carrying a 6- or 8-inch artillery shell that exploded when it hit—and yes, the hole was sizable.

The plane hit a fuel bunker, and the explosion started a fire; but seawater flowed in to put it out. Since this was the bunker that was on line the boiler fires went out, and we went dead in the water. Shock knocked out all the ship's communications, so we ran sound-powered phones to emergency steering stations in the stern, hooked up a battery to a radio so that we could report our condition, put a clean fuel oil bunker on line, fired the boilers, and got under way for Kerama Retto for emergency repairs. The total time that elapsed from when we first sighted the planes to when we got under way again was fifty-six minutes, according to the ship's log. Our only casualty was the doctor, who suffered minor injuries when the concussion knocked him off his feet. Well, some of the men below decks did get shaken up somewhat, but not seriously. We had lived through a few more of the *Sterett's* many magnificent moments, but once again I had been reminded that death and destruction could visit us without warning, and that we could not drop our guard for an instant.

A day or two later we were moored at Kerama Retto, getting a patch put on our side. The island looked as if a load of otherworldly rocks had been dumped there. Everything had a weird shape and color; there were unexpected crevices, a stone arch reaching down to the water, red and brown lichen-splotched stones, and practically no vegetation. In the morning and evening, the way shadows and colors shifted was fascinating. There were always some off-duty men standing mesmerized at the rail as they watched the scene. If a gnome or a kobold had hopped out and scurried around, no one would have been surprised; we might have said, "Well, what d'ya know, a gnome." I can understand how the old windjammer sailors came back with their tall tales. . . .

We were at anchor watch at night in Tacloban harbor when word came that the Japs were moving down from the hills to swim out and blow up the ship, or to climb aboard and run amok. Our anchor watch had handguns, but some of the nearby ships had tommy guns and twitchy trigger fingers. My watch and I agreed that it would be best to lie flat on the deck and peer over the side. I don't know if any swimmers showed up, but there was an awful lot of promiscuous gunfire.

Once when we lay off an island—Saipan, I think—some of the men were sunbathing, while others were just being lazy. But a few who had access to binoculars were watching some Marines who were backed up on a nearby point of land and engaged in a desperate firefight. (They did eventually win out.) Those of us who watched got a strong feeling of being disconnected from reality.

We swam in Sunlight Channel in the Russels with the ship's gig on shark picket, tommy gun at the ready. The channel was just wide enough for two ships to pass each other and yet was deep water. The water was nearly the temperature of blood, and swimmers got so sapped that it became hard to climb back aboard.

For decommissioning we took the ship from Hawaii to Brooklyn via Panama. The convoy commander stretched things too far en route, and we had to refuel on the fringes of a hurricane. We popped hoses and sprayed oil all over our ship as well as the fueling ship alongside. It was so rough that we had to pump ballast to maintain our stability. It was miserable and dangerous. One moment we on the fantail would look up at the ship alongside as if we were staring up at a cliff, and the next moment we were level with the other ship's weather deck. The helmsman had a rough time trying to keep the hoses from breaking—and trying to keep us from crashing into the fueling ship. I experienced a number of bad fueling attempts at sea, but this was the worst. At the time the *Sterett*'s topside weight was a big concern, and it made for a wild ride around Hatteras. We were on our beam ends most of the time until the convoy commander "got the word," reduced speed, and changed course to quarter the seas somewhat.

When we sat around at officers' clubs, one of our games was to spot the communications officer in a group of new arrivals. He usually looked pretty haggard.

When securing from general quarters, Ens. Otis Erisman would always begin to sing sotto voce: "Sunday school is over, and we are going home. Good-bye-y, good-bye-y, we are going home." I don't think he realized what he was doing.

From Leonard Woods—

After being hit, we steamed slowly into Kerama Retto. I was detached and sent by air to the Puget Sound Navy Yard with all the data that shipyard personnel would need in order to decide (with some assurance of accuracy) exactly how to repair our damage. I arrived on 1 May, and the *Sterett* came in on the tenth. The yard was well prepared. They went right to work on the repairs and also removed our torpedo tubes; in their place they installed additional 40-mm guns in preparation for the kamikaze attacks that were expected to greet us when we invaded Japan. Fortunately, President Truman ordered the delivery of atomic weapons on selected targets to convince the Japanese military that further resistance was futile. We were sent to San Diego for trials and were there when Japan surrendered. We then went to Hawaii and spent about a month there. Next we were ordered to New York for Navy Day.

The *Dictionary of American Naval Fighting Ships* has this to say about the *Sterett's* last days: "On 25 September, she set sail with *Mississippi* (BB 41), *North Carolina* (BB 55), and *Enterprise* (CV 6). *Sterett* transited the Panama Canal on 8 and 9 October, and after a three-day stay in Coco Solo, C.Z., proceeded north. She arrived in New York on 17 October and was decommissioned there on 2 November 1945. Her name was struck from the Navy list on 25 February 1947, and she was sold on 10 August to Northern Metal Co. of Philadelphia for scrapping."

On 3 November 1945 Lieutenant Woods was ordered to supervise the stripping of the *Sterett* prior to her disposal for scrap. He carried out those orders until she was towed up the Hudson on the ninth to a reserve fleet anchorage. Of course, he did not live aboard—the ship was an empty hulk, without even the most rudimentary services. But one crewman did remain aboard until the end. Charles H. "Frenchy" LeFebvre joined the *Sterett* as an apprentice seaman on 5 December 1942. He had served his ship well as a radioman striker and later a radioman 3/c. He was officially detached on 2 November 1945. But apparently Frenchy decided that the ship was a better shelter than any offered by the streets of New York, and as of the ninth he was still sleeping on board. This is his account of his last day on the *Sterett*:

By this time there was only one person left—the captain. Me. Frenchy. This was good. I slept in, and had liberty any time. My time was my own. Guess what? That only lasted as long as my money held out. But, being captain, I held on. After each and every liberty I'd check the ship fore and aft. The damage from pilferers and vandals would be apparent each time. There were broken light fixtures, and many things were missing. All kinds of brass and copper fittings as well as piping and instruments and gauges were being removed. It sure made me feel bad, and it also made me mad. However, I had to stay with the old fighting ship. It had saved my life more than once, so I was going to try to save her life. At this point, I felt that she was all mine. I would like the world and all my shipmates to know that I did try to save her. One day, before I got up, I felt the ship rocking and moving in a way that told me we were no longer tied up. I went to the bridge, where a good captain should be when his ship is under way, and found civilians all over the bridge of *my ship*. With great authority, I asked, "Where are you taking my ship? What are you doing on my ship?" They ignored me—even laughed at me—and at that moment I knew I had lost her.

Even though Frenchy (whom I recall pleasantly from my days on the *Sterett*) wrote his account with tongue in cheek, I am sure he really did wish to save her from being cut up into chunks of metal and sold off to the highest bidder. It seemed like an ignominious end for such a heroic veteran.

Another *Sterett* sailor now appeared on the scene. Earl J. Andrews had come aboard as a fireman 2/c on the day the ship was commissioned, and he served with distinction as our log room yeoman while I was the assistant engineering officer. He remained aboard until after the Third Battle of Savo Island on 13 November 1942. His 1988 letter picks up the narrative where Frenchy left off: "When I was engineering officer of a Navy tug (ATR 8) in New York harbor I was privileged to tow the *Sterett*, following her decommissioning, to her assigned nest of reserve ships at Jones Point, up the Hudson River. While we had her in tow, which was a matter of several hours, I wandered the ship with a flashlight and toured the spaces. What memories flashed back—what voices I heard—what smooth-running turbines and quiet machinery! It was all quite melancholy. That was the last time I saw the *Sterett*."

Summarizing his article "*Sterett* Revisited," which records the experience of reading through the *Sterett's* logs over an eight-day period in July 1988, J. D. Jeffrey remarks:

> Upon first reading, the log of the *Sterett's* final day, 2 November 1945, was disappointing. To go along with the necessary stereotyped phraseology, it seemed there should be some words of praise or perhaps regret, some accolades for feats accomplished and disasters overcome. On second thought, though, maybe the most appropriate entries were the simple ones made. "Moored starboard side.... Mustered crew at quarters, no absentees. Transferred [listed officers and men]. Decommissioning board number two came aboard.... Commission pennant and colors hauled down. . . . *Sterett* decommissioned." The record speaks for itself.
>
> The *Sterett* handled everything the Japs could throw at her. I choose to think that, having proved herself a proud first-line warship, she was spared the indignity of old age and a second-class existence in an alien peacetime Navy.

So ends my history of the USS *Sterett;* in the words of Secretary of the Navy James Forrestal, she was "a gallant fighting ship, superbly handled by her officers and men." The description was penned to characterize her conduct on 13 November 1942 in the Third Battle of Savo Island, but in reality it applies to the *Sterett's* performance in each of her actions against the enemy. She repeatedly demonstrated magnificent courage, and—like everyone who was privileged to serve her—I am proud to have been a *Sterett* sailor.

EPILOGUE

THE STERETT, OR AT LEAST HER REPUTATION AND HER PEOPLE, continued to influence events in my life long after my detachment. It started with Watso Singer, who visited me in Espíritu Santo a few days after my arrival at the hospital on 10 April 1943. He said he would speak with the commanding officer of the hospital and determine when I was to be evacuated. That same afternoon I received a note reporting the results of his inquiry. I was scheduled to depart two days later aboard the *Pinckney* (APH 2), a hospital transport. No doubt my *Sterett* shipmate had a hand in effecting that early departure.

After a short voyage to Nouméa, New Caledonia, I was transferred to the hospital ship *Solace* (AH 5)—a welcome change from the austere facilities at Espíritu Santo. The ship's entire surgical team had come from the University of Pennsylvania Hospital. The medical care was excellent, as were the living conditions. In late May I was one of several *Solace* patients to be transferred to the Matson passenger liner SS *Lurline* for the return trip to the United States. She stopped briefly en route at Melbourne and Wellington to pick up two thousand Marine ambulatory patients; then she proceeded to San Diego at a comfortable 21 knots, under clear and sunny skies. It was a pleasure cruise by comparison with my four years of destroyer duty.

The *Lurline* arrived in San Diego in early June and delivered her patient-passengers to the San Diego Naval Hospital. Among the doctors who greeted us on our arrival was a Navy captain (Medical Corps) who had sailed with us on the *Sterett's* shakedown cruise. A friend of Captain Macondray, the doctor was a plastic surgeon. Reminding him of his cruise aboard the *Sterett*, I asked if he would examine Ensign Blackwell, a friend and fellow patient whose ship—the oiler *Kanawha* (AOG 31)— was sunk in the same attack in which I was injured. "Blackie" had suffered disfiguring wounds to his face. The doctor gladly accepted Blackie as a patient and expertly repaired the scars, so that they were almost invisible. Again a *Sterett* shipmate had played the role of the good Samaritan. A couple of weeks later, with the same doctor's assistance, I managed to transfer to Oak Knoll Naval Hospital in Oakland. My family then lived in Santa Cruz, and I was able to stay at home and commute to Oak Knoll as necessary for physical therapy.

A letter from Frank Gould and a visit to Santa Cruz in August by Ens. Perry Hall, en route to submarine school in New London, Connecticut, enabled me to keep up with the *Sterett's* experiences. From Perry I learned of the Vella Gulf battle and Frank's Navy Cross. I could not have been any prouder of my old ship, or wanted to go back to her more. There was no chance of realizing that desire, but still the *Sterett's* esprit de corps was very much a part of my consciousness. It was a supplemental tonic to my own mood and outlook.

Meanwhile I was anxious to get out of the hospital and back to sea duty. My buddies were all out there fighting a war, and I wanted to join them. But my doctor at Oak Knoll did not think I was ready for sea duty and made it clear that he would recommend against it. As far as I could tell, my only physical deficiency was a wrist-drop in my right arm, and the only negative aspect of that was a very limp salute. It certainly did not affect my capacity to make decisions or issue orders. When I pressed my point, the doctor made a small concession: he would be willing to recommend my assignment to limited duty ashore. Any kind of duty that would get me out of the hospital was a welcome prospect. I asked if I could appear before a Board of Survey to determine my fitness for return to active duty. The answer was yes, and I was scheduled for examination by the board the following week. Meanwhile, my doctor conveniently went on leave.

When I went before the Board of Survey, the *Sterett's* reputation preceded me. All five board members had heard of the destroyer and its encounter with a Japanese battleship. They were not concerned about my injured arm—they wanted to hear an account of the Third Battle of Savo Island. When I finished, the senior member of the board asked what they could do for me. I told him I wanted to be ordered to full active duty at sea, in a command billet if one was available. Presto! The answer was definitely in the affirmative. The *Sterett's* aura was still with me.

As I drove away from the hospital that afternoon I filled the car with hitchhiking sailors, all hospital patients on their way into town. One had his arm in a sling, and all wore the ribbon of the Purple Heart. We had gone only a hundred yards when I recognized a lone sailor on crutches standing along the roadside. Bringing the car to a stop, I said, "OK, fellas, I have to ask one of you to get out. This sailor is an old shipmate, and he takes priority." To a man, they realized that this might be a special moment. They all piled out, saying that they understood. Two of them helped the new passenger into the car. It was Hawkins. The last time I saw him he was being carried down the accommodation ladder in a stretcher, bound for the *Solace* in Espíritu Santo. Now he wore a patch over his blind eye and walked with crutches, although he had been fitted with a new leg. His face was one big smile as he came into the car, and I reached over and gave him a hug. He was in very good spirits and gave me a rundown on everyone who had left the ship with him. They had all survived and had been transferred to hospitals near their homes. He was about to be transferred to the Naval Hospital at Philadelphia, where amputees were usually sent to learn how to use their new artificial limbs. I drove him to his destination in Oakland and dropped him off with a handshake and my best wishes. The encounter brought back a flood of memories, and I marveled at the caliber of the young men who were fighting for America's freedom. They asked for nothing in return.

My orders to sea duty came in early January. I went to Oak Knoll to check out for the last time and had just completed the departure process when I recognized the ward doctor who had told me I was fit only for limited duty. He was walking directly toward me. My heart sank. Would he now interpose some objection to my release? He greeted me pleasantly and asked, "Where are you off to?"

"I've been ordered to command a high-speed minesweep, and I'm on my way to join her in San Diego," I told him.

"Well, that's just fine," he said. "Best of luck to you." I thanked him and, with a sigh of relief, walked away. Apparently he had accepted the Board of Survey's recommendation without question.

In short order I was on my way to the USS *Lamberton* (DMS 2), my first command. The reputation of the *Sterett* had paved the way. On 14 January 1944 I relieved Lt. Comdr. B. M. McKay as commanding officer of the minesweeper. Because I was only a lieutenant, the men of the *Lamberton* probably thought that the Navy Department had just downgraded their ship to some kind of second-class status. Their new skipper, however, was very happy to be chosen for a command billet, no matter what type it was. The ship was a converted World War I destroyer—a durable old veteran—and her company took pride in her as though she was the newest destroyer in the fleet.

The *Lamberton* was under the control of the Training Command of the Pacific Fleet, led by Rear Admiral Braisted. I made a courtesy call on the admiral in San Diego. He explained that our role was to provide target services for any and all fleet units, and that although the duty was not glamorous it was important. After serving on the *Sterett* I understood the importance of this task perfectly. The *Lamberton* towed targets in the San Diego area from January to March, and in April she was ordered to Pearl Harbor.

As soon as we arrived in Hawaii we were besieged with orders to provide target services for all kinds of ships. Now we were part of the Service Force of the Pacific Fleet, which was then engaged in the Marianas campaign. The intensity of gunnery training exercises in the Hawaiian area can be judged by the *Lamberton's* record for May 1944: she provided towing services for forty-one destroyers, two destroyer-escorts, one attack cargo ship, two high-speed minesweeps, four cruisers (the *Indianapolis, Miami, Houston,* and *Vincennes*), and three battleships (the *North Carolina, Tennessee,* and *Washington*). One of the destroyers was the *Sterett,* but we were never in close proximity and I have no record or recollection of any exchange of messages.

After six months I began to grow restless. There were a lot of big Pacific operations on the horizon, and it looked as though I would not get a chance to participate. That did not seem like the best way for a line officer to fight a war. I began to look for a way to effect another move—this time to a first-line destroyer. Lt. Ed Hunt was the *Lamberton's* executive officer; he was an exceptionally talented ship handler, and oftentimes I turned over the conn to him for coming alongside and close maneuvering. He was well qualified for command, a fact that I entered on the official record. I knew that having a qualified relief on board made my transfer more feasible from a detailer's standpoint.

One morning as we moved out the channel with our target in tow, a whole squadron of new destroyers approached from the south at high speed. It was one of those magnificent Hawaiian days with clear blue skies and a gentle breeze. I watched the ships through binoculars, admiring their sleek lines and the white "bone in the teeth" that accentuated their speed and power. As they drew closer I was able to read the bow numerals of the lead ship and discovered that she was the *Remey* (DD 688), flagship of Destroyer Squadron 54—the one to which former *Sterett* skipper Jess Coward had been ordered. I prepared a message for transmission to the *Remey* by flashing light: "For Commodore Coward—Congratulations on your fine command. They look as ready as the *Sterett* was. New subject: Please get me back in the destroyer navy.—Cal." The destroyers passed us rapidly, and by the time my message went out there was only time for the *Remey* to reply, "Roger. I'll see what I can do.—Coward."

We spent the next week towing targets for a number of cruisers and destroyers. On the way back to Pearl Harbor we sighted the ships of Squadron 54 again. As soon as we got within easy signaling range the *Remey* sent a message: "Have you gotten your copy of my letter yet?"

"Negative," I replied.

"Check with the flag secretary at Commander Destroyers Pacific Fleet Headquarters. Good luck.—Coward."

There was barely time to send "Thanks. Smooth sailing.—Cal" before the destroyers disappeared over the horizon. As soon as we anchored I made my way to ComDesPac headquarters, went to the office of the flag secretary, and asked if he had a letter from Commodore Coward about Calhoun. He did, and he gave it to me to read. It recommended that Lieutenant Commander Calhoun (I had been promoted while on the *Lamberton*) be reassigned to command a destroyer. I asked if the letter could be placed at the top of the admiral's in-basket. "No sweat!" the secretary replied. I returned to the *Lamberton*, my hopes high.

The author, then a lieutenant commander, in September 1944. (Author's collection)

On 28 August 1944 I was detached from the *Lamberton* and directed to proceed on the first available government flight to a U.S. port and to report to the Naval District Commandant there for temporary duty, pending further assignment. I left the next morning via a Navy patrol bomber and was in San Francisco that night. On 4 September the long-awaited additional orders arrived. I was sent to Seattle to take command of the USS *Dewey* (DD 349). At last I had my own destroyer. And once more the *Sterett* had acted as my guardian angel: without Jess Coward's help, I would have towed targets for the rest of the war.

THE DEWEY AND HER MEN SPENT AN ACTION-PACKED YEAR with the Third and Fifth fleets in the western Pacific. She participated in the Philippine campaign as well as the invasions of Iwo Jima and Okinawa, and she performed escort duties with logistic support forces. She and the *Aylwin* (DD 355) were the two *Farragut*-class destroyers that survived the typhoon of 17–18 December 1944; two others, the *Hull* and the *Monoghan*, capsized and sank. During the first few months of 1945 the *Dewey* also rescued survivors from LCI 600 when that craft struck a mine and rendered fire-fighting assistance to the USS *Patuxent* (AO 44) after an internal explosion and fire. In the course of her travels she once passed the *Sterett* at sea while Gordy Williams was the *Sterett's* skipper. We exchanged messages of some sort, but apparently they contained no golden prose since I have no recollection of their exact content.

On 28 January 1945 the *Dewey*, then the flagship of Commander Destroyer Squadron 1 (Capt. Preston V. Mercer), moored alongside the *Remey* to expedite the relief of Commander Destroyer Squadron 54 (Capt. Jesse G. Coward) by Captain Mercer. It was a sad moment for me. Jess Coward was our guest in the wardroom that evening, and memories of the *Sterett* were reawakened when he told us about his squadron's night torpedo attack against Japanese battleships in the Battle of Surigao Strait (24–25 October 1944). My old skipper was tired, and he suffered from severe arthritis. When I delivered him to the Ulithi airstrip the next day he was the picture of dejection. He did not want to relinquish his command, and Preston Mercer asked me to "talk sense" to the old warrior. I was able to convince him that he had to leave, but the experience was disturbing for all of us.

After the war ended I brought the *Dewey* through the canal and up to New York. She was decommissioned at the Brooklyn Navy Yard on 19 October 1945. I served for a few months at Purdue University's NROTC unit and then transferred to the unit at the University of Mississippi. In June 1946 I became administrative aide to the commander of the Norfolk Naval Base, Rear Adm. Emmet P. "Savvy" Forrestel.

One morning a few months later I was in my office when Capt. Charlie Chillingworth, the chief of staff, came to the door and said, "Cal, the boss wants to see you." I followed the captain into the admiral's office. I could see that Admiral Forrestel had what looked like a letter in his hand. He looked up and said, "Cal, why didn't you tell us that the *Sterett* won the war?" Then he began to read: "The Secretary of the Navy, Washington. The President of the United States takes pleasure in presenting the Presidential Unit Citation to the United States Ship *Sterett....*" (The full text of the citation appears in Appendix 1.)

When he finished he handed me my copy of the citation. I thanked him and remembered Captain Coward's words after the battle, when he assured us that we would hear more about awards and decorations. This Presidential Unit Citation was exactly what he had envisioned. The only trouble was that the men of the *Sterett* had dispersed long before—some of them might never hear about the award. I also thought of the twenty-eight shipmates who had given their lives to earn it. No, the *Sterett* had not won the war, but she had certainly upheld the highest traditions of the naval service. Her reputation and her special spirit remain engraved in the hearts of all who had the honor to serve her.

APPENDIX 1
PRESIDENTIAL UNIT CITATION

THE SECRETARY OF THE NAVY
WASHINGTON

The President of the United States takes pleasure in presenting the
PRESIDENTIAL UNIT CITATION
to the
UNITED STATES SHIP STERETT
for service as set forth in the following
CITATION:

"For extraordinary heroism in action against an enemy Japanese Task Force during the Battle of Guadalcanal on the night of November 12–13, 1942. Fighting boldly and with determination against units of the powerful enemy Fleet intent on bombarding our airfield at Guadalcanal, the U.S.S. STERETT successfully engaged three Japanese vessels at close range during the thirty-four minutes of furious action. Scoring numerous hits on an enemy light cruiser, she then closed range to 3000 yards and fired a full salvo of torpedoes to cause two large explosions and assist in sinking a battleship. When an enemy destroyer was sighted at 1000 yards from her starboard bow, she immediately took it under fire and, with two torpedoes and two five-inch salvos, exploded and sank the vessel before it could open fire. With her after section severely damaged and burning and with both after guns disabled as the remaining enemy ships concentrated their gunfire on her, she fought desperately to control the damage and succeeded in retiring from the battle area under her own power. A gallant fighting ship, superbly handled by her officers and men, the STERETT rendered invaluable service in defeating a major enemy attack at this crucial point in the Solomon Islands Campaign."

For the President,

James Forrestal

Secretary of the Navy

APPENDIX 2

Compiled by Joseph D. Jeffrey from the original ship's logs as preserved in the National Archives, Washington, D.C., July 1988 (revised January 1990). His explanation of the roster follows.

At first this seemed like a straightforward task: to sort through the *Sterett*'s logs and itemize personnel movements. After all, the logs should show the exact date on which a member of the ship's company reported aboard, and the exact date on which he was detached. But nothing is as simple as it appears.

Early on it became clear that the logs (and this compiler) were not infallible. Some people were never logged aboard, while others were never logged out when they transferred. Further discrepancies resulted when crew members left the ship temporarily for school or hospitalization and never came back for whatever reason. Other inconsistencies were the result of confusion among similar names and rates and must be attributed to fleet and yard personnel offices that apparently went out of their way to assign people that were stacked close together alphabetically. The great majority of errors and omissions, however, must be attributed to this compiler and his log transcriptions.

This summary shows that 832 persons called *Sterett* home during its short life of seventy-five months. For 171 of these, the record contains some blanks. It is disturbing that the transfer record is incomplete for some plank owners, and that the on-board date is missing for some of those who departed the ship on its last day. I particularly regret that I could not locate the on-board date for a few of those killed in action on 13 November 1942.

This roster purposely omits those who came aboard temporarily as observers or for transportation only. My apologies to any member of the ship's company who were omitted by being mistakenly placed in that class.

The letters and symbols used in the roster are explained below. Some of this supplementary information is derived from sources other than the logs. Ranks and ratings are consistent with log nomenclature.

*   Killed in action—night surface engagement, 13 November 1942
- B   Awarded Bronze Star Medal
- C   Received Commanding Officer's commendation
- D   Died under honorable conditions while serving aboard (not as a result of combat)

F   Flag complement aboard *Sterett* as Commander Destroyer Division 15 and staff

M Missing after night surface engagement, 13 November 1942

N   Awarded Navy Cross Medal

S   Awarded Silver Star Medal

W Wounded as a result of enemy action

Apparently no one served aboard for the entire life of the ship, but log entries indicate that some plank owners came close:

- Buford Daniels transferred on 8 September 1945 (less than two months before the *Sterett* was decommissioned)
- Willie "Red" Hammack transferred on 6 August 1945
- Fred Gibson and Charles McVicker both transferred on 31 July 1945
- Vernon Fray transferred on 25 May 1945

Of the four men lost over the side on 13 November 1942, Clarence Simmons returned to the ship and served aboard until transferred as chief gunner's mate on the last day of the *Sterett*'s commissioned life, 2 November 1945. William H. Cartwright returned aboard and served until transferred as gunner's mate, first class, on 12 March 1945. The logs contain no further entries for Hubert Godecker, bos'n's mate, second class, or James Grann, seaman, first class.

From left to right, the columns read as follows: name, date first reported aboard, rank or rate on arrival, date last transferred or detached, rank or rate on detachment, and special comments. Plank owners are denoted by the on-board date of 15 August 1939; those detached when the ship was decommissioned have the departure date 2 November 1945.

The compiler welcomes corrections, clarifications, additions, or deletions to be included in a future updated edition. This revised roster was completed 8 January 1990 and includes twenty-four names omitted initially. These added names were kindly furnished by Felix Gebert, who is doing a valiant job keeping lists of reunion attendees and ever-changing current addresses.

A

Name	Date	Rank	Date	Rank
Adamson, Milton N.	10/6/44	S1c	6/21/45	S1c
Aikins, Norman L.	12/1/41	SM3c	12/6/42	SM2c
Aley, Ray C.	2/18/43	S2c	10/13/44	SM3c
Anderson, Emil C.	2/18/43	S2c	11/2/45	S1c
Anderson, H. L.	9/13/39	Sea2c	8/23/40	Sea1c

Anderson, Howard L.	12/10/40	Sea2c	7/5/41	QM3c	
Anderson, Robert L.	2/9/40	Sea2c	3/12/45	MM1c	
Anjal, Curtis C.	12/5/42	F1c	11/2/45	CMM	
Andrews, Earl J.	8/15/39	F2c			
Apple, L. E.			10/18/41	EM1c	
Armstrong, Tim H.	10/6/44	S1c			
Arnold, Oval R.	5/30/45	S2c	10/29/45	S2c	
Arnold, Vernon J.	8/15/39	GM3c	1/22/43	GM1c	
Ash, Paul R.					
Awbrey, Allen G.	10/6/44	S1c	10/30/45	S1c	

B

Bacarella, Ralph	1/21/44	S2c	7/19/45	F1c	
Baer, Robert B.	8/15/39	SM1c	3/27/40	SM1c	
Bailey, Tron F.	10/6/44	S1c	10/17/45	SM3c	
Baker, William J.	8/15/39	CQM			
Barcus, LeRoy W.	12/11/40	AS	3/18/42	F2c	
Barrera, Gilbert J.	12/5/42	AS	10/17/45	S1c	
Barron, Walter J.	8/15/39	BM1c	12/14/40	BM1c	
Barry, David J. Jr.			10/18/40	RM3c	
Batts, Ross F.	5/30/45	S2c	10/29/45	S2c	
Baumgardner, Frank Jr.	2/18/43	S2c	5/21/44	S1c	
Baumgartner, S. M.	5/8/41	Sea2c	8/13/41	Sea1c	
Beck, Robert P.	10/6/44	S1c	10/29/45	S1c	
Bell, Louis R. Jr.	9/16/44	F2c	11/2/45	F1c	
Bell, R. W.	3/19/42	SK2c			
Bennet, Esau Jr.	9/16/44	StM2c	10/13/44	StM1c	
Bently, Phillip M.	2/7/43	MA2c	5/21/44	StM1c	
Bernaldes, Valentine	8/15/39	OC2c	7/3/40	OC1c	
Berry, Thomas F.	9/16/44	F2c	11/2/45	EM3c	
Betker, Robert E.	1/21/44	S2c	12/7/44	RM3c	
Bigi, Louis F.	9/16/44	F2c	11/2/45	MM3c	
Bivens, Donold H.	8/15/39	F1c	3/27/40	WT2c	
Bjork, Edward W.	8/15/39	S1c	12/8/40	S1c	
Black, Joseph N.	8/15/39	F2c	12/24/40	F1c	
Blakely, Silas M.	11/28/41	SM1c	9/17/43	CSM	F
Blankenship, Elbert	8/15/39	CM1c			
Blouin, Francis J.	1/13/44	LtComdr	1/27/45	Comdr	C†
Boland, J.	1/11/41	RM2c	10/2/41	RM1c	
Bolster, Theodore A.			5/18/45	CPhM	
Bostick, William C.	9/16/44	F2c	10/30/45	F1c	
Botkin, James T.	9/28/42	FC3c	12/28/43	FC2c	

†Commendation by a senior unit commander.

Boudreaux, Preston A.			3/14/44	SC2c	C
Bourgeois, Walter L.	10/28/43	S1c	10/26/45	S1c	
Bowers, Charles N.	8/15/39	MM1c	8/11/41	CMM	
Bradley, William L.	11/22/42	AS	11/2/45	GM2c	
Breder, George F.	11/22/42	AS	10/17/45	SSML2c	
Brehio, Edward D.	9/16/44	F2c	10/29/45	F1c	
Brewer, Edward J.	11/12/44	S2c	10/31/45	S1c	
Brown, Charles A.	8/15/39	WT1c	6/1/43	CWT	
Brown, Chester W.	8/15/39	SC2c	7/16/41	SC1c	
Brown, H. H.	11/8/41	BM2c	3/16/42	BM1c	
Brown, L. E.			7/2/40	CQM	
Brown, Peter M.	8/15/39	SF1c	12/24/40	SF1c	
Brown, W. E.	1/7/41	Matt1c	3/30/41	Matt1c	F
Bryan, Brady L.	8/15/39	F1c	3/25/41	MM1c	
Bryant, Christial C.	8/15/39	BM2c	3/27/40	BM1c	
Buckelew, Robert E.	2/18/43	S2c	1/13/44	QM3c	
Bunn, Raymond W.	8/15/39	F3c	6/24/41	F3c	
Burke, William T.	8/15/39	F2c	2/25/41	F1c	
Burns, Gurvis H.	2/18/43	S2c	5/21/44	S1c	
Burns, Robert L.	1/14/44	S2c	10/30/45	TM3c	
Burns, Wallace R.	10/28/43	S1c	10/17/45	S1c	
Burris, George G.	2/22/42	Sea2c	2/6/45	GM2c	C
Byers, Robert O.	8/15/39	Cox	9/20/43	CBM	W, S
Bynum, J. W.	11/19/41	OS3c			
Byrd, Charles W.	2/18/43	S2c	5/21/44	S1c	

C

Caddell, Kenneth E.	1/21/44	S2c	11/2/45	S1c	
Cafferata, Joseph T.	1/21/44	S2c	11/2/45	SK3c	
Cain, N. R.	5/8/43	S1c	5/21/44	TM3c	
Calhoun, Charles R.	8/15/39	Ens	4/10/43	Lt	B, W, C
Caloway, Elmer P.	5/23/43	F1c	11/2/45	MM1c	
Campbell, Wilson H.	11/22/42	AS	11/2/45	SkD2c	
Capps, A. R.	7/5/40	CWT	8/15/41	CWT	
Carberry, P. A.	12/23/40	BM2c	3/22/42	BM1c	
Carel, Davidson	11/22/42	AS	11/2/45	WT1c	
Carlquist, Robert A.	8/15/39	RM3c			
Carmichael, Quintus E.	2/18/43	S2c	10/17/45	WT3c	W
Carnes, J. H. Jr.	12/24/41	RM1c	3/22/42	RM2c	
Carrol, Donald L.	11/22/42	AS	12/4/44	FCO3c	
Carter, A. H.					
Carter, Robert L.	11/22/42	AS	1/18/45	S1c	
Cartwright, William H.	12/11/40	AS	3/12/45	GM1c	M, W
Cauley, J. B.	10/23/39	RM1c	12/14/40	RM1c	

Cedenio, Clemente	8/15/39	OS3c	7/3/40	OS2c	
Ceryan, Joseph C.	1/21/44	S2c	11/2/45	MM3c	W
Chaisson, Joseph G.	10/6/44	S2c	10/17/45	S1c	
Chaney, J. C.			10/20/44	RM3c	
Channery, James C.	6/25/43	S2c			
Chapman, Edward F.	8/15/39	FC1c	10/26/43	CFC	
Chapman, Frederick W.	9/16/44	S2c	9/16/45	S2c	
Cheek, Vernice T.	8/15/39	Y2c	12/25/40	Y1c	
Chenez, Raymond J.	10/6/44	S2c	10/29/45	S2c	
Childress, Clovis C.	10/21/44	CPhM	10/17/45	CPhM	
Choban, John Jr.	8/15/39	F2c	2/26/41	F1c	
Clark, Harry D. Jr.	5/30/45	S2c	8/11/45	S2c	
Clark, Robert D.	7/13/45	Ens	10/31/45	Ens	
Cleere, I. J.			7/14/43	BM	
Cleere, Timothy J.	1/7/41	SM1c	3/30/43	CQM	F
Clute, James M.	8/15/39	Lt(jg)	2/12/42	Lt	
Cochran, William J.	8/15/39	QM2c	2/25/42	QM1c	
Cochran, William J.	8/15/39	BM2c	9/8/41	BM1c	
Colburn, Calvin D.	2/18/43	S2c	10/17/45	SM2c	
Colburn, Douglas C.					
Cole, Albert B.	12/23/40	F1c	5/13/41	F1c	
Collier, Oscar A.	2/18/43	S2c	12/18/43	SC3c	
Combs, Carl E.	8/15/39	FC3c	11/13/41	FC1c	
Conn, Coleman E.	9/13/39	Sea2c	8/20/45	Sm1c	C
Connor, James D.			11/2/45	GM1c	
Connors, William P.	12/17/40	F3c	2/6/45	CMM	
Cook, James B.	8/2/44	RdM2c	10/29/45	RdM2c	
Cook, Joseph W.	12/12/43	Ens(SC)	6/5/45	Lt(jg)(SC)	
Coppola, Edward	8/15/39	MM2c	2/18/43	CMM	
Cotten, Thomas M. Jr.	8/15/39	Matt1c			
Coughlan, Thomas P.	5/10/45	Ens(SC)	11/2/45	Ens(SC)	
Coward, Jesse G.	4/30/41	LtComdr	1/18/43	Comdr	N
Cowdrey, Roy B.	10/24/43	Ens	5/19/45	Lt(jg)	C, C
Cox, Robert H.	8/18/39	MM2c	1/2/40	MM2c	
Cox, William V.			10/17/45	RM2c	
Cribbs, William T.	12/5/42	AS	2/6/45	GM3c	
Cross, Junior L.	8/15/39	Sea2c			
Crowley, John F.	8/15/39	MM2c	7/21/43	CMM	
Cruickshank, C. E.					
Cunningham, Grover D.	7/25/41	PhM3c	9/23/44	PhM1c	

D

Dale, Ernest J.			12/9/40	Prtr1c	
Dallas, Dewey Jr.	9/16/44	S2c	10/31/45	RdM3c	

Daniels, Buford N.	8/15/39	Sea2c	9/8/45	CWT	
Dantinne, Emil E.	10/19/40	F3c	8/21/44	MM1c	
Davis, William L.	8/15/39	EM1c	10/12/40	EM1c	
Dawson, Gilbert D.			11/2/45	EM3c	
Dean, John D.	2/21/42	MM2c	12/12/42	MM2c	
Declusin, L.			10/20/44	EM2c	
Denny, John T.	9/16/44	F2c	10/30/45	F2c	
Denuson, Rudolph	5/23/43	F2c	9/29/43	F2c	
Dernehl, Howard G.	11/21/41	BM2c	6/1/42	BM1c	
Deuel, William H.	12/5/42	F1c	11/2/45	WT1c	
Dewey, R. E.			6/6/42	PhM1c	
Didonna, R.	5/30/45	S2c	10/26/45	S2c	
Doan, Clifford	12/5/42	AS	3/6/44	S1c	D
Donnelly, James R.	12/5/42	F2c	9/29/43	F1c	
Doty, Charles P.	12/5/42	AS	12/4/44	SoM2c	
Dolson, Max T.	7/13/43	Lt(jg)			
Douglas, Ralph L.	12/5/42	AS	10/17/45	F1c	
Draper, James A.	1/14/44	S2c	8/14/45	S2c	
Drost, Stephen A.	9/16/44	F2c	10/30/45	F1c	
Dukes, Jack	5/30/45	S2c	11/2/45	S2c	
Dunlap, Chester N.	8/15/39	CCStd	5/4/44	CStd	W
Dunnaway, James L.	9/29/39	F2c	11/2/41	F1c	
Durant, Johnny F.	8/15/39	Sea1c	10/20/41	BM2c	

E

Early, Arthur L.	10/18/45	CPhM	11/2/45	CPhM	
Eberhardinger, Joseph W.	8/15/39	Sea1c			
Eberhart, G. L.			12/7/44	RM3c	
Ebert, Ralph R.	6/23/41	AS	2/5/43	F1c	
Edwards, L. F.			10/18/41	EM1c	
Ellis, Marion W.	8/15/39	Sea2c	5/29/42	RM3c	C
English, Rowland H.			7/30/40	CRM	
Erisman, Otis W.	8/3/44	Ens	10/31/45	Ens	
Ertenberg, Vincent G.			10/23/44	CEM	
Everett, Gordon S.	3/28/41	Lt	10/31/41	Lt	

F

Fairchild, Edward	9/7/45	S1c	10/31/45	S1c	
Farmer, Freddie K.	8/15/39	Sea2c	12/23/40	FC3c	
Fedder, Anthony J.	8/15/39	MM1c	9/5/40	MM1c	
Felton, Raymond			12/2/44	StM1c	
Ferrone, Anthony J.	2/5/43	EM3c	1/13/44	EM2c	
Field, Oliver F.	12/4/42	Ens(SC)	1/13/44	Lt(jg)(SC)	

Fink, Aaron G.	12/25/40	Cox	8/6/45	CBM	C
Finley, Hercules			11/2/45	CK3c	
Flack, Perry C.	6/23/41	AS	11/13/42	Sea1c	*
Fletcher, Albert E.	8/15/39	MM1c	3/30/40	MM1c	
Flinn, Joseph F.	8/15/39	EM2c	11/5/43	CEM	
Fobes, Vernon H.			10/30/45	Lt(jg)	
Force, Aubrey I.	12/5/42	AS	2/17/43	Sea2c	
Forsman, Charles L.	8/15/39	Sea2c	8/13/43	Cox	C, W
Franks, Doyle D.	1/14/44	MM3c	9/17/45	MM3c	
Fray, Vernon W.	8/15/39	F1c	5/25/45	Mach	
Frazier, Julius G.	8/15/39	Matt1c	7/1/42	OC3c	
Fredrickson, Stanley V.	2/21/42	SK3c	8/6/45	SK1c	
French, Lloyd J.	3/31/41	AS	11/13/42	Sea2c	*
Friest, William J.	1/14/44	F3c	5/21/45	F1c	
Frilling, Edwin C.	5/30/45	S2c	10/29/45	S2c	
Fry, Rufus G. Jr.	8/15/39	Sea1c			
Fudge, John C.	8/15/39	CGM	5/30/40	CGM	
Fugate, Neale T.	5/13/44	Ens	10/29/45	Lt(jg)	

G

Gaffney, Thomas P.					
Gallagher, Melvin	8/15/39	F2c			
Gamble, John T.	8/15/39	F2c			
Gardner, Harry J.	10/19/40	CGM	3/5/42	CGM	
Garn, Harold L.	10/13/44	CCS	11/2/45	CCS	
Garretson, Leslie L.	3/30/43	S1c	10/29/45	TM2c	
Garrison, Thomas M.	12/21/40	Sea2c	12/6/42	SM2c	
Gates, William B.	10/6/44	S2c	11/2/45	S1c	
Gebert, Felix K.	4/4/41	Sea2c	11/2/45	CEM	
Gee, Wallace T.	2/20/43	TM3c	4/27/44	TM1c	W
Gendreau, Antoine P.	8/15/39	Sea1c	12/23/40	SF3c	
George, Ernest F.			11/2/45	S1c	
Gerszewski, R. F.			7/30/40	SM2c	
Gibbs, George M.	10/21/41	WT2c	10/2/43	WT2c	
Gibson, Fred Q.	8/15/39	Sea2c	7/31/45	Gunner	
Gibson, Leslie T.	12/5/42	AS	10/17/45	Bkr3c	
Giffen, Ronald H.	2/21/42	Y3c	11/2/45	Y1c	W
Gillick, John E.					
Glatzer, Seymour	10/6/44	S2c	10/31/45	S1c	
Glowacki, Raymond	5/12/44	S2c	11/2/45	RM3c	
Godecker, Hubert T.	8/15/39	Sea2c	11/13/42	BM2c	M
Goforth, Warren H.	12/5/42	AS	3/12/45	SoM3c	
Goings, Elmer G.	12/5/42	AS	10/26/45	S1c	
Goldwasser, Samuel N.	12/5/42	AS	10/31/45	Cox	

Gomes, Eugene L.	12/5/42	AS	10/17/45	Cox	
Gooch, Charles B.	2/5/43	S2c	10/17/45	QM1c	
Goodson, William A.	3/31/41	AS	11/13/43	SM2c	
Gott, Edward B.	12/5/42	AS	11/2/45	S1c	
Gould, Frank G.	2/9/42	Lt	1/14/44	Comdr	N
Graca, Steve T.	12/5/42	AS	10/30/45	GM2c	
Graham, Kimball E.	8/15/39	EM3c	2/24/41	EM2c	
Grann, James I. Jr.	6/23/41	S2c	11/13/42	S1c	M
Graves, John J. Jr.	6/23/41	AS	8/12/41	AS	
Gray, Raleigh S.	8/15/39	Sea2c			
Greenbank, Chester G.	2/20/43	TM3c	9/1/44	TM1c	
Greenlaw, William C.	10/6/44	S2c	10/29/45	S1c	
Greenwood, Edward R.	12/5/42	AS	9/30/44	BM2c	
Gremli, Kenneth J.	12/5/42	F2c	12/7/44	B2c	
Griffin, Omer L.	2/10/43	Ens	5/23/45	Lt(jg)	C
Grimm, William B.	3/31/41	AS	5/9/43	S1c	
Groce, Raymond E.	6/23/41	AS	10/26/45	S1c	W
Grogan, Thomas F.	6/25/43	MoM2c			W
Gurnicz, Eugene H.	6/23/41	AS	12/7/44	MM2c	

H

Haas, Walter H.	8/15/39	CMM	12/17/40	CMM	
Hagan, Joseph M.	11/22/42	Matt2c			
Haines, Richard E.	5/8/43	SoM3c	11/2/45	SoM1c	
Halford, Malcolm T.	8/15/39	Sea2c	3/23/42	Bmkr2c	
Hall, Jesse J.	2/9/42	S2c	1/13/44	S1c	
Hall, Perry	9/19/42	Ens	8/11/43	Lt(jg)	B
Halliday, Joseph L.			4/7/43	TM3c	W
Hambsch, Philip P.	5/11/45	Lt	11/2/45	Lt	
Hamilton, Claud L.	5/23/43	Y2c	9/17/43	Y2c	F
Hamilton, D. L.	1/17/41	Y3c	2/22/41	Y3c	F
Hammack, Willie R.	8/15/39	Sea2c	8/6/45	CSF	W, C, C
Hammonds, Lowell R.	8/15/39	Sea2c	8/21/44	SM1c	
Hanna, Gordon W.	8/19/42	Ens	9/15/43	Lt(jg)	C
Hantleman, Eldon E.	12/5/42	Sea2c	6/26/45	BM2c	
Harbison, Paul P.	12/8/41	Sea1c	12/7/44	SC1c	
Harding, Harry Jr.	5/4/44	StM2c	10/13/44	StM1c	
Harm, Harry H.	6/23/41	AS	11/13/42	Sea1c	*
Harmon, Robert K.	5/23/43	RM2c	10/8/44	RM1c	
Harmsen, John O.	3/31/41	AS	6/3/42	F2c	
Harrington, Martin	3/31/41	AS	3/12/45	SC1c	W
Harris, Walter I.	9/16/44	F2c	10/30/45	F1c	
Harrison, W. W.	12/24/40	BM2c	4/30/41	BM1c	
Harvard, Henry E.	12/5/42	TM3c			

Name	Date	Rate	Date	Rate	Note
Haslett, Franklin L.	6/23/41	AS	2/6/43	TM3c	
Hass, Charles E.	12/12/43	S2c	3/12/45	FC3c	
Hass, W. H.	12/ /39	CMM			
Hawkins, E. J.			11/14/42	TM3c	W
Hayden, Paul G.	12/29/40	Ens	6/19/42	Ens	
Haynes, Charles D.	10/19/40	S2c	7/20/43	MM2c	
Hazard, Edward S.	12/11/40	AS	11/13/42	F2c	*
Hedges, H.	3/31/41	AS	7/3/41	Sea2c	
Heiden, George J.	3/24/45	F1c	11/2/45	F1c	
Heideman, Alfred C.	8/15/39	F1c			
Henderson, Albert J.	4/4/41	RM3c	10/17/45	RM2c	
Herman, Jacob W.	8/15/39	MM2c	12/11/39	MM2c	
Hewitt, Arlee T.	2/9/42	CMM	8/21/44	CMM	
Heywood, W. B.					
Hibben, Carl B.	5/27/42	Ens	1/14/44	Lt(jg)	
Hicks, Evan B.	6/23/41	AS	2/14/42	Sea2c	
Higbie, William A.			8/9/40	CPhM	
Higgs, Robert H.	9/7/45	S2c	11/2/45	S2c	
Hightower, Robert H.	1/25/43	Ens	2/20/45	Lt(jg)	
Hildreth, R. R.	10/18/39	SK3c			
Hilliard, Glenn E. Jr.	5/23/43	Sea1c	9/5/44	TM3c	
Hillman, Leo					
Hilton, Robert D.	8/15/39	Sea2c	5/9/43	S1c	
Hines, Dale L.	2/5/43	CM3c	10/31/45	CM2c	W
Hinrichs, William H.	10/17/45	Lt(jg)(MC)	11/2/45	Lt(jg)(MC)	
Hittle, E.	1/7/41	Y2c	1/20/41	Y2c	F
Hobgood, Seabern F.	8/15/39	F1c	1/2/40	MM2c	
Hodge, Hiram J.	8/15/39	GM1c	8/25/44	CGM	S, C
Hodge, James C.	8/15/39	WT1c			
Hoeltzel, L.			12/8/40	CBM	
Hoffman, Richard F.	9/16/44	S2c	10/30/45	S1c	
Hoft, Carl U.	12/19/42	CPhM			
Holden, Weldon W.	2/11/40	AS	3/22/43	Sea1c	
Holland, Jerome D.	8/15/39	F1c			
Hollingsworth, George W.	8/15/39	Sea2c	5/29/42	TM3c	
Holloway, William M.	8/15/39	Sea2c			
Holmes, Roscoe C.	3/31/41	AS	6/3/42	F2c	
Howard, Harry E.			11/2/45	TM1c	B
Howe, Herb H.	10/6/44	FC3c			
Huff, A. Jr.					
Hughes, Robert B.	8/15/39	Ens	6/24/40	Ens	
Hurst, Claude R.	1/21/44	S1c	12/4/44	FCO3c	
Husband, Raymond J.	12/5/42	AS	10/25/45	WT2c	
Husby, Gordon S.	12/12/43	Ens	7/24/45	Lt(jg)	
Hutchins, J. L.	12/20/39	S2c	6/2/42	Matt3c	
Hutchins, Jacque L.			12/10/41	GM3c	

I

Ivie, Harold V.	2/8/41	Sea1c	12/31/42	TM2c	

J

Jackson, Albert	8/15/39	WT2c	7/3/40	WT1c	
Jackson, George R.	8/15/39	CTM	11/13/42	CTM	*
Jackson, Willie	1/14/44	StM2c	10/13/44	StM1c	
James, Robert F.	8/15/39	TM2c	12/12/42	CTM	
Janzen, Fred E.	12/11/40	AS	1/30/43		
Jedziniak, Joseph J.	2/7/43	RT2c	10/31/45	CRT	
Jeffery, Kenneth	8/15/39	SM1c	11/13/41	SM1c	
Jeffrey, Joseph D.	2/21/42	Ens	3/14/44	Lt	C, W
Jeffries, George E.	8/15/39	EM1c	12/17/40	EM1c	
Jencks, Claude D.	3/24/45	CBM	11/2/45	CBM	
Jennings, Horace R.	1/14/44	StM2c	10/13/44	StM1c	
Jenson, Hilbert	8/15/39	TM1c	12/12/42	CTM	
Jervey, Harold E. Jr.	10/12/41	Ens	4/10/43	Lt(jg)	
Johnson, Arthur S.	10/6/44	GM3c	11/2/45	GM3c	
Johnson, Clarence	8/15/39	Matt2c			
Johnson, Davis H.	3/30/43	S1c	10/17/45	TM2c	B
Johnson, Donald R.			11/2/45	SoM1c	
Johnson, William T.	8/15/39	Sea2c	5/13/41	Sea1c	
Jones, Bobby L.	9/16/44	S2c	10/26/45	S2c	
Jones, James G.	8/15/39	SM3c	12/23/40	SM2c	
Jones, Paul F.	12/5/42	AS	10/31/45	SC1c	W
Jones, Raymond L.	8/15/39	MM1c	6/3/42	MM1c	
Jones, Robert N.	8/15/39	WT1c	3/25/40	WT1c	

K

Kandarian, Mark M.	6/2/43	S2c	11/2/45	MM2c	
Karstens, Gordon E.	3/31/41	AS	12/6/42	SM3c	
Keefe, Fred A.	2/4/43	GM1c	9/23/43	GM1c	
Keenum, Luther G.	8/15/39	TM2c	10/2/43	Ens	S
Kelley, John P.	5/30/45	S2c	10/26/45	S2c	
Kelley, Bruce A.	12/10/40	Sea2c	2/21/43	TM3c	W
Kelly, G. W.	12/11/40	AS	11/15/42	Sea2c	W
Kelly, Robert P.	2/9/42	AS	8/21/44	MM3c	
Kensler, George W.	2/9/42	AS	1/18/45	FC3c	
Kiehna, Earl	11/22/41	SC3c	6/1/42	SC2c	
Kilham, R. A.	2/9/42	AS			
Kilmon, Charles A.	1/13/41	Sea2c	2/19/43	RM3c	
King, Cecil L.	2/18/43	S1c	10/17/45	FC2c	
Klepacki, A. B.	2/9/42	AS	11/13/42	SC3c	*

Klosky, Simon P. III	9/5/43	Ens	7/7/44	Ens	
Knapp, Elwin C.	2/9/42	AS	7/28/45	WT1c	
Kochenburg, Charles M.	3/7/42	AS	10/26/45	S1c	
Konzal, Thomas F.	2/18/43	S1c	11/2/45	FC1c	
Koproski, L. J.	2/9/42	AS	11/13/42	Sea2c	*
Kosalko, John P.	2/9/42	AS	10/17/45	GM2c	
Koss, Clifford W.	2/9/42	AS	11/13/42	Sea2c	*
Kozak, Jacob J.	2/9/42	AS	5/21/44	Cox	
Kozma, L.	2/9/42	AS	10/9/44	B3c	
Kraetsch, Richard E.	5/30/45	S2c	9/16/45	S2c	
Krahel, W. W.	2/9/42	AS	3/12/45	WT2c	
Kramer, Howard J.	3/20/42	AS	1/13/44	S1c	
Kreilick, Kenneth L.	2/9/42	AS	11/13/42	Sea2c	*
Kress, Albert E.	10/6/44	S2c	10/31/45	S2c	
Kriger, H. H.			9/8/41	RM3c	
Kruithof, Vernon F.	2/9/42	AS	9/19/44	SM2c	
Kudla, Robert					
Kukich, Louis	2/9/42	AS	11/2/45	M3c	W
Kula, Matthew A.	9/20/41	SC1c	11/13/42	SC1c	*
Kuryllo, Barnard J.	8/15/39	WT2c	12/31/43		

L

Lachapelle, H. G.	2/9/42	AS	11/13/42	F2c	*
Lachtara, Edward J.	3/20/42	AS	9/30/44	SC2c	
Lafleur, Louis G.	8/14/45	SoM2c	10/31/45	SoM2c	
Lambie, William D.	2/9/42	AS	6/25/43	S1c	
Lamm, Paul E.	8/15/39	Sea2c	12/6/42	B2c	
LaMotte, Edwin N.	8/15/39	F2c	4/7/41	F2c	
Lancaster, Estle P.	2/18/43	F1c	3/12/45	MM2c	
Lanczak, Chester J.	3/20/42	AS	11/13/42	F2c	*
Land, Carl W.	3/20/42	AS	1/13/44	S1c	
Landers, Charles C. Jr.	8/15/39	MM1c	12/12/42	CMM	
Lane, Cary E.	8/15/39	F1c	9/4/40	F2c	
Lane, Joseph D.	8/15/39	Sea1c	8/4/41	Cox	
Lang, James W.	3/20/42	AS	8/21/44	Cox	
Langford, Woodie W.	5/8/43	TM3c	8/21/45	TM1c	
Lapinski, John	3/20/42	AS	12/4/44	GM3c	
Lastra, Louis J.	3/20/42	AS	10/17/45	BM1c	
Laughlin, Adelbert L.	12/5/42	AS	12/11/42	AS	
Laurent, George L.	8/21/44	Ens	11/2/45	Lt(jg)	
Layton, Stephen R.	8/15/39	Sea1c	11/15/42	Cox	W
Laws, Louis L.			10/17/45	MM3c	
Lea, Austin W.	9/5/43	Lt(jg)MC	6/11/45	Lt(MC)	W
Lebo, Charles A. P.	5/31/45	Lt(jg)MC	10/19/45	Lt(jg)MC	
Ledgerwood, Leo M.	12/5/42	AS	9/8/43	F1c	

Lefebvre, Charles H.	12/5/42	AS	11/2/45	RM3c	
LeMay, Raymond J.	8/15/39	SK1c			
Lemmonds, Joe L.	8/15/39	Sea2c	2/21/43	SK3c	
LeMonds, Charles E.	2/5/43	S1c	12/4/44	TM3c	
Lester, Alvin	12/5/42	AS			
Lettino, Robert I.	7/11/41	Ens	11/8/41	Ens	
Lewis, Charles R.	10/27/44	SoM3c	11/5/44	SoM3c	
Lewis, J. C.	5/30/45	S2c	10/26/45	S2c	
Liesinger, Andrew	2/18/43	F1c	10/17/45	MM2c	
Light, James D.	8/15/39	TM3c	1/17/41	TM2c	
Lillard, Reese W.	8/15/39	CRM	4/29/41	CRM	
Lineberry, Herbert E.	8/15/39	TM3c	10/29/41	TM2c	
Lipsche, Stephen Jr.	3/13/44	Bosn	9/11/44	Bosn	
Lisle, Samuel T.	2/23/45	S2c	11/2/45	S2c	
Litchfield, Herman L.	8/15/39	MM2c	10/18/44	CMM	
Livingston, Claude Jr.	9/16/44	S2c	10/30/45	S1c	
Long, William H.	2/23/45	S2c	11/2/45	S2c	
Lopes, LeRoy A.	9/16/44	StM2c	11/2/45	StM2c	
Lopez, Refugio	2/23/45	S2c	11/2/45	S2c	
Lopez, Vincent M.	2/23/45	S2c	10/26/45	S2c	
Lorton, Warren L.	9/16/44	S2c	10/26/45	S1c	
Louis, C. R.			11/5/44	SoM3c	
Lovas, George A.	8/15/39	F2c	12/12/42	MM2c	C
Lowery, Raymond E.	5/30/45	S2c	10/29/45	S2c	
Lowry, Ford W.	3/30/43	EM3c	11/2/45	EM2c	
Lund, Clifford E.	10/27/44	SoM3c	10/31/45	SoM3c	
Lundy, George N.	12/28/42	MA2c	1/13/44	StM1c	
Luongo, Frank P. Jr.	8/15/39	Lt	2/11/42	LtComdr	
Lynch, John W.	4/4/41	WT1c	9/19/43	CWT	
Lynn, Irvin G.	12/5/42	AS	8/20/45	MM3c	

M

MacArthur, Russel B.	8/18/39	TM3c	12/23/40	TM3c	
Mack, Daniel A.	9/16/44	S2c	10/26/45	S1c	
Mackabee, William E.	9/16/44	F2c	11/2/45	F1c	
Mackey, Kenneth M.	8/15/39	TM1c	8/14/41	CTM	
Macondray, Atherton	8/15/39	LtComdr	5/2/41	LtComdr	
Mahoney, Melvin G.	5/30/45	S2c	10/29/45	S2c	
Mahoney, Raymond J.	12/5/42	Sea1c	3/12/45	TM2c	
Malinowsky, John H.	8/15/39	F3c	9/20/42	MM1c	
Manganello, L. A.			10/18/41	SC1c	
Mann, John P.	8/15/39	Sea2c			
Mansfield, Albert W.	8/15/39	GM2c	3/29/41	GM1c	C
Marden, John A.	2/19/43	RM1c	10/17/45	CRM	
Marrs, Arthur W.			11/2/45	MM1c	

Marsh, Dannie			10/17/45	RdM2c	
Marsh, Glen L.	2/5/43	EM3c			
Martin, Fred F.	2/5/43	S2c	2/6/45	GM3c	
Martin, Harry I. Jr.	8/15/39	Sea2c	8/21/44	GM1c	
Martin, Kenton J.	12/5/42	AS	10/15/43	HA1c	
Martin, L. A.	12/24/40	Sea2c	11/14/42	F2c	W
Martin, R. C.	11/28/41	Matt3c	5/24/43	Matt3c	F
Martin, Vernon R. E.	8/15/39	Sea2c	11/13/42	GM2c	*
Marver, Hillard M.	4/26/41	Ens	6/3/42	Ens	
Masland, J. W. Jr.	3/20/42	AS	3/22/42	AS	
Mason, Arthur C. H.	11/8/43	Ens	11/2/45	Lt(jg)	
Mast, Dennis D.	12/5/42	Sea1c	10/17/45	TM2c	
Matson, Harvey N.	5/30/45	S2c	11/2/45	S2c	
Mauldin, Olaf F.	12/5/42	AS	1/13/44	S1c	
May, Daniel L.	5/30/45	S2c	10/26/45	S2c	
May, Earl	8/15/39	MM2c	3/27/40	MM1c	
May, Herbert A.	3/19/42	Ens	5/25/45	Lt	S, C
Mayefsky, Joseph	3/20/42	AS	1/13/44	S1c	
Mayfield, Joseph E.	8/10/44	Lt(jg)	10/31/45	Lt	
McCall, F. C.	5/27/40	SK1c	12/10/40	SK1c	
McCallion, William J.	8/15/39	SC3c			
McCardy, Gordon J.	10/28/43	S2c	11/2/45	S1c	
McCarroll, Verlon O.	12/5/42	F1c	7/7/44	MM2c	
McCullough, Henry O.	12/31/42	MM2c	12/7/44	MM2c	
McCullough, William E.	5/17/44	S2c	8/20/45	HA1c	
McGee, James H.	11/8/43	Ens	10/29/45	Lt(jg)	
McGillicuddy, R. W.	2/9/42	MM2c			
McInnes, George F.	2/9/42	Lt(jg)MC	3/21/42	Lt(jg)MC	
McIntyre, John L.	12/5/42	AS	11/2/45	Cox	
McKenna, T. M.	9/16/44	S2c	3/17/45	S2c	
McKenna, William C.	2/19/43	PhM3c	7/26/43	PhM3c	
McKenzie, Leonard M.	12/5/42	AS			
McRill, Chandos J.	12/5/42	AS	10/17/45	Y3c	
McVicker, Charles K.	8/15/39	Sea2c	7/31/45	Bosn	
McWhorter, Thomas O.	3/13/41	Ens	1/5/43	Lt	
McZeal, Robert	12/12/43	StM2c	4/30/44	StM2c	
Means, Allen L.	12/10/40	Sea2c	6/2/42	SC2c	
Meek, Burton	6/4/42	CPhM			
Meier, Robert A.			10/26/45	QM3c	
Meierding, Bennie R.	12/5/42	AS	11/2/45	SSML3c	
Mercuri, Antonio J.	8/15/39	Sea2c	10/19/40	Sea2c	
Meredith, Dean D.	12/5/42	AS	12/7/44	Cox	
Merritt, Neil L.	12/5/42	AS	10/29/45	S1c	
Messier, Henry C.	8/15/39	F3c	3/14/44	MM1c	
Metcalf, Kenneth E.	5/23/43	S2c	10/17/45	FC2c	
Metheny, Junior R.	12/5/42	AS	10/17/45	GM3c	

Meyer, William J.	10/6/44	S2c	10/26/45	S1c	
Midkiff, Dennis C.	8/18/39	Sea2c			
Miller, David C.	6/25/43	Lt	7/3/44	LtComdr	
Miller, James E.	8/15/39	MM2c			
Miller, Ivy J.	9/16/44	S1c	10/31/45	RM3c	
Miller, Manley L.			10/17/45	QM2c	
Mills, Harold W.	8/15/39	Sea2c	1/16/41	F1c	
Miner, Frank U.	6/25/43	S2c	11/2/45	MM3c	
Mioni, Joseph C.					
Mitchell, George E.	5/30/45	S2c	10/17/45	S2c	
Mitchell, N. G.			2/9/43	MA1c	
Montenegro, Salvador	5/8/43	S1c	11/2/44	FC3c	
Moody, William G.	12/5/42	AS	8/17/45	QM3c	
Moon, Don P.	5/31/40	Comdr	3/28/42	Comdr	F
Moore, L. R.			5/23/40	MM1c	
Morgan, Blaine K.	8/15/39	F2c	8/13/41	F1c	
Moring, Maxwell T.	8/15/39	EM2c			
Morley, Richard P.	6/30/45	PhM2c	8/17/45	PhM2c	
Morris, Donald B.	1/13/41	F2c	9/17/45	CMM	
Moynihan, Francis W.	12/5/42	AS	10/29/45	S1c	
Muleski, Walter R.	12/24/42	Y1c	8/6/45	CY	
Mullen, Joseph Jr.	3/4/45	Ens	11/2/45	Ens	
Musgrove, Lewis W.	12/5/42	AS	10/17/45	SF3c	
Mynarzy, Edward G.	5/30/45	S2c	10/30/45	S2c	

N

Nacelli, William	8/15/39	TM2c	12/25/40	TM2c	
Nagy, Julius G.	12/5/42	AS	11/2/45	SSML3c	
Nelson, Ardean J.			10/27/44	FC1c	
Nelson, F. L.	8/15/39	Matt2c	1/18/41	Matt1c	
Nelson, George	3/24/45	StM2c			
Nelson, Virgil A.	8/15/39	F2c	1/16/42	MM1c	
Newcomb, Richard					
Nice, Orville G.	8/15/39	Sea2c	6/4/43	EM1c	
Niziolek, Anthony Jr.	12/5/42	AS	5/21/44	SM3c	
Norcross, David N.	10/2/41	AS	11/15/42	Sea2c	W
Normandie, Arthur	10/2/41	AS	11/13/42	Sea1c	*
Nyce, Harry C.	6/22/42	Lt(jg)MC	9/6/43	Lt(MC)	

O

O'Briant, Kenneth G.	8/15/39	CPhM	6/3/42	CPhM	
O'Connell, Arthur J.	3/7/42	AS	5/27/42	AS	
O'Connor, Kenneth J.	10/2/41	AS	10/25/43	F1c	
O'Daniel, Elvie J.	8/15/39	TM3c	1/8/41	TM2c	

O'Daniel, R. W.					
Odell, Claude W.	8/15/39	Sea2c	7/16/41	SC3c	
Odom, E. B.					
Oldenburg, Harold A.			10/31/45	SoM2c	
Olson, Alvin H.	12/5/42	AS	1/13/44	WT3c	
Olson, Robert J.	11/1/41	Bmkr2c	8/20/45	CWT	
Omelan, Leo A.	12/5/42	AS			
O'Rourke, William J.	12/5/42	AS	1/18/45	S1c	
Ortner, Glen E.	5/23/43	Sea2c	1/13/44	S1c	
Otis, Frank L.	8/21/43	StM1c	9/17/43	StM1c	F
Otto, C.					
Overvold, Lee M.	12/5/42	AS	11/2/45	Cox	
Owens, Adolph C.	8/15/39	FC1c	9/29/40	FC1c	
Owens, Andrew C.			10/31/45	S1c	

P

Pace, William R. Jr.	10/21/44	RdM3c	10/30/45	RdM3c	
Palmer, Donald W.			10/30/45	S2c	
Palmer, Roy L.	6/23/41	AS	1/13/44	S1c	
Palmier, Bert					
Parker, Donald E.	10/2/41	AS	5/9/43	S1c	
Parkis, Barnum H.	8/15/39	Sea2c	11/15/42	MM1c	C, W
Parmentier, Henry N.	3/13/44	S1c	4/27/44	S2c	
Patman, Bill			10/31/45	WT3c	
Payne, Joel D.	8/15/39	F2c			
Peck, Joseph D.	2/25/45	S1c	10/17/45	S1c	
Peloquin, Albert J.	8/15/39	CMM	12/16/40	CMM	
Perkins, Eston E.	8/15/39	Sea2c			
Perry, Carmen S.			11/13/42	Sea1c	*
Pessina, William E.	9/16/44	S2c	11/2/45	S2c	
Pete, Leo J.	10/2/41	AS	11/13/42	F2c	*
Peters, Richard A.	3/7/42	AS	6/26/45	GM3c	
Peterson, Gerald T.	3/7/45	Bosn	4/28/45	Bosn	
Peterson, Richard	8/15/41	Matt3c	1/15/44	CK3c	
Pfeffer, Charles E.	3/7/42	AS	12/11/42	AS	
Phillips, J. W.			8/9/40	EM1c	
Phillips, John H.	8/15/39	Sea1c	8/13/41	Sea2c	
Pianfetti, Matt	8/15/39	F1c	11/3/40	MM2c	
Piche, Marc					
Pierce, Oliver H.	8/15/39	F2c	5/13/41	F1c	
Pike, Amos F.	10/2/41	AS	11/13/42	F2c	*
Pinzon, Dimas	10/2/41	AS	6/25/43	S1c	
Plecker, Owen	8/15/39	MM2c	3/15/44	WMach	
Plumley, George					

Pomerance, Sherman	4/4/43	Ens	10/28/44	Lt(jg)	
Poor, Daniel G.	1/25/43	Ens	6/14/44	Lt(jg)	
Poppen, Floyd	12/5/42	GM3c	12/4/44	GM2c	
Poschke, R. D.			11/13/42	Sea2c	*
Poscus, John A.	3/7/42	AS	11/2/45	EM2c	
Pray, P. L.	10/21/41	CMM	5/29/42	CMM	
Price, Dennis E.	8/15/39	F2c	7/16/41	F1c	
Priest, Robert H.			1/13/44	S1c	
Pritchett, Frank N.	8/29/45	StM1c	11/2/45	StM1c	
Probst, H. O.	9/16/44	S1c	2/25/45	S1c	
Provow, Ralph E.	9/29/40	AS			
Pszczola, Edward			7/31/45	S2c	
Purcell, John W.	5/12/43	RM3c	10/2/43		

Q

Quillian, Hubert T.	2/17/45	Lt(jg)	11/2/45	Lt	C

R

Rafferty, J. P.	10/21/40	CMM			
Rajcevich, Eli			10/29/45	S1c	
Rancourt, Archie J.	8/15/39	CFC	1/18/41	CFC	
Ray, Arthur J.	9/29/40	AS	11/2/45	MM1c	
Ready, William J.	3/7/42	AS	5/3/44	Cox	
Reames, Alvin R.	5/30/45	S2c	10/17/45	S2c	
Reese, C. R.	10/23/40	BM1c	12/12/42	CBM	
Reid, James V.	12/5/42	AS	6/8/43	AS	
Reider, Freeman R.	10/19/40	F2c	11/8/41	EM3c	
Respess, George M.	8/15/39	MM1c	10/1/41	CMM	
Rhode, Elmer			10/31/45	EM2c	
Rhodes, Harry G.	12/10/40	Sea2c	11/15/42	TM3c	W
Rhoten, Lawrence Q.	6/29/45	S1c	11/2/45	S1c	
Rhudy, F. W.			5/23/40	CRM	
Riccuito, George	2/21/42	AS	7/28/45	F1c	
Rich, J. E.	2/21/42	AS	11/15/42	Sea2c	W
Rich, James W.			10/26/45	S2c	
Richard, Charles S.	10/19/40	AS	8/20/45	B1c	
Ritter, Vernon H.	11/10/44	RT3c	11/2/45	RT2c	
Roark, James B.	8/15/39	SC2c	5/13/41	SC1c	
Roberts, Augustine J.	12/15/43	S2c	10/29/45	GM3c	
Roberts, M. B.					
Robinson, J. E.	10/19/40	AS	11/13/42	SC2c	*
Robinson, James A.	8/22/40	SF3c	12/12/42	SF1c	C
Rogers, Alton H.	8/15/39	CWT	8/30/40	CWT	

Rogers, Ivan G.	12/12/43	MM2c	11/2/45	MM2c	
Rohrer, O. D. Jr.			12/8/40	RM2c	
Roll, Andrew J.	9/4/40	MM2c	4/17/41	MM2c	
Rose, Elmer J.	8/15/39	Sea2c	1/13/44	B1c	
Rossman, H. M.					
Rowe, Charles B.	9/16/44	F2c	10/30/45	F1c	
Royce, Wallace F.	12/15/43	S2c	10/31/45		
Rueda, Peter R.	5/23/43	Sea2c	5/21/44	S1c	
Ruh, Charles F.	8/15/39	Sea1c	2/25/42	GM2c	
Rupert, Meredith D.	9/16/44	S2c	10/17/45	S1c	
Russel, Raymond	2/13/42	MM2c			
Ruth, Charles D.	3/7/42	AS	11/13/42	F2c	*

S

Sanders, Anthony	8/15/39	Sea2c	5/3/40	Sea2c	
Sanders, Hugh B.	7/2/40	Ens	1/18/43	Lt	
Sapalo, Ruperto	6/3/42	OS2c	1/15/44	St1c	
Saucier, Henry F.	2/21/42	AS	1/13/44	S1c	
Saunders, A.					
Sawyer, Leslie R.	2/18/43	F2c	3/9/45	MM2c	
Saye, J. J.	10/19/40	AS	3/2/41	Sea2c	
Schaepers, Joseph J.	2/18/43	F2c	10/31/45	RT3c	
Scharbius, Alfred A.	3/19/42	Lt(jg)MC	6/25/42	Lt(jg)MC	
Scheiderer, W.	10/1/41	RM2c			
Schissler, William P.	8/15/39	Sea2c			
Schoen, Ellis R.	10/19/40	AS	10/29/45		
Schoenberg, L. G.					
Schofield, E. K.	6/15/40	Lt(jg)SC			F
Schugerl, Theodore W.	2/5/43	MM2c	1/13/44	MM2c	
Schurig, William E.	12/15/43	S2c	10/26/45	FC3c	
Schwartz, John J.	8/15/39	MM2c	5/1/41	MM1c	
Sciarini, John J.	3/7/42	AS	3/12/45	WT2c	W
Scorel, Edward J.	2/18/43	F2c	9/17/45	MM2c	B
Scott, Reginald L.	8/15/39	MM1c	8/15/41	CMM	
Scovel, Roy	8/15/39	CY			
Segerson, Hans C.	6/5/44	MM1c	9/8/45	MM1c	
Setterquist, Leslie M.	10/6/44	FC3c	11/2/45	FC3c	
Seymour, Henry A. Jr.	10/19/40	AS	11/15/42	Sea1c	W, S
Shadel, Theodore J.					
Shaffer, William H.	3/24/45	MM3c	9/17/45	MM3c	
Shannon, V. L.			6/2/40	F1c	
Sharley, Chester W.	12/5/42	MM2c	9/30/44	MM1c	
Sharp, Paul E.	8/3/45	WT2c	9/17/45	WT2c	
Shaw, Ezekiel			10/31/45	RM3c	

Shaw, Leland R.	2/21/41	RM3c	6/24/42	RM2c	
Shaw, Richard H.	9/2/44	Ens	10/29/45	Lt(jg)	
Shelton, J. W.	8/16/39	Sea2c	7/14/43	CFC	W, S
Shelton, Jean A.	8/15/39	F2c			
Shelton, L. L.	12/10/40	AS			
Shennick, T. P.	1/11/42	F3c			
Shepard, G. S.	12/10/40	AS			
Sherer, N. R.	12/10/40	AS	4/9/41	Sea2c	
Sherman, Frederick J.	3/7/42	AS	1/13/44	SM3c	
Shirley, Houston I.	3/19/42	Ens	12/22/43	Lt(jg)	
Shoemate, James W.	5/30/45	S2c	10/26/45	S2c	
Shook, J. D. C.	8/15/39	Sea1c	3/11/42	SM2c	C
Shorr, Henry F.	11/8/43	Ens	10/31/45	Lt(jg)	
Shrieves, Douglas F.	12/10/40	Sea2c	11/15/42	TM3c	W
Silvis, Joseph E.	9/13/44	PhM3c	10/31/45	PhM3c	
Simmons, Clarence M.	12/10/40	AS	11/2/45	CGM	M
Simmons, D. H.					
Simmons, Lloyd D.	10/19/40	AS	12/12/42	MM2c	
Simpkins, Donald E.	9/16/44	S2c	11/2/45	S1c	
Simpson, Roger W.	5/23/43	Comdr	9/17/43	Comdr	F
Sims, Doyle C.	6/28/45	MaM3c	11/2/45	MaM3c	
Singer, Watson T.	8/15/39	Lt	3/20/41	LtComdr	
Skutely, Richard L.	12/10/40	AS	11/15/42	Sea1c	W
Slayton, R. G.	12/10/40	AS			
Smallhausen, Morris B.	10/25/43	CSM	2/28/44	CSM	F
Smies, Joseph H.	11/8/43	Ens	2/14/45	Lt(jg)	
Smilek, John	3/7/42	AS	11/2/44	FC3c	
Smith, Dale R.	6/27/42	AS	11/13/42	Sea2c	*
Smith, Francis P.	8/15/39	Bmkr1c	9/3/41	CWT	
Smith, Frederick W.	2/18/43	F2c	10/31/45	MM2c	
Smith, George B. Jr.	9/16/44	S1c	7/28/45		
Smith, Joseph	3/10/42	AS	11/13/45	RM3c	*
Smith, J. L.			6/2/42	SM3c	
Smith, Lester F. Jr.	8/15/39	Sea1c	6/19/41	RM3c	
Smith, Morris E.	3/7/42	AS	11/13/42	Sea2c	*
Smith, Ralph	5/30/45	S2c	10/30/45	S2c	
Smith, Thomas R.	6/27/42	AS	6/25/43	S1c	
Smith, William K.	8/2/45	StM1c			
Smith, Wylie R.	5/30/45	S2c	10/29/45	S2c	
Smitherman, Lee R.	9/29/40	AS	11/13/43	SF2c	
Soelch, Charles L.	8/15/39	GM3c	6/1/43	GM1c	
Solloway, John E. Jr.	8/15/39	Sea2c	2/15/43	TM1c	
Sommers, Francis A.	3/7/42	AS	8/21/44	Cox	
Sotak, John W.	5/25/45	Lt	11/2/45	Lt	
Sova, Joseph A.	3/7/42	AS	3/24/42	AS	

Spaulding, Ronald G.	12/10/40	AS	11/13/42	Cox	*
Spence, M. R.	12/10/40	AS	12/7/44	SF2c	
Speyer, Arthur J.	2/18/43	F2c	10/17/45	MM2c	
Spicer, Herbert F.	12/8/41	Sea1c			
Sprinkle, Carl C.	3/12/41	Y3c	8/25/41	Y3c	
Sproat, D. A.	12/10/40	AS	6/23/42	S2c	
Standridge, Elmer L.	8/15/39	Sea2c			
Stapleton, James P.			11/13/42	Sea2c	*
Starr, Donald J.	12/10/40	AS	12/18/43	FC1c	
Stegall, J. W.	9/16/44	S2c	3/17/45	S2c	
Stella, William J.	2/18/43	F2c	11/2/45	MM2c	W
Steller, E. G.	8/16/39	F3c	5/30/42	EM2c	
Stenslie, Harry	8/15/39	CEM	12/6/42	CEM	
Stephens, Thomas M.			10/22/43	Lt(jg)	
Sterchi, Ralph	11/26/40	SC1c	12/23/40	SC1c	
Sterk, L. E.	4/15/41	RM2c	10/29/41	RM2c	
Stevens, Charles L.	5/30/45	S2c	10/26/45	S2c	
Stevens, Walter L.	6/5/44	CMM	11/2/45	CMM	C
Stinson, Troy L.	1/11/42	F3c	7/26/43	MM2c	
Stokes, Charles W.	8/15/39	Sea2c	5/9/43	S1c	
Stoneburner, Melvon L.	1/14/44	F2c	11/2/45	WT3c	
Stout, R. H.			5/23/40	CMM	
Strawder, I. N.			3/8/42	Matt3c	
Strickland, Raymond L.	9/16/44	F2c	9/3/45	F1c	
Strickland, Will V.	8/15/39	MM1c			
Stricklin, C. C.			9/15/40	CWT	
Strochine, Donald C.	1/14/44	F2c	11/2/45	WT1c	
Stuart, Charles J.	10/24/43	Comdr	2/28/44	Capt	F
Stump, Calvin J.	3/7/42	AS	8/21/44	SF3c	
Sudnick, Edward A.	1/14/44	F2c	11/2/45	MM3c	
Sukley, Joseph F.	9/16/44	S2c	10/31/45	S2c	
Summers, A. V.	12/20/39	F3c			
Summers, Robert W.	12/8/41	Sea1c	2/15/42	SM1c	
Svizeny, Joseph W.	3/8/42	AS	11/2/45	RdM2c	
Swanberg, Carl W.	5/30/45	S2c	10/30/45	S2c	
Swope, George A. Jr.	8/15/39	MM2c	3/27/40	MM1c	

T

Tadevich, Walter	1/21/44	S2c	10/31/45	S2c	
Taffe, Gerald E.	1/21/44	S2c	11/2/45	SK3c	
Talbot, Warren W.	8/15/39	EM2c	2/7/43	CEM	
Tanner, Raymond M.	1/21/44	S2c	11/2/45	S1c	
Tapia, Carl N.	12/21/41	Sea2c	11/15/42	F2c	W
Tarnoff, Nathan	1/14/44	F2c	11/2/45	WT3c	

Taylor, Caleb J.	9/16/44	F2c	10/31/45	EM3c	
Taylor, Henry E.	11/10/44	Y1c	8/21/45	Y1c	
Taylor, Eric	9/15/44	CPhM	10/27/44	CPhM	
Teator, Homer	1/21/44	F3c	5/3/44	F1c	
Terrano, Richard R.	8/15/39	Sea2c	11/15/42	EM3c	W
Thames, Dee C.	9/16/44	F2c	11/2/45	F1c	
Thomas, James S.			12/28/43	RM3c	
Thomas, Robert E.	1/21/44	S2c	10/30/45	TM3c	
Thomas, Winfred E.	1/21/44	S2c	10/29/45	S1c	
Thompson, Raymond F.	9/16/44	F2c	11/2/45	F1c	
Thompson, Thomas C.	1/21/44	S2c	10/31/45	S1c	
Thompson, Weldon L.	1/21/44	S2c	11/2/45	SM3c	
Thorne, James A.	9/16/44	F2c	11/2/45	SSMB3c	
Thurman, Marion E.	8/15/39	WT2c	4/28/44	CWT	
Tice, Dale W.	1/21/44	S2c	11/2/45	S1c	
Titzer, Glen F.	1/21/44	S2c	3/17/45	S1c	
Toerner, Chester A.	10/25/43	CY	2/28/44	CY	F
Tomkins, T. O.			10/18/41	FC1c	
Tomko, Michael Jr.	3/7/42	AS	9/23/43	TM3c	
Trauscht, John V.	2/25/45	S2c	10/26/45	S1c	
Traweek, Bert L.	8/15/39	Sea1c	6/2/42	Cox	
Tsolakos, Sam J.	5/23/43	Sea2c	1/13/44	S1c	
Turley, Robert L.	3/25/42	RM1c	1/14/44	CRM	
Turner, Lawrence W.	1/21/44	F3c	9/17/45	WT3c	
Turovsky, Michael	1/21/44	S2c	6/14/45	S1c	
Tuttle, Harry O.	1/21/44	F3c	11/2/45	WT2c	
Tynan, Joseph M. Jr.			11/13/42	Sea2c	*
Tyner, Charles R.	5/17/44	S1c	1/23/45	S1c	

U

Ulmer, Vernon D.	5/30/45	S2c	9/16/45	S2c	

V

VanEtten, Harry C.	8/15/39	MM2c	12/11/39	MM2c	
VanMill, Donald A.			10/26/45	RdM3c	
Varner, Earl	8/15/41	Matt3c	11/2/45	St1c	W
Veer, William W.	3/24/45	S2c	10/26/45	S2c	
Verdugo, Ernest F.	5/23/43	Sea2c	1/13/44	S1c	
Vestal, David	5/23/43	S1c	10/26/45	TM3c	
Villareal, Ramon A.	3/24/45	Bkr2c	11/2/45	Bkr2c	
Violette, Clinton J.	8/15/39	RM2c	1/8/41	RM1c	
Visconti, George J.	1/13/41	F1c	12/18/43	MM1c	
Visser, Bernard D.	10/21/44	RdM3c	10/31/45	RdM2c	

Name					
Waddell, Charles A.			8/9/40	Bosn	
Wadsworth, J. K.	3/19/42	SK1c			
Wagner, Marland M.	6/2/43	S2c	2/6/45	MoMM2c	
Waldron, Willard J. Jr.	5/30/45	S2c	10/29/45	S2c	
Walker, James A.	1/13/41	Sea2c	5/21/44	BM2c	
Walker, John L.	8/15/39	Sea2c	11/13/43	EM2c	
Walker, Vernon H.	8/15/39	Sea2c	11/24/41	GM3c	
Walker, W. S.	3/7/42	Matt3c	11/13/42	Matt2c	*
Wall, Walton C.	12/19/42	S2c	10/26/45	S1c	
Wallace, James F.	12/19/42	S2c	11/2/45	S2c	
Wallace, R. J.	3/19/42	SK3c			
Walls, Alfred O.	12/24/40	Sea2c	8/21/44	S1c	
Walters, John K. Jr.	12/19/42	S2c	5/5/42	Bkr3c	
Walther, Joseph A.	12/19/42	S2c	11/2/45	MoM3c	
Ward, Athan	12/19/42	S2c	9/30/44	Cox	
Ward, Clarence C.	12/19/42	S2c	5/21/44	S1c	
Ward, John H.	12/19/42	S2c	12/4/44	GM3c	
Ward, Malcolm D.			4/4/41	RM3c	
Warden, J. A.	10/1/41	RM2c			
Warlick, W. W.	11/28/41	Comdr	5/29/42	Capt	F
Waters, Oris L.	12/19/42	S2c	8/21/44	GM3c	
Watkins, Kern J.	11/2/44	Y2c	11/2/45	Y2c	
Wauhop, Charles S.	5/17/44	S2c	10/30/45	F2c	
Weatherby, Floyd J.	8/15/39	F1c	6/24/40	F1c	
Weddington, Robert E.	8/15/39	Sea2c			
Weitz, Carl L.	8/15/39	Msmth1c	2/12/41	Msmth1c	
Weller, Lawrence A.	12/8/41	Sea1c	12/13/43	SF2c	
Welna, Jerome S.			10/31/45	TM3c	
Welsh, Thomas J.	8/15/39	CBM			
Welsh, Thomas M.	12/5/42	EM3c			
Wessendurk, George E.	9/27/44	S2c	2/25/45	S2c	
West, Louis	9/27/44	St1c			
Wheelhouse, Franklin T.	3/24/45	SoM2c	8/20/45	SoM2c	
White, Charles L.	9/16/44	S2c	11/2/45	S1c	
White, Delbert R.			12/2/44	F1c	
White, George R.			2/27/44	SK1c	
White, William J.	3/7/42	AS	11/13/42	Sea2c	*
Whiteacre, Billie M.	2/18/45	Ens	10/29/45	Ens	
Whiting, Clinton L.	5/17/44	S2c	9/17/45	Y3c	
Whitney, Roger R.	5/30/45	S2c	11/2/45	S2c	
Wholley, Joseph B.			1/13/44	EM2c	
Wilder, Jack L.	8/15/39	Sea2c	8/26/41	Sea1c	
Wilk, Edwin H.	8/15/39	Sea2c	4/7/41	F1c	
Wilken, Richard F.	3/31/41	AS	5/14/44	SC1c	

Williams, Gordon B.	1/27/45	LtComdr	11/2/45	LtComdr	N
Williams, John A.	10/6/44	S2c	12/4/44	S2c	
Williams, Purvie	5/30/45	S2c	10/17/45	S2c	
Williams, S. K.					
Williams, Sostan	7/5/41	Matt3c			
Williams, Sylvester			5/18/45	CK1c	
Williams, W. T.	2/9/42	MM2c	1/14/44	MM1c	
Williams, William H.	9/3/39	Cox	3/27/40	BM2c	
Wilmot, Byron E.			5/29/42	RM2c	
Wilson, H.	2/21/42	AS	10/20/44	B3c	
Wilson, James D.	5/30/45	S2c	10/29/45	S2c	
Wilson, Russell S.	2/7/43	MM2c			
Winant, F. I. Jr.	8/15/39	Lt	4/26/41	Lt	
Wise, Howard A.	5/30/45	S2c	10/29/45	S2c	
Withey, Leroy L.	5/30/45	S2c	10/30/45	S2c	
Wofford, James W.	5/30/45	S2c	10/30/45	S2c	
Wood, J. J.	2/5/43	EM3c			
Woods, Edward C.	1/21/44	F3c	5/13/44	F2c	
Woods, Glen R.	5/13/44	Ens	7/2/45	Ens	
Woods, Joseph J.			6/25/43	CM3c	
Woods, Leonard D.	10/11/43	Ens	11/2/45	Lt(jg)	
Woods, Walter L.	1/21/44	F3c	10/31/45	MM3c	
Woolard, Frazier T. Jr.	8/15/39	Sea2c	1/29/41	EM3c	
Worth, Thomas C.	3/19/42	Ens(SC)			
Worthington, Robert E.	8/15/39	Sea2c	6/19/42	F1c	
Wrenn, Alva B.	2/22/41	Y2c	3/21/42	Y2c	F

Y

Yezzi, Emmett J.	10/19/40	F2c	9/30/44	WT2c	
Young, Edward	8/15/39	MM1c	10/13/40	CMM	
Young, Tommie	10/25/43	StM2c			F

Z

Zabriskie, John P.	1/14/44	S2c	10/30/45	GM3c	
Ziegler, Warren H.	12/10/40	Sea2c	12/4/44	MM2c	

INDEX

ABOUT THE AUTHOR

After World War II, C. Raymond Calhoun served as executive officer on the flagship of the Atlantic Fleet and had command of the destroyer USS *Moale*. He received a commendation for outstanding performance of duty as commander of Destroyer Squadron 6 during the Cuban missile crisis. He also served as deputy chief of staff for U.S. Naval Forces Europe and as director of research at the National War College, where he earned the Legion of Merit. He was vice chancellor of the Minnesota state university system from 1968 until his retirement ten years later. He is the author of *Typhoon: The Other Enemy*, also published by the Naval Institute Press. He and his wife, Betsy, now reside in Wilmington, North Carolina.